Unwoke

UNWOKE

How to Defeat Cultural Marxism in America

TED CRUZ

Regnery Publishing
WASHINGTON, D.C.

Regnery® is a registered trademark and its colophon is a trademark of Salem Communications Holding Corporation

Cataloging-in-Publication data on file with the Library of Congress

Library of Congress Control Number: 2023941990

ISBN hardcover trade: 978-1-68451-362-8
ISBN hardcover signed: 978-1-68451-545-5
eISBN: 978-1-68451-477-9

Published in the United States by
Regnery Publishing
A Division of Salem Media Group
Washington, D.C.
www.Regnery.com

Manufactured in the United States of America

10 9 8 7 6 5 4 3 2 1

Books are available in quantity for promotional or premium use. For information on discounts and terms, please visit our website: www.Regnery.com.

This book is dedicated to my Father, my Tia Sonia, and my Abuela—in my family, the original freedom fighters.

Contents

PROLOGUE

His white linen suit was stained red with blood. Blood that had been beaten out of him with a club, regularly each hour. Breaking his nose. Shattering his teeth. Scarlet red blood, as if his suit were emblazoned with the color of the Marxist revolution of which he was a part.

As my father lay on that prison floor, crumpled and broken, not a spot of white was visible on the now torn and tattered suit he had been given for his seventeenth birthday. Instead, mud and dirt and grime and blood.

To this day, my dad remembers what he was thinking in that dark hole: "Nobody depends on me. I have no wife, no children. It doesn't matter if I live or I die."

Three years earlier, when he was just fourteen, my father had made the fateful decision to join up with the revolution in his homeland of Cuba. To follow Fidel Castro. My dad was young and ignorant and naïve. Rafael Bienvenido Cruz didn't know Castro was a communist. He didn't know the horrors that would befall the Cuban people at the hands of his new comrades. He just knew that the then dictator of Cuba, Fulgencio Batista, was corrupt and cruel and oppressive. As Francis Ford Coppola immortally chronicled in the *Godfather* saga, Batista was in bed with the American mafia, enjoying wealth and power purchased with the blood beaten out of the Cuban people.

Born in Matanzas, a small Cuban town named for the brutal massacre carried out by the Spaniards more than four centuries earlier, my father grew up in an idyllic island paradise. My grandfather, my *abuelo* Rafael Cruz, had grown up as an indentured servant on a Cuban sugar plantation. In 1918, at eighteen, Rafael left the plantation, accepting the offer of five dollars and a sandwich to board a bus and go vote for a local politician. He slept on the floor of a fruit stand on the beach, where he got a job sweeping the floors. As the years passed, he became a salesman for RCA, the American company selling the new and miraculous inventions called televisions. Over time, he would become the top-producing RCA salesman in Cuba.

He met a fetching girl, Laudelina, who was eleven years his junior. She was a sixth-grade teacher, beloved by her students for her compassion and meticulous care in teaching them each day. Together, their first-born son was my father, who arrived in 1939.

My dad was an excellent student like his mother, with a natural gift for math. By the time he was fourteen, he had been elected to the student council and was a leader in his school. Years later, I too was on the student council. But we concerned ourselves with school dances and the food in the cafeteria. In Cuba, in the 1950s, the concerns of student council members were more fundamental: revolution. Fidel Castro, the charismatic revolutionary guerilla, had been a student council leader at the University of Havana. The children who followed him were, as my dad puts it, "fourteen- and fifteen-year-old boys who didn't know any better."

Marxist revolutions have always begun with the children. Young and idealistic and passionate and oh-so-unaware of the vicious perils that await them, teenagers can easily be swept up in the currents of revolution.

My father joined up and began doing acts of sabotage—burning government buildings, throwing Molotov cocktails, whatever he could to undermine the oppressive regime.

That's what had landed him in prison at seventeen. Batista's police had caught him, and they were extracting their brutal revenge.

The next day he was dragged into the office of a colonel, who told him, "I'm letting you go. But if another bomb goes off, if another fire starts, I'm blaming you."

"How can I be responsible for every bad thing that happens in the city?" my father asked.

"I don't care," replied the commandant. "I'm holding you responsible."

When my father returned home, my *abuela* wept. Her eldest child had walked in the door beaten, covered in his own blood. As she told me when I was a child, that image from that day was seared into her mind forever.

My *abuelo* told him, "Get out of the country. They know who you are now. They'll just hunt you down and kill you."

Nevertheless, my father wanted to stay. His revolutionary comrades were preparing a military assault on the government, and he wanted to participate. But a young woman, a fellow guerilla, came by his house that night, slipping in unseen. She told him, "Stay away from the rest of us now. Batista's police are following you. You'll lead them to us."

So he did. He applied to college in America. To the University of Miami, to LSU, and to the University of Texas. Texas was the first one that let him in. And that's how I came to be a Texan.

In the summer of 1957, my eighteen-year-old father boarded a ferry boat to Key West. He watched his homeland recede and wondered if he would ever see his beloved Cuba again. When he landed, he bought a ticket on a Greyhound bus and began the lonely trek to Austin. When he arrived, he had nothing but one hundred dollars sewn into his underwear and a slide rule in his suit pocket. He knew no one, and he spoke no English.

He found a place to live—a boarding house that catered to impoverished students—and he got a job as a dishwasher, making fifty cents an hour.

Enrolled at UT, he began his freshman classes—all of which were in English. Since my dad couldn't speak English, he sat at the back of the class wondering what his professors were saying. But, thankfully, he learned English quickly. My dad had an acute incentive to do so—if he didn't, he would flunk out; if he flunked out, they would revoke his student visa; if they revoked his visa, they would send him back to Cuba; and if he went back to Cuba, the government would kill him.

So he signed up for Spanish 101 and reverse-engineered the course. When the professor said, "'milk' is '*leche*,'" my father wrote down, "'*leche*' is 'milk.'" And he went to movies. All day on Saturday, he would go see the same movie over and over again. The human mind is marvelously intuitive, and after the third or fourth time in a row watching a movie, he would start to get a sense of what the actors were saying, and then to understand it.

Once he learned English, my dad began giving talks around Austin. He'd go to Rotary Clubs and other gatherings of businessmen in town, and he'd speak about the revolution. He'd sing the praises of Fidel Castro, describe the corruption and abuse of Batista, and urge Texans to support the guerillas.

Then the revolution succeeded. On December 31, 1958—New Year's Eve—Batista fled Cuba, boarding a plane to escape certain death. And a triumphant Fidel Castro, with his ragtag band of revolutionaries—mostly children—entered the city of Havana.

For a moment, there was widespread celebration. Castro was seen by many as a liberator, and his victory was celebrated in many quarters in the United States. When Castro began naming fellow revolutionaries to his cabinet, *Time* magazine, one of the most influential publications in the United States at the time, reported that they were "mostly responsible, moderate men, ready to get to work."[1]

But early hopes were quickly shattered. Now victorious, Castro declared to the world that he was a Marxist, a communist. And his revolution became a dictatorship.

Batista was bad. Very soon, it became clear to almost anyone watching that Castro was much, much worse.

He seized people's lands. He seized their homes. He arrested any who dared to speak up, who dared to oppose him. His bloodthirsty lieutenant, Che Guevara, lined up dissidents before firing squads, executing hundreds. Anyone who resisted faced prison and torture and murder.

For me, Castro's Marxist brutality was not abstract. It was personal.

As Cuba descended into vicious oppression, my father's kid sister, my Tia Sonia, was still there, as were my grandparents. My Tia Sonia, whom I adore, is fiery and passionate and irrepressible. She was just a teenager, but she was horrified by what was happening.

And so she fought back.

Like her brother before her, she joined a revolution, this time the counter-revolution against the Castro regime. She, too, began committing acts of sabotage, burning sugar cane fields and working to topple the oppressive regime. And, like her brother before, she too was caught and imprisoned.

They threw my Tia Sonia in jail, and they did horrible, unspeakable things to her. Communist regimes are always evil and oppressive, but they reserve unique brutality for women. My Tia Sonia endured their worst.

In prison with her were my Tia Miriam and my Tia Mela. (In Spanish culture, you can have lots and lots of *tias*. They weren't actually my blood relatives, but they were my Tia Sonia's best friends, and so I grew up with them both, and they were my *tias* as well.) The three of them had been volleyball players together in high school, spirited athletes, and together they fought ferociously against Castro's barbarity. My Tia Miriam was thrown in a hole—a cell that was just a couple feet wide—where she was left for days in darkness lying next to the rotting corpse of another prisoner they had already murdered.

In 1960, my father returned to Cuba, the only time he has ever been back. He saw first-hand the misery, the suffering, the poverty, the brutality. With his own eyes he observed the devastating reality that his former comrades—the Marxists who had filled the minds of idealistic teenage boys with grand promises of liberty and justice and equality—were in fact liars and murderers and tyrants. He saw the savage abuse his little sister had faced.

And he saw the crushing impact on his own mother. For decades, my *abuela* had taught sixth grade, and she loved her students. When Castro took over, one of the very first priorities of the revolutionaries was to target the youth, to indoctrinate the children. Abuela told me that, shortly after Castro took over, they sent soldiers into the elementary schools. The soldiers instructed the kindergartners to close their eyes and pray to God. To ask for candy. They did; they opened their eyes, and there was no candy. Then, they told the children to close their eyes and pray to Fidel Castro for candy. They did. And when they opened their eyes, each child had a piece of candy on his or her desk, quietly slipped there by the soldiers.

Marxism always begins that way. By destroying allegiance to anything other than the state, Dear Leader, El Comandante. Faith in God must be destroyed. Devotion to family must be destroyed. Children are taught to betray their parents, to report what they said at home if it differs from the views mandated by the government. Anything that might get in the way of complete and absolute loyalty and obedience to the revolution must be eradicated.

The communists demanded the same of my family. They ordered Abuela to begin teaching her children Marxism. And so she faced a choice. She could be complicit in poisoning the minds of her beloved students. Or she could refuse, and face prison or worse, be forcibly removed from her own family and subjected to who knew what horrors. She chose a third option. She feigned insanity. One day in class, she began foaming at the mouth, tearing out her hair, screaming and wailing like a madwoman. They removed her from class, and she escaped her dilemma. But the price she paid—willingly—was the stigma and scorn of her neighbors' thinking she was a crazy lady.

My father returned from Cuba profoundly troubled and permanently changed. And then he did something I deeply admire. He sat down, and he made a list of every place he had spoken in Austin in support of Castro. Then he went back, to each and every one of them, and stood before the same people to make amends.

"I am here to apologize," he told them. "I misled you. I didn't do so knowingly, but I did so nonetheless. I urged you to support an evil man and an evil Marxist regime. And for that I'm truly sorry."

The Long, Slow March through the Institutions

M y father admitted he was wrong.

After spending his early years devoted to a cause that he did not fully understand, Rafael Cruz looked around him, saw the terror that Marxism had wrought in his home country, and changed his mind.

Most Marxists can't bring themselves to do that.

In the late 1960s various left-wing groups sprung up in the United States, many of which attempted to bring Karl Marx's dream of a socialist utopia to life. These groups, including terrorist organizations such as The Weather Underground, were strikingly similar to the bands of left-wing radicals my father had known in Cuba. Like Castro and Che Guevara, the members of these groups were mostly young. They did their recruiting on college campuses, and they believed deeply in the principles of Marxism.

Sometimes they were peaceful. Many groups held demonstrations and spoke out against the war in Vietnam, among other things.

Most photographs people see today of the New Left are of skinny, stoned-looking hippies in flowery outfits and tie-dye shirts. Anyone looking at your average high school history textbook might believe that your average 1960s leftist just wanted to listen to Jimi Hendrix, lie on a blanket, and talk about *the government, man*.

But that is far from the whole story. Throughout the 1960s, members of the New Left terrorized innocent people in pursuit of their political goals. They threw bricks through windows, planted bombs in restaurants, and lit whole city blocks on fire to get their message across. Anyone who asked what that message actually *was* would get slogans and impassioned speeches, nearly all of them derived from Karl Marx and his many disciples.

The movement came to a climax at the 1968 Democratic Convention, which was held at the International Amphitheatre in Chicago in August of that year. As various speakers took the stage and outlined their vision for the nation, radical left-wing protestors clashed with police in the streets outside. Watching from home, millions of Americans saw how unruly and insane the left wing of American politics had become. By the time the convention was over, left-wing rioters had done millions of dollars' worth of damage, injured hundreds of people—and turned the public against their cause.

Standing amid this carnage, the key figures of the New Left had the chance to rethink their devotion to the twisted, half-baked ideology of Marxism—which, as many of them surely knew, had already been responsible for the deaths of millions of people around the world by the late 1960s. If nothing else, they might have taken to heart the fact that public opinion had turned sharply against them.

It turns out, beating up police officers and burning down buildings tend to make people *less* likely to support your cause, not more.

I'm sure at least some of these activists realized that the writings of Karl Marx were nonsensical and that his ideas were not worth implementing. I'm sure that some of them looked up from the smoldering wreckage of their movement and were horrified, as my father had been, at what they'd supported, even if they had done so unwittingly. They may have looked back through the writings of Karl Marx and Friedrich Engels and discovered that the propositions they contained were stupid, backward, and evil.

All they had to do was read.

Anyone who reads even the most charitable biography of Karl Marx will find that the man was hardly a good example for anyone, let alone someone whose ideas should serve as the basis for a global political movement. From the moment Marx was old enough to be responsible for himself, he refused to—instead taking advantage of everyone in his life, refusing to work or become a productive member of society. He lived in a series of squalid apartments in different parts of Europe, writing poetry about the allure of Satan (yes, seriously) as well as the long, turgid pieces of political philosophy for which he would soon become a household name.

He was often drunk (which explains quite a bit), and he rarely bathed. His children went hungry because of their father's refusal to get a job to support his family. The little money they did have came, at first, from Marx's parents. Then, when his parents died, Marx began mooching off a series of wealthy benefactors, most notably Friedrich Engels, who would serve as a co-author of Marx's most famous work, *The Communist Manifesto*. The few friends Marx had remembered that even on the most solemn of occasions he would find a way to ask for money, which he'd later spend on alcohol and other vices.

Anyone who met the man came away feeling confused, unclean, and worried. The following passage from Paul Kengor's excellent book *The Devil and Karl Marx* quotes from the account of a Prussian police-spy report that was commissioned on Marx in the mid-1840s. As the officer assigned to Marx found, "'Washing, grooming, and changing his linens are things he does rarely, and he likes to get drunk.... He has no fixed times for going to sleep or waking up.' As for the family apartment, 'everything is broken down,' busted, spilled, smashed, falling apart—from toys and chairs and dishes and cups to tables and tobacco pipes and on and on. 'In a word,' said the report, 'everything is topsy-turvy.... To sit down becomes a thoroughly dangerous business.' Quite literally, the chair you chose to sit upon in the Marx household could collapse."[1]

As if that weren't enough, the man was also ferociously racist—something that the modern left-wing activists who constantly cite his work seem to have brushed aside. They ignore, for instance, the fact that Marx used the n-word constantly in letters to friends. In one exchange he seemed to agree with Engels's assessment that Black people were "a degree nearer to the rest of the animal kingdom than the rest of us."[2] He also objected fiercely when one of his daughters sought to marry a man from Cuba, denigrating her suitor as a "Negillo" and calling him "the Gorilla" because of his race.[3]

As a Cuban American myself, that gives me yet one more reason to loathe Karl Marx and everything he stands for (not that I needed another). And I'm not alone. In his other writings, Marx denigrates Mexicans, whom he believed were inferior, and Jews, whom he (like all conspiracy theorists, and too many members of today's Democratic Party) believed were somehow both an inferior race and simultaneously evil masterminds who control the global banking system in a conspiracy to keep workers down.[4]

Marx was, in short, not the kind of person you'd want to be stuck on an elevator with for a few minutes, let alone someone you should look up to and trust to solve the world's problems. But for over a century left-wing activists have looked to his dense, borderline-unreadable works and found the blueprint for a revolutionary worker's utopia—one that they have tried, with absolutely no success, to bring about in countries all over the world. Despite ending every time in failure, they keep trying again, hoping that *this* time they get it right, finally bringing about a world where people like Karl Marx are free to lie around, get drunk, and have the government pay for it all.

The writings they look to, much like the furniture in Karl Marx's house, are built on the flimsiest foundations imaginable. Rather than data and solid reasoning, Marx uses poetic language and rhetoric to make his grand claims. Perhaps that is why his work has appealed to wayward English majors and self-serious left-wing activists for generations. It would certainly help explain why so many people throughout history who have become committed to Marxism refuse to give up on the idea even when presented with incontrovertible evidence that it doesn't work.

This is exactly what happened to many members of the New Left in the early 1970s. Like so many Marxists who had come before them, they did not admit that they were wrong. The most devoted among them did not simply turn in their bricks and torches, buy suits, and get respectable jobs. Instead, they returned to their sacred texts with more fervor than ever, attempting to figure out why Marxism had failed so badly in the United States. They read the words of *The Communist Manifesto* and other works by Marx and his disciples, putting their heads together to find new ways of implementing these ideas in the United States.

They knew they could not continue to mount a violent revolution against the government. Not if they wanted to be successful. They could no longer throw bricks through windows, scream at police officers, and hold unruly demonstrations in the public square if they wanted to win hearts and minds to their cause—at least not yet.

For now, they had to take the ideas of Marx, the ones that they had worked so hard to bring to the United States, and quietly slip them into the minds of people in some other way.

The question was: How?

The answer, oddly enough, came in part from an obscure series of political essays called *Prison Notebooks*, selections from which had just appeared in translation in the United States, in 1971.

These notebooks had been written by a man named Antonio Gramsci, who had been imprisoned in the last years of his life, from 1926 to 1937, by Benito Mussolini shortly after Mussolini became dictator in Gramsci's home country of Italy. For years, Gramsci had been an active member of the Italian Communist Party, attempting to overthrow the government and bring about a worker's paradise on earth just as his hero Karl Marx had envisioned.

But he kept hitting walls. The society Gramsci and his comrades were living in seemed especially resistant to the doctrines of communism that they were pushing—not to mention that their Marxist groups kept splitting apart on account of infighting and poor organization.

But Gramsci didn't blame himself or his fellow communists for their constant failure. He certainly didn't blame the bad ideas of Karl Marx. Instead, like so many Marxists before and after him, he blamed society. In his view Italy, and other societies in the West, were especially resistant to Marxism because they were made up of institutions that were not connected to the government: universities, schools, churches, and newspapers, as well as publishing houses and other means of distributing popular culture. This made implementing Marxism, which relied on the central power of the government to control everything, extremely difficult.

"In the East," Gramsci would write in his *Prison Notebooks*, describing his moment of epiphany, "the state was everything, civil society was primordial and gelatinous; in the West, there was a proper relation between state and civil society, and when the state trembled a sturdy structure of civil society was at once revealed. The state was only an outer ditch, behind which there stood a powerful system of fortresses and earthworks."[5]

According to Gramsci, the only way to truly change society was not by violent revolution, but by infiltrating the institutions that make Western society unique. If Marxists could get inside the universities, for instance, where knowledge is effectively "made," or get jobs at publishing houses, which were the main avenues through which ideas were distributed at the time, they might be able to change the ways people thought in subtle ways, rather than having to resort to the kind of outward revolution that Karl Marx had planned on.

As the writer Nate Hochman recently described in *National Review*, Gramsci set out a plan that would require any would-be Marxist revolutionaries to "engage in a longer, more covert counterhegemonic struggle, waged via a 'war of position' against the ruling cultural consensus. That war of position would not, as in the East, culminate in a single violent, cathartic victory. It would require a protracted, multifront battle for control of the civic structures that form the social consciousness."[6]

Antonio Gramsci died before he could begin that struggle in his home country. Unlike many reformed revolutionaries, my father among them, he died without ever seeing the error of his ways. And the writing he had done in prison eventually made it out to the world, where it was picked up by young Marxists eager to conduct exactly the kind of covert war he'd described.

One of these people was Rudi Dutschke, a student activist in Germany who had already achieved considerable success by the 1960s, when he encountered Gramsci's ideas. Using these ideas as well as the work of other Marxist scholars, Dutschke proposed what he called "the long march through the institutions." According to this vision, Marxist revolutionaries would no longer simply protest in the streets and try to tear down existing structures. They would, rather, infiltrate those existing structures in an attempt to change them from within. Given his talent as a public speaker and a campus organizer, Dutschke was able to spread his ideas quite widely across the globe.

At some point in the 1960s, they reached the United States, and by the end of the decade the New Left in America was already beginning to burn out. The primary means of transmission was a professor named Herbert Marcuse, who had done some organizing with Dutschke before coming to the United States and who'd grown to admire Dutschke's plan for the "long march through the institutions." In a letter to Dutschke written in 1971, Marcuse said that the long march would be "the only effective way" to bring about a true left-wing revolution in the United States.

Marcuse described the strategy in detail in a book published the next year. He described how leftists would now work "against the established institutions while working within them, but not simply by 'boring from within,' rather by 'doing the job,' learning (how to program and read computers, how to teach at all levels of education, how to use the mass media, how to organize production, how to recognize and eschew planned obsolescence, how to design, et cetera), and at the same time preserving one's own consciousness in working with others."[7]

In other words, the activists who had once planted bombs in buildings and torched cars to bring about revolution would now have to calm down, get jobs, and pretend to be productive members of society ("doing the job"). All the while, though, they would maintain their revolutionary ideas ("preserving one's own consciousness") and work to insert those ideas into the work they did, indoctrinating as many people as possible in the process. Those who became university professors would treat figures like Karl Marx kindly while attacking capitalists and other revered figures from American history. Those who went into information technology would design systems with a subtle liberal bias. Those in journalism would work to transform the newspapers—and, eventually, the cable news networks and internet startups—into propaganda organs for the Left.

Marcuse also wrote about the need to develop "counterinstitutions," especially when it came to the media. He noted that these "must be made competitive."

"This is especially important," he wrote, "for the development of radical, 'free' media. The fact that the radical Left has no equal access to the great chains of information and indoctrination is largely responsible for its isolation."[8] (Ironically, Marcuse's call for effective "counterinstitutions" is today mirrored by many on the Right's call to create the same, now that the Left has captured the original institutions wholesale.)

In the years immediately following the tumultuous events of 1968, which turned public opinion sharply against the radical Left, the new revolutionaries began implementing the long march through the institutions, carefully following the instructions of Gramsci, Dutschke, and Marcuse. For the most part, they worked slowly. Sometimes they stumbled. In the process, many of the revolutionaries actually became what they were pretending to be, throwing off the ridiculous revolutionary ideas of Marx and becoming genuinely productive members of society.

But enough of these leftists remained committed to the project that it began to succeed. Over the course of several decades, this group of revolutionary professors, journalists, film writers, and others began slowly to change the way Americans thought about culture. They exploited their new avenues of transmission to great effect. Along the way, the original tenets of Marxism—which, in the beginning, applied mostly to economics—began to mutate. The new revolutionaries found that the core idea of Marxism—namely, that the world was a battleground between oppressed people and their oppressors—could be mapped not only onto warring economic classes (what Marx called the "proletariat" and the "bourgeoisie") but onto races as well.[9]

Today, many Americans are so used to this idea that they don't wonder where it came from. But its origin is worth investigating. You might wonder why, in the year 2023, with the long shadow of overt racism receding further into the past every day, we constantly hear stories about "racial tension" in the media. Why is it that there is seemingly no news story that the radical Left cannot twist to fit the narrative of racial oppression?

The answer is that the long march through the institutions has finally paid off. Today, ideas that were once peripheral to American life are at the forefront. Notions like White supremacy, class warfare, and internalized racism are now discussed on major news networks as if they have always been with us. Few people stop to wonder how these concepts, which seem to have come straight from a college literature seminar, have ended up ubiquitous throughout American culture.

The term "Cultural Marxism" refers to this transition. Over the past several decades, Marxists took Marx's communist teachings, which were originally applied to economics and to property, and applied them to culture instead. Using the same Marxist framework—a never-ending struggle between victims and oppressors that can only be corrected through force by the government's punishing the oppressors and rewarding the victims—they extended the oppression matrix to race, gender, sexual orientation, transgenderism, and disability. And they expanded their weapons to enforce Marxism: no longer is it imposed just through government policy, but now also through education, journalism, Big Tech, Big Business, sports, music, and Hollywood.

Whenever he's asked to explain this shift, my friend Christopher Rufo—whose work on Cultural Marxism, particularly Critical Race Theory, has proven extremely influential—references a book from the 1970s called *Prairie Fire*. Reading this book today, he notes, you can see all the terms that would eventually become familiar to American audiences: systemic racism, White privilege, and post-colonialism. The book describes the plight of oppressed classes in the United States, saying that the only way to end the oppression of these people is to mount a revolution against the ruling capitalist class.

What's notable about it, according to Rufo, is that in 1974, when it was written, the book needed to be printed in small batches by left-wing presses all over the nation. Mainstream publishers would never have touched such garbled nonsense. The fact that it was written and endorsed by The Weather Underground, one of the most famous left-wing terror groups in American history, would alone have been enough to keep this book off the shelves at any major bookstore.[10]

Today, books like it appear regularly, published by major mainstream publishers. The reading lists of many Fortune 500 companies include them, as do the syllabi of many colleges and high schools. In fact, I'm willing to bet that if you're currently reading this introduction while standing in front of the "Current Events" shelf at your local Barnes & Noble, you'll notice that many of the other books in front of your face contain the same radical Marxist ideas as the ones in *Prairie Fire*. Within your grasp, I'm sure there is a book about how to be an "anti-racist," or one that defends looting. You might even see books written by people who are members of Black Lives Matter, an outwardly Marxist organization that explicitly stated its desire to "disrupt the Western-prescribed nuclear family."[11]

The fact that these books are widely available today, and that they no longer need to be printed by crazy people in basements, speaks to how successful the long march through the institutions has been. Today, ideas that were once (rightly) considered insane are mainstream. This has happened because the radical Left has systematically seized control of the organs of the transmission of ideas.

They began with the universities. Then they expanded to K–12 education. Then came science and journalism and Big Business and Big Tech.

Even entertainment was not exempt. Today, in fact, the radical Left exerts more control over entertainment than virtually anything else.

Within these institutions—and, consequently, in the United States in general—if you think wrong, you will be reprogrammed. If you

speak wrong, you will be silenced. If you act wrong, you will be cancelled, eliminated, fired, destroyed.

Many today are still wondering how the hell this happened. The
brief outline of events in this introduction, while a good place to start,
does not quite capture just how insidious the infiltration has been.

Reading it, I'm sure many people still wonder how the storied institutions of America, many of which used to be bastions of conservatism,
went so stark raving nuts in such a short amount of time. How, you
might wonder, did they become uniform and brutal enforcers of such
an evil, misguided orthodoxy?

This book will endeavor to answer that question. It will walk you
through precisely how anti-American Marxists have systematically
worked to destroy our nation, to capture our institutions, and to turn
them against us. To turn them against America, so that they have literally become organs of hate undermining our history, our Constitution,
our Bill of Rights, our founding, and our fundamental liberties.

And, critically, it will lay out specific steps for how we stop it: how
we defeat Cultural Marxism.

How we retake our institutions, and how we retake America.

CHAPTER ONE

The Universities:
The Wuhan Labs of the Woke Virus

E arly in the spring of 2007, the heads of the government program at
the University of California at Berkeley realized they had a problem.

As part of their jobs, these professors—who worked at one of
the most rabidly far-left universities in the country—were obliged to
select a commencement speaker for the political science department's
upcoming graduation ceremony, which was held every year at the
Hearst Greek Theatre on campus. Reviewing the list of speakers who
had been invited in the past, these professors saw the names of senators, statesmen, and former White House officials; they saw lawyers
and legislators of all kinds.

What they didn't see was a single Republican.

At the time, Republicans had controlled the White House for almost
seven years. Whatever the students thought about them, there was no
doubt that Republicans had actual experience in governing. Yet for
some reason, not a single one had ever been invited to address a class

of students who were preparing for careers in government—the people who might someday run Congress, the White House, or any one of the numerous under-the-radar federal agencies in Washington. This year, likely still believing that universities were places where students should encounter ideas they might disagree with, at least one Berkeley professor resolved to invite a Republican to address the university's political science students for the first time in many years, if ever. This, presumably, is when they began to understand the scope of their problem, which was a big one, considering the circumstances.

They didn't know any Republicans, and neither, it seemed, did anyone they worked with.

To anyone familiar with the political landscape of UC Berkeley, this probably doesn't come as a shock. Known the world over for its student protests and far-left politics—not to mention vegan food, Birkenstocks, and copious amounts of marijuana—the university was practically a parody of a liberal bubble. It was easier to find self-produced chapbooks of lesbian poetry there than a copy of the morning newspaper; joint-rolling and hacky sack were practically D-1 sports. It was not, to say the least, the kind of place where buttoned-up Bush-era conservatives were likely to gather. (In truth, it was somewhere they were likely to go only in their most vivid nightmares.)

For the next few days, I'm sure that these professors searched far and wide for even a single Republican who had been tangentially involved in national or state-level politics. They might have grown desperate enough to try the rifle range a few towns over, or even perhaps a restaurant that served meat. I don't know. What I do know is that, eventually, one of them called a professor at the University of Texas, likely assuming that a political scientist in Texas would have more luck tracking down an actual Republican.

Even that, I'm told, almost didn't work. Only at the end of the call did the UT professor think to suggest the young government official who had given a commencement address at his school the previous spring.

"We had this guy last year at our school of government," he said, "the solicitor general of Texas. He did a pretty good job. His name was Cruz."

And that is how, by being the only Republican whose name was proffered as a possibility, I was invited to give a commencement address at UC Berkeley in the year 2007. I still remember sitting in my office and taking the call from the UT professor, who happens to be a friend of mine, and wondering what in the hell I would be getting myself into if I accepted the offer. In my mind I saw the images I had associated with Berkeley for years: burning flags, student protests, and mass walkouts that often ended in drum circles or poetry slams. I wondered if I would step onstage and be greeted by nothing but boos and flying vegetables.

But I had never backed down from a challenge before.

So I accepted.

For the next few weeks, primarily at night when my work as solicitor general was done, I began scratching out some ideas for a commencement address on yellow legal pads. At the time, it was my job to represent the state of Texas before all the state and federal appellate courts, including the U.S. Supreme Court. This meant that I was no stranger to defending my views in front of a hostile audience—an audience that predictably included some of the sharpest legal minds in the country. Arguing on behalf of my home state in front of the Supreme Court, I had often felt like chopped tuna thrown to a group of hungry sharks, forced to come up with answers instantaneously to questions being fired from all directions.

Compared to that, I assumed that speaking to a bunch of tired (and probably hungover) college seniors would be fairly manageable.

Still, I couldn't deliver the same speech at Berkeley that I had delivered to the graduating seniors in the government department at the

University of Texas one year earlier. This group of students would be different, to say the least, and the advice that I gave them would need to be tailored to make the greatest impact. I wrestled with this dilemma for quite some time, trying to figure out what message I should deliver to the students of Berkeley. I spent long hours at night wondering what they and I might have in common. And in doing so, I reflected on my own time in college two decades earlier.

◆ ◆ ◆

I arrived at Princeton in the fall of 1988, a seventeen-year-old kid who felt completely out of place in those hallowed halls. Nobody in my family had ever been to an Ivy League school. This was not my world. My dad had been a penniless immigrant from Cuba; my mom came from a working-class family and was the first person in her family ever to go to college.

I came from a small Christian high school in Houston, Second Baptist High School, with a graduating class of just forty-three. At the time, the school itself was less than a decade old, and the academic standards there in the 1980s left much to be desired.

And my family didn't come from money. To the contrary, just a year earlier my parents' small business had gone bankrupt. We lost our home, our business, and all our savings.

There I was, surrounded by kids who had gone to the best schools across America: elite boarding schools, with storied names that I had never heard of. My classmates were scions of wealth and power, kids with trust funds and yachts and jets and mansions.

Lyle Menendez was a classmate—the Cuban American who with his brother was later convicted of murdering their parents in their Beverly Hills mansion. As was MacKenzie Bezos, who later married Jeff and became one of the richest women on earth. So was a Greek princess named Olga. I remember finding it really funny that she was listed in the class directory under "O"; the entry simply read, "Ofgreece, Olga."

I never met any of them.

My randomly assigned roommate was an angry, entitled, liberal kid from New Jersey who has since become a relatively successful Hollywood screenwriter. His sense of humor was rude, juvenile, and prurient; it didn't surprise me that he later wrote films in that spirit, including *The Hangover Part II* and *The Hangover Part III*.

The day we met, he took an immediate dislike to me; he looked down on me and ignored and insulted me for the entirety of my freshman year. The freshman roommate from hell is a cliché, but I couldn't wait to get away from him.

I haven't spoken to the guy in over thirty years, but decades later he was still regularly taking to Twitter to lob nasty insults my way.[1] I guess Warhol was right about everyone's fifteen minutes.

Thankfully, I made lifelong friends at Princeton, including someone who would become my very best friend (other than Heidi): David Panton.

David was from Jamaica. He was tall and confident and immensely charming. He was in my Resident Advisory group freshman year, and he walked into the room and greeted every person there with a handshake, saying with a lilting Jamaican accent, "Hello, my name is David Keith Panton; it is a *pleasure* to meet you." It reminded me of Eddie Murphy's character in *Coming to America*—that same effortless grace.

David was just sixteen at the time, the second-youngest person in our class. And, as I would soon learn, he too felt scared and out of place at Princeton. His country school in Mandeville, Jamaica, didn't have remotely the academic rigor that most of our classmates had experienced.

We almost immediately became best friends. We were roommates the next three years of college, and then roommates again in law school. After his first year at Harvard Law School, David won a

Rhodes scholarship and went on to get a doctorate at Oxford. When he returned to law school (right after I graduated), he was elected president of the Law Review. Just a few years earlier, Barack Obama had become the first Black president of the Harvard Law Review; David was the second.

In college, David and I together ran the student government at Princeton; he was the president of the student body, and I was the chairman of the university council. And we were debate partners as well.

Virtually every weekend, David and I would travel to debate tournaments at schools all up and down the Eastern Seaboard. We worked tirelessly at debate, staying up until three or four in the morning after debate tournaments analyzing how we could have done better. And, over time, we did well. By our senior year we ended up as the top-ranked team in the United States. I was the number-one ranked speaker in the country, and David was number two.

One of the reasons David and I liked debate is that it was a meritocracy. As a Black man and an Hispanic man, we both faced regular aspersions from other students and even professors that we were only at Princeton because of affirmative action. Ironically (or perhaps not), most of those slights came from supercilious liberals who were offended that two minorities would dare to be conservative. Debate largely eliminated those concerns: two teams walked into a room, and whichever team performed better won.

My sophomore year, I was the chairman of the Cliosophic Party, the conservative party in our college debating society. David was my whip. The Clios, as we were called, comprised half of the American Whig-Cliosophic Society, an organization that had been formed from the merger of two parties originally formed in the 1760s: the American Whig Society, founded by James Madison (our fourth president and the father of our Constitution), and the Cliosophic Society, founded by William Paterson (later the second governor of New Jersey, a signer of the Constitution, and an associate justice of the Supreme Court). Among the first Clios was Aaron Burr (who was vice president to Thomas Jefferson, and responsible for the death of Alexander Hamilton).

Today, the Whigs are liberals and the Clios are either conservative or libertarian. I found it ironic that I couldn't lead the Whigs, given that I agree emphatically with virtually every idea espoused by James Madison, but the party he founded had over time abandoned Madison's political philosophy and embraced the Left.

For the last debate David and I had leading the Clios, we proposed that "Princeton should abolish racial affirmative action." We pointed out that racial discrimination is wrong, it is pernicious, and it leads to harmful stereotypes. Instead, we argued, Princeton should shift to giving a preference for low-income students. That would likewise result in a diverse student body, and it would recognize students who had overcome real adversity, *without* discriminating based on race. At the end of our debate, all the students who attended voted. Even though Princeton was a very liberal school, that night at least, the students voted with us by a significant margin.

Late in our senior year, David and I both thought it would be fun to compete in a "hybrid" tournament where the two members of each team came from different schools. I teamed up with a fellow named "Slash," who went to UMBC, the University of Maryland, Baltimore County. "Slash," who wore long hair and a beard, got his nickname because he wore a leather jacket festooned with razor blades, "one for every woman who'd broken up with him and cut his heart." He was a very talented debater, and very much from the other side of the political aisle from me. We debated under the team name "Armageddon A."

In the fifth round of the tournament, Slash and I came up against David and his partner. We were the ones presenting the affirmative case. In college debate, sometimes the opposition team will whine about the side of the argument they have to defend, saying it's unfair, it's a truism, it's a tautology. Neither David nor I liked rounds that consisted of nothing but whining, so we had adopted an unusual practice to eliminate it: at the very beginning of each debate round, we would give the other side the choice of which side of the debate to take. Typically, a minute or so into my opening speech, I'd turn to the opposition and ask them, "Which side do you want?" Once they chose, the whining stopped.

So Slash and I presented the following case: "The United States is/is not the greatest country in the history of the world." And we allowed David and his partner to choose the side they wanted. David immediately chose "is," which forced me to argue that the United States was *not* the greatest country ever. Before the round, Slash had expressed to me that he considered the affirmative proposition to be a "falsism"; he believed it was obviously incorrect and indeed indefensible to say that the United States was the greatest, because he considered our country so deeply and inherently flawed.

There was some irony that David—a Jamaican, and not an American—would choose to argue the side he did. Afterwards, he laughed and said he had picked that side because he knew how thoroughly and completely I believed it, and he wanted to force me to argue a position I hated and fully disagreed with. And, I'm proud to say, I lost that round; David and his partner mopped the floor with us, as they argued compellingly for America's greatness.

◆ ◆ ◆

Encountering ideas you disagree with, even passionately, used to be an integral part of education. It certainly was when I was in college. Though I suspect many people would never guess it, I always respected the left-wing radicals I attended school with—at least the ones who appeared to have thought through their arguments in a serious way, and to have considered the real-world implications of their ideas. In fact, two of my closest friends at Princeton were the successive heads of the liberal Whig party, even though we disagreed on just about every major issue of the day.

At the time, of course, the phenomenon known as "political correctness" was still in its infancy. The ideology had not yet made its way from Harvard and Yale down to campuses across the nation. That is, students who called themselves "liberal" at the time were still somewhat tethered to reality. They could reliably define basic terms such as "woman" if called upon to do so, and you didn't have to worry about being hauled into the dean's office for messing up their they/them pronouns during a debate. It might surprise some people to learn that liberals in the late '80s *could* debate without breaking down in tears or resorting to accusations that their opponents were "mansplaining," committing "microaggressions," or "enacting White supremacy" by disagreeing with them too vigorously.

My liberal classmates and I could go back and forth for hours about everything under the sun—voting rights, economics, even the politics of films we'd seen recently. Nothing was off the table, and everything was permissible so long as it was backed up with reason, data, and a good argument. Usually, after a long night of verbal jousting in Whig Hall, I would call my opponent a communist, he'd call me a fascist, and then we'd all laugh and go grab a beer. We understood that no matter how many jabs were hurled in either direction, a debate over ideas was no reason to end a friendship. In fact, debates of this kind were what kept our friendships interesting.

Being a college debater meant not just that you would encounter ideas that you might find abhorrent; it also meant that at times you were forced to argue the other side, to articulate persuasively the reasons for a position with which you strongly disagreed.

Reflecting on this experience so many years later, I decided that I would speak to the graduating students at UC Berkeley about diversity—not the identity-obsessed, check-the-boxes kind of diversity that would soon sweep colleges and corporate boardrooms across the country, but *intellectual* diversity. I wanted to impress upon these students the importance of speaking with and to people with whom they vehemently disagreed, and of listening to viewpoints that were radically different from their own. Only through rigorous argument and respectful dialogue could they ever hope to persuade anyone that their views were correct.

As it turned out, this was a message that many students desperately needed to hear.

Sometime in early May, when I was putting the finishing touches on my address, I learned that a small group of students at Berkeley had begun an online protest against me on a new website called Facebook. I had no idea how to log onto this website at the time, so I asked a friend to create an account so I could see what all the fuss was about.

Logging on for the first time, I found a group titled "Official Protest to Remove Ted Cruz as the Commencement Speaker," which is still public as of this writing. The group's main objections were listed at the top of the screen, written out as a letter to the university's political science department.

"Mr. Cruz stands for everything that the fine institution of higher learning, UC Berkeley does not," they wrote. "The accomplishments that Mr. Cruz are so proud of are not accomplishments that we the students of UC Berkeley respect and would like to honor with the tremendous privilege of speaking at the UC Berkeley political science department's graduation ceremony. Therefore the students of UC Berkeley respectfully request the reconsideration of Mr. Cruz as the political science key note commencement speaker."

From there, they listed a few of my "accomplishments" (sarcastic quotation marks theirs, not mine), first noting that I had worked with the George W. Bush campaign in Florida after the election of 2000, a race that was decided by the Supreme Court after multiple Florida recounts. For this work, they accused me of "helping to disenfranchise millions, upon millions of American voters and install an unelected President."[2]

Today, of course, any self-respecting member of the Left would call such rhetoric a dangerous denial of election results, and an "assault on Democracy." But back then, it was a common talking point among young, deluded Democrats—and old ones with high-rating cable news shows, for that matter—who couldn't deal with the fact that their candidate had lost the race in a stunning upset.

The remainder of the post was an attack on the work I had done as the solicitor general of Texas. Oddly enough, the students chose to include only cases in which I had prevailed at the Supreme Court, which was an interesting touch given the group's overall aim.

The list of complaints, reprinted in full:

His representation of the State of Texas includes:
* Successfully defending the constitutionality of the Texas Ten Commandments monument before the Fifth Circuit and the U.S. Supreme Court; (explicit violation of the first amendment)
* Authoring a U.S. Supreme Court brief on behalf of all fifty States and successfully defending the words "under God" in the Pledge of Allegiance; (another violation of the first amendment)
* Serving as lead counsel for the State and successfully defending the multiple litigation challenges to the 2003 Texas congressional redistricting plan in district courts and before the U.S. Supreme Court; (violation of each citizen's right to fairly elected and representative government)
* Successfully defending the constitutionality of the Texas Sexually Violent Predator Civil Commitment law before the

Texas Supreme Court; (violation of the constitutional protection against cruel and unusual punishment)

* Successfully representing Texas before the U.S. Supreme Court in a case resisting efforts by the International Court of Justice to order reconsideration of U.S. death penalty jurisprudence. (Another violation of the constitutional right from freedom of cruel and unusual punishment)[3]

I suppose I should note that while I did indeed do all of these things, more or less, the statements in parentheses about how my actions violated the United States Constitution are not accurate. If my positions *had* been unconstitutional, one might think the United States Supreme Court would have said so at the time. (They tend to be sticklers about that sort of thing.)

Aside from the law and politics, there seemed to be a more general distaste for me and everything I stood for.

One student summed it all up rather eloquently, writing: "i almost cried when i found out this guy is speaking at our graduation. he sucks."

Scrolling around, I could see that a few other students had voiced objections to my speech—in one case, on the grounds that I was "non-famous"—but there wasn't much more to it than that.[4] It seemed that a few students had gotten together, written a virtual letter to the administration, and received nothing in response. I had seen more than my fair share of similar letters during my own career as a student, so I didn't think much of it.

I was also gratified that one liberal Hispanic woman—who had been a student of mine when I taught Supreme Court litigation at UT Law School—posted something to the effect of, "You've got this all wrong. I'm very liberal, and I disagree with Ted on just about everything, but when I was his student he was very respectful of opposing views and ensured we had a full and fair opportunity to discuss and debate what we believed and what was right." Alas, I can't quote her comment verbatim, because the Berkeley students were such passionate believers in free speech that they deleted her comment the very next day.

I hoped their dismay wouldn't spill over into the real world and become a serious, in-person protest. When I mentioned the small Facebook group to my wife, Heidi, she laughed and reassured me, sort of.

"Oh my goodness," she said. "You're not nearly important enough to protest."

As I would learn many times throughout the years, there are few things better for a person's humility (involuntary or otherwise) than marriage (and children).

A few days later, Heidi and I arrived on Berkeley's campus and found that the protest had indeed become a little bigger than anticipated. A small crowd of students held signs on the street outside the Greek Theater, chanting some slogan that was supposed to scare the university officials into disinviting me. I felt bad for the parents, friends, and other relatives who had come out to see students graduate in peace, but I decided not to say so in my speech.

Instead, I stepped up to the stage, which was built to resemble an actual amphitheater where Greek tragedies would have been staged, and began with the phrase "Friends, Romans, countrymen, lend me your ears," a reference to Mark Antony's famous speech in Shakespeare's *Julius Caesar.* There was a small wave of laughter from the crowd, presumably from people who wanted to show that they understood the reference. (No one seemed to care that I was mixing my Greek and Roman history, which made me hopeful right from the start.)

Around the room, I could see the students who were unhappy at my presence quite clearly; they were instantly recognizable by their slumped shoulders, their crossed arms, and the exaggerated scowls on their faces.

I decided to aim every joke in the speech (there were several) right at those folks.

Right away, I praised the students of Berkeley for their university's long tradition of student activism. This, I could tell, surprised many people in the crowd. I'm sure many of them believed that I thought they were a bunch of hippies who should be thrown in jail.

But I didn't.

Quite the opposite, in fact.

For the next few minutes, I implored the students not to give up that spirit of activism, but rather to nurture it and preserve it as they grew older. Too often, I said, when students grow up and get a job, a mortgage, and more responsibilities, that fire they once felt to change the world fades into middle-aged acquiescence and complacency. I had seen it happen to people too many times, and it was a tragedy every time, even when the politics of the person in question were in direct contradiction to my own.

However, I emphasized to the students that there was a caveat. To paraphrase Spider-Man's Uncle Ben, with great activism comes great responsibility—in this case, a responsibility not to judge our enemies too harshly, and to keep our minds open to opposing points of view.

"Too often," I said, "we tend to characterize those who disagree with us as either stupid or evil. We believe that our opponent is either too dumb to know the right answer, or that they know what is right but they want people to suffer, making them evil. Are there some evil people? Yes. Are there some stupid people? Of course. But most people don't fall into either of those two categories."

I went on to say that until these students could take the issue they cared most passionately about and understand how someone of good intelligence, good faith, and good morals could look at that very same issue and come to the exact opposite conclusion—until they could genuinely understand how their mother might come to the exact opposite conclusion from the one they had—they would be utterly ineffective at persuading anyone—in law, in politics, in business, or in life.

Above all, I implored them to go into the world with a sense of open-mindedness and generosity, to treat others with decency and respect.

By the end of the speech, I noticed that a few of the intentionally aggrieved people in the audience were beginning to crack smiles. Once or twice, I saw students laugh at a joke involuntarily, then catch themselves and double down on the scowling, as if to signal to their protestor buddies in the crowd that they really didn't think whatever I'd said was funny. But there was applause at the end nonetheless, and after the speech I had the pleasure of speaking with several students who seemed to appreciate the importance of civility, argument, and listening to people on the other side with an open mind.

When I got back to my office in Texas, a few of my colleagues asked how the speech went. Several of them were surprised to learn that the protest had amounted to very little and that I'd been able to deliver my full speech to polite applause without much trouble.

Looking back, I can see why they might have been concerned. Just a few months before I gave my own speech, Senator John McCain was invited to give a commencement address at the New School in New York City, an institution that ranked just behind Berkeley in terms of how far-left it was at the time. When he stepped onstage to speak, the audience erupted into a chorus of boos and insults, making it very difficult for the senator to get through his remarks.

Even in the small Facebook group about my own speech, a student from UMass Amherst had commented on a successful protest of Andy Card, the former chief of staff to President George W. Bush, who was set to receive an honorary degree during the university's commencement. "We've already had two large rallies," he wrote, "the second one with about 500 people, shutting down the entire administrative building!"[5]

In the years to come, the instances of Republicans giving speeches at colleges would shrink almost to nothing. There was good reason for this. People were surprised in 2014 when the students of Rutgers protested Condoleezza Rice's scheduled commencement address so vigorously that she backed out of giving it—not for anything she might say during the speech, but simply because she had worked for a Republican president. The fact that she was an historic figure, and the first African-American woman ever to serve as secretary of state, mattered not one whit to the angry mob.

Even at universities in middle America, where you might expect students to be slightly more open-minded than on the coasts, the reception for anyone who leans even slightly conservative can be extremely hostile. When Cynthia Lummis, a first-term senator from Wyoming (and a good friend of mine), was invited to deliver the commencement address at the University of Wyoming, I'm sure she believed she would be speaking to a sensible crowd. She quickly learned that this was not the case when she commented, almost as an aside, "Even fundamental scientific truths, such as the existence of two sexes, male and female, are subject to challenge these days." Suddenly, jeers and boos came from every corner of the stadium, right there in bright-red Wyoming,[6] indicating that a) this basic scientific fact was indeed under attack, and b) the campuses of our major universities had become hostile places for anyone who held even the mildest conservative views (such as believing that women actually exist).

When I first arrived in the Senate in 2013, it was almost a spring rite of passage that my colleagues and I would be asked to deliver commencement addresses at colleges all over the country. That first year, I gave the commencement address at Hillsdale College, a wonderful, small liberal arts school in Michigan that leans significantly more conservative than most. In the two years that followed, I gave commencement speeches at Texas Tech University and Stephen F. Austin State University.

But in the years since then the invitations have disappeared. Likewise for all of my Republican colleagues. Even though we have all been elected by majorities of people in our respective states and our views align with at least half the people in this country, we have been deemed by the academy too dangerous to put in front of the average crowd at a university commencement ceremony.

In other words, the protestors have won, effectively exercising a heckler's veto over half the country. If we want to keep colleges safe from tyranny and censorship—if we want them actually to educate rather than indoctrinate—it's critical that we override this effective veto and begin speaking and listening to one another again.

First, though, we need to figure out what the hell happened to get us here.

Mutations

Looking back on the small protest that occurred when I stepped onto the campus of UC Berkeley in 2007, I'm filled with a strange sense of nostalgia. It's not because I liked getting protested or having an online group dedicated to making me go away (although I'm sure there are many more of those today). Rather, it's because, on that day, the system worked exactly the way it was supposed to. A group of angry radical students tried (albeit not very hard) to get me disinvited from giving a speech because they didn't like my ideas, the university administrators refused to succumb to the mob, and I came anyway, because that's what grown-ups who've been invited to give speeches do.

Once these students actually heard my ideas—which, fittingly, happened to be about the importance of listening to those who disagree with you—at least some of them may have come around; even some of the ones who weren't persuaded maybe, just maybe, realized that I was not the great Republican Satan they had believed me to be. Then they graduated, I left campus, and we all moved on with our lives.

Today, this sequence of events has become incredibly rare—and I use "incredibly" here in its original sense, meaning "literally impossible to believe." Looking around at the shout-downs and outbreaks of violence that regularly occur on college campuses today, one is shocked not only by the intolerance and arrogance of these student protestors but by just how much power they wield. We have reached a point where even a small group of students, often even smaller than the few hundred students who wanted to stop me from coming to Berkeley, can successfully cancel an event, silence a speaker, and—most important—send a message to all similar speakers that coming to a college campus is simply not worth the trouble.

Consider what happened at Yale University in 2016, when a group of student protestors successfully drove a professor named Erika Christakis out of her job because of an email she had sent criticizing the efforts of students to erect a "safe space" to protect them from "offensive" Halloween costumes (an email which, it shouldn't surprise anyone to learn, was extremely respectful). During that incident, groups of students gathered outside on the quad in an attempt to get Christakis fired and screamed in the face of her husband, who had come out to try to make peace with the mob.[7]

Even when these protests are not successful in shutting down the events they oppose, they can cause enough trouble to intimidate people into silence. I'm sure that anyone who watched protestors harass the many conservative activists who had their events shut down on campuses—from Ben Shapiro and Michael Knowles to Steven Crowder and Charlie Kirk, all of whom were forced to cancel speaking engagements because of the mob—got the message that similar views would not be welcome on campus anytime soon.

You'll notice, of course, that this intimidation only goes in one direction. Despite searching for many years, I've been unable to find an instance of a left-leaning speaker—Elizabeth Warren, for instance, or

Ibram X. Kendi, the author of a book on how to be an "antiracist"—who has been attacked or intimidated by a right-wing mob on a college campus. If that ever did happen, I'm sure that the Biden Department of Justice would have a team of federal agents, all armed with machine guns, rolling down the campus's quad in armored vehicles before the protestors could even raise their signs.

It's worth stopping for a moment to consider how the current state of affairs transpired. In other words, how did the major universities of this country—the places where students once went to learn new things and have their old ideas about the world challenged and tested—descend into left-wing mob rule, right there in plain sight, while we were all watching? How did it become impossible for speakers and professors who lean even slightly to the right to express their ideas without fear that they'll be shouted down, canceled, or even physically harmed?

The answer is that the Cultural Marxists deliberately decided to begin their "slow march through the institutions" of the United States at universities—places that have historically been siloed off from the rest of society, where even the worst ideas can develop and mutate without being subject to any outside influence. The Cultural Marxists have been able to spread these ideas largely thanks to an administrative structure (which they control) that typically protects them from the consequences of their censorship, intolerance, and abuse.

It has never been a big secret that university professors tend to lean left. I'm sure most people wouldn't be surprised to learn that many of them see no problem describing themselves as outright socialists and Marxists. Given that these people typically have life tenure—removing some of the pressure to make money that drives the rest of us—that is only natural.

But for most of the twentieth century, college professors at least understood that the objective of education was to...well, educate. They would take young people who didn't yet know how to think critically and give them the skills that they needed to succeed in life, get a job, and become productive members of society. In some disciplines, this involved filling students' heads with facts and equations, then rigorously testing the ability of those students to use the equations and recall the facts. In others, professors would show their students how to construct arguments and persuade people, then assign papers and essays to see how well the students could do it.

But the coin of the realm, so to speak, was ideas. Professors were supposed to take kids from all over the country who hadn't previously heard of thinkers such as Herodotus, Aristotle, and Tolstoy and present the ideas of those thinkers in a way that was neutral and, ideally, intellectually stimulating. Some of those ideas would come as a shock. Students who'd come to the East Coast after a childhood spent at some hippie commune in San Francisco would be forced to wrestle with the ideas of free-market economists such as Adam Smith and Milton Friedman, while the sons and daughters of East Coast bankers would be confronted with Karl Marx, Friedrich Engels, and the legion of left-wing imitators who came in their wake.

Ideally, the professors would not push the ideas of one group over another—or even one thinker over another. Even academics who'd spent their entire careers studying a single year in the life of the poet John Milton, for instance, would generally not claim that Milton was a better poet than Shakespeare; they would simply present the works of both men, give the students the tools to analyze and interpret those works, and then get out of the way.

One notable exception to this rule was the field of economics, a discipline that sits somewhere between the hard sciences—given its reliance on numbers, equations, and hard data—and the social sciences, given how much it also relies on theory and unknowable variables such as human behavior. On the rare occasions that well-known professors of economics actually taught undergraduates (rather than delegating that work to teaching assistants), it wasn't uncommon for them to push a particular point of view or fully formed philosophy from the beginning.

A handful of right-wing academics would tell the story of economics as a struggle of the free market against government constraints and central planning, claiming that a free market combined with only occasional intervention from the government was the way to run an effective society. This philosophy, which became known as "neoliberalism," was popular at schools such as the University of Chicago, which trained some of the most prominent free-market thinkers in the world.

On the other side, there were Marxist economists who would teach students that the opposite was true. In the seminar rooms of Berkeley and Harvard, students learned the story of economics as a continual battle between the haves and have-nots. The bourgeoisie owned the factories and the "means of production," while the proletariat were forced to work in those factories forever, making too little money and slowly dying inside every day. The goal of economics was to help the proletariat—also known as the "workers of the world," the Left's first class of permanent victims—to seize the means of production by armed revolution, uniting all the workers of the world in the common cause of toppling the oppressor class.

By the middle of the twentieth century, multiple governments around the world had been organized around this principle. From the Soviet Union to China to Cuba to North Korea, everywhere that Marxism was implemented in the real world the result was poverty, suffering, torture, imprisonment, and death.

For a long time, countries that had adopted Marxist principles were nevertheless able to hide the rot at the core of this ideology. They were able to cover up the horrible effects that central planning and a command economy have on a society. But they couldn't keep it hidden forever. In the late 1980s, when I was coming to the end of my time at Princeton, the Soviet Union—then, by far the most significant and powerful communist country in the world—began to crumble. On December 31, 1991, the Soviet Union voted itself out of existence, leaving the United States with its capitalist economy as the lone remaining superpower in the world.

For Marxist academics, this should have been the ultimate ideological death blow. The collapse of the most important country to have implemented their twisted, wrongheaded ideology was as close as economists ever get to the kind of hard proof more typical of hard science and mathematics. One system, capitalism, had produced the largest expansion of wealth and opportunity in the history of civilization, while the opposite system, communism, had led repeatedly to totalitarianism, corruption, mass starvation, and financial ruin.

The game, so to speak, was over.

In the private sector, such a "proof of concept" failure would result in the people responsible filing for bankruptcy, packing up their offices, and moving on to other things. But that's not what happened at our universities in the late 1980s and early 1990s. Rather than shifting gears and finding something else to study—or at least another historical figure on whom they could base their entire philosophies—Marxist professors grew more emboldened than ever.

In October of 1989, less than a month before the fall of the Berlin Wall knocked out one of the last major vestiges of communism, a reporter named Felicity Barringer traveled to college campuses on behalf of the *New York Times*, intending to investigate what would happen to all the professors and graduate students who had been pushing Marxism for years. The answer, she found, was that these people were getting better jobs and bigger offices, becoming more and more accepted by their traditionally liberal peers.

Remarkably, it was a time when the *New York Times* was still practicing journalism. On October 25, 1989, Barringer's article ran under the headline "The Mainstreaming of Marxism in U.S. Colleges." In it she noted that "as Karl Marx's ideological heirs in Communist nations struggle to transform his political legacy, his intellectual heirs on American campuses have virtually completed their own transformation from brash, beleaguered outsiders to assimilated academic insiders." However, the study also noted that the "excitement" about Marxism "[had] not brought increased enrollment in courses that focus on Marxist analysis.... Where Marxism is thriving, scholars say, is less in social science courses, where there is a possibility of practical application, than in the abstract world of literary criticism."[8]

Rather than pushing the classic form of Marxism that sought to overthrow capitalism, the new Marxists decided to get more theoretical and abstract, applying Marx's ideas to stranger things every year. The first time these strange ideas found their expression was in the phenomenon known as "political correctness," which swept campuses in the early 1990s. Anyone who was ever told to call manhole covers "personhole covers" in order to root out sexism in our language will remember how silly this first foray into identity politics was.

But to its proponents at the time, there was nothing silly about it. I still remember the seriousness with which many on the Left began to demand absolute conformity when it came to matters of political correctness. And I recall being in classrooms at Harvard Law School, which I attended from 1992 to 1995, and listening to professors actively pushing their ideology. My torts professor, for example, a young, earnest liberal who dressed up socialism in the language of economics, argued to us 1Ls that if a person made the moronic choice to use a lawn mower to shave—and he was horribly injured as a result—then the company who manufactured the lawn mower should be forced to pay for that idiot's medical care because it was a big bad corporation and therefore could better bear the costs. Even then, that sounded pretty loopy.

And yet there were some left-leaning members of the faculty who still believed in the principles of free speech and open debate. I learned this quite early in my law school career, when I walked into my criminal law classroom and first met Alan Dershowitz, then and now one of the most famous law professors in the world. Right away, Professor Dershowitz—or "Dersh," as he was known to his students and fellow faculty members—impressed the class with his dry wit, vast intellectual capacity, and deep love for argument. As best I can recall, whenever a student in one of his classes would begin a sentence with "I feel like," Dersh would interrupt almost immediately.

"Oh," he'd say, angling his head and raising his voice. "You feel, do you? You're emoting? I'm sorry. I thought we were in law school. I thought we were learning to marshal an argument using facts and logic, not merely…feelings."

To this day, the disdain with which Professor Dershowitz pronounced this final word echoes in my mind. So do the arguments that he and I often had, in the classroom and then back in his office when class had wrapped up for the day. To him, argument was both an art form and a blood sport. Although he was a passionate, bleeding-heart liberal, fond of going on long tirades against conservative justices on the Supreme Court in the middle of his lectures, he never shied away from an intellectual challenge from students who disagreed with him.

In fact, from what I observed, there was nothing Dersh hated more than a liberal student who agreed with him on substance but could not articulate why he or she agreed.

In the spring of 1995, two years after I had taken Professor Dershowitz's class, I learned that a group of conservative students had come together to challenge him. After hearing Dersh go on one of his many tirades against Justice Antonin Scalia, one of the most brilliant and conservative justices in the history of the Supreme Court, these students had written a letter to Justice Scalia himself. They let the justice know that one of their professors, Alan Dershowitz, was constantly attacking his opinions in the classroom, and they asked if he might come to Harvard and debate the liberal professor in their classroom.

To everyone's surprise, Justice Scalia accepted.

At the time, I was dating a woman two years behind me in law school, who learned that this debate was happening. Knowing that I had an eight-hour written take-home final exam on the afternoon that the debate was scheduled to take place—and knowing further that I would have been stupid enough to skip one hour of that exam to go see Justice Scalia debate my old professor—she managed to keep the whole thing secret from me. But she did smuggle in a tape recorder, preserving the debate for posterity. (As a condition of his acceptance, Justice Scalia had insisted that there be no media in the room.)

Listening to these two giants of the law go at it for about sixty minutes, I was amazed, not only at their ability to craft and counter arguments, but at the extent to which they could listen respectfully to one another, carrying on a contentious conversation without ever resorting to name-calling, cheap politics, or ad hominem attacks. I'm sure that sitting in the audience and watching this conversation take place was enlightening for the hundred or so students who were fortunate enough to see it live. Knowing the capacity of both men to persuade and reason, I wouldn't be surprised if a few liberals in the audience became a bit more conservative, and vice versa, that day.

Unfortunately, events like this one became much less common as the left wing of Harvard Law School drifted even further to the left. This is something that Alan Dershowitz, who has since become a good friend, saw coming before most people. As a man of the Left, he seemed to be deeply concerned at the increasing radicalism on his own side. Even when I was in his class, he would often remark on this strange fact.

He would say something like, "It's funny. Almost anywhere in the country, I would be in the most liberal 1 percent of people on almost any issue. But here at Harvard Law School, compared to some of the faculty, I am practically a Republican."

Sadly, Dersh was more right than he knew. A year after I took his class, I joined the staff of the Harvard Law Review, where I was surprised to find several outspoken Marxists. These people would talk, usually without any hint of embarrassment, about how much they hoped for a communist government in America one day.

But as bad as it was at the time, the neo-Marxist ideology was still largely contained on the college campuses where it had started. Only occasionally did we see it spread to government, entertainment, or other forms of media. If Marxism was a virus, to use a popular analogy, it remained "in the lab" for about two decades, causing the occasional flare-up that made national headlines and died down quickly.

Perhaps this is why, when we began to see evidence of increasingly radical and violent behavior by left-wing mobs on campuses near the end of President Obama's second term, most commentators dismissed it as just another passing fad. When the first mobs formed over "microaggressions," for instance, serious people compared them to the student protests that had been happening on campuses for decades. I must admit that even when I saw the videos of students screaming at deans and demanding "safe spaces" where they could hide away from evil members of the Bush administration, I didn't think the hysteria was likely to spread much beyond college campuses.

I remembered the student activism I had witnessed during my own time in college and law school, and even thought back to the vivid portraits of student radicalism I had read in works such as *Demons* by Fyodor Dostoyevsky, which paints a satirical portrait of crazed activists on a university campus.

But it soon became clear that this new group of campus radicals was much different from anything that had come before. In part, this was explained by the advent of new social media sites such as Twitter, which allowed echo chambers and outrage mobs to form with a speed that had previously been unthinkable. Suddenly, it was possible for a group like the one that had protested me at Berkeley to go from ninety members to nine thousand members in a matter of hours. It was also possible for the members of the group to whip each other up into a frenzy using the language of neo-Marxism and social justice, claiming that the presence of a Republican on campus would do literal harm to vulnerable communities.

The virus of Cultural Marxism had mutated and spread.

The Juice and the Squeeze

On the afternoon of March 9, 2023, a federal judge named Stuart Kyle Duncan arrived on the campus of Stanford University, where he had been invited to speak by a group of students at the law school. Like any conservative speaker who arrives on a college campus in the year 2023, I'm sure that somewhere in the back of his mind, Judge Duncan anticipated that there might be a protest of some kind. I'm sure he'd seen videos of conservatives being shouted down in seminar rooms or read reports of speeches by right-leaning thinkers being canceled for fear of mob violence.

Still, I'm sure he had no idea what was coming.

In terms of jurisprudence, Judge Duncan was not some far-right provocateur. He was a sitting judge on the U.S. Court of Appeals for the Fifth Circuit. If anything, the opinions he had delivered from the bench had been well-reasoned and relatively mild. Before he was appointed a judge by President Trump and confirmed by the Senate, he had been an accomplished litigator, arguing dozens of cases in appellate courts across the country, including two before the U.S. Supreme Court. He was a sitting federal judge, not a man who posed a serious threat to anyone.

But you never would have known it from the scene he walked into at Stanford.

Walking through the halls of the building where he was scheduled to speak, Judge Duncan passed a group of students dressed all in black. They lined the hallways on either side of him, subjecting the judge to a strange walk of shame not unlike something you might see on *Game of Thrones*. As he passed them, they yelled vile things at him. According to the president of the Federalist Society's Stanford chapter, one student shouted, "We hope your daughters get raped."

By the time Judge Duncan reached the room where he was going to deliver the speech—modestly titled "The Fifth Circuit in Conversation with the Supreme Court: Covid, Guns, and Twitter"—he must have realized that he would not be able to give his prepared remarks. After what he had been forced to endure in the hallways outside the room, I'm not sure anyone should have expected him to do so. Still, according to reports from those who were present, he tried as best he could.

But it was no use. While some seats in the room were filled with students eager to hear what the judge had to say, most of them were taken up by protestors. There were also dozens of flyers on the wall, most of which shouted some variation of "YOU SHOULD BE ASHAMED." This was nothing new on college campuses. Neither were the high-pitched screams that began as soon as Judge Duncan opened his mouth to speak (again, presumably to deliver a mild-mannered academic address on important legal issues of our time).

It was a scene that, sadly, has become all too familiar over the past decade. A group of students who had organized primarily on social media came together to shout down a speaker whose views they found objectionable. As they did so, they reinforced the mistaken idea—which, thanks to the spread of neo-Marxist wokeness, was already quite strong—that this speech was not only bad or incorrect; instead, it was literally *harmful* to them and the people they cared about.

This language of "harm" ran all through the heckles that flew at Judge Duncan from the crowd. One student claimed that she felt "unsafe" listening to the talk (which, by the way, she had voluntarily attended).[9]

This is a fantasy—nothing more than wish fulfilment on the part of these woke neo-Marxists to portray themselves as victims engaged in an eternal struggle against their oppressors. Despite, I might add, living in the most affluent society in the history of the world, attending one of the most elite law schools in America, sitting in an air-conditioned room, and listening to a talk that *no one forced them to attend in the first place.*

I hardly need to point out that if this had gone the other way—if Justice Sonia Sotomayor, for instance, had come to give a talk at Stanford Law School and members of the Federalist Society had screamed that she was "literally harming them" with her opinions—the entire campus would enter lockdown mode. The names and pictures of every person who had screamed at her would appear in the next day's *New York Times*, and they would be tarred as racists and bigots for the rest of their lives.

As usual, free speech does exist on college campuses, but it exists only for people who express the pre-approved leftist views shared by the college faculty and administrators—which, as many people have pointed out, makes a mockery of the whole concept.

Still, Stanford does employ countless administrators who are supposed to ensure that its free speech code is not broken. A code that, by the way, can still be found on the university's website. It reads, verbatim:

It is a violation of University policy for a member of the faculty, staff, or student body to:
Prevent or disrupt the effective carrying out of a University function or approved activity, such as lectures, meetings,

interviews, ceremonies, the conduct of University business
in a University office, and public events;

Obstruct the legitimate movement of any person about
the campus or in any University building or facility.[10]

Judge Duncan knew that there had to have been some policy like
this that should have prevented him from being shouted down. That is
why he asked for the intervention of a university administrator almost
as soon as the shouting began—a decision he came to regret almost
immediately, for reasons anyone who watches the footage of this catastrophe on YouTube can see.[11]

Unfortunately, the administrator who arrived was Tirien Steinbach,
the law school's associate dean for diversity, equity, and inclusion.
Rather than doing her job as a representative of the university, following
Stanford's free speech code, and telling the offending students to either
shut up or leave the room—thus allowing the university's invited guest
to speak—she stepped up to the podium and began to deliver her own
speech, a seven-minute diatribe that she had carefully written out for
the occasion.

A partial transcript of that speech, which was interrupted several
times by snapping fingers from the students, is below:

> STEINBACH: I want to give you space to finish your remarks
> too, Judge Duncan. I'm also uncomfortable because many of
> the people in the room here I've come to care for and in my
> role at this university my job is to create a space of belonging
> for all people in this institution. And that is hard and messy
> and not easy and the answers are not black or white or right
> or wrong. This is actually part of the creation of belonging.
> And it doesn't feel comfortable and it doesn't always feel safe.
> But there are always places of safety. And there is always

an intention from this administration to make sure you all can be in a place where you feel fully you can be here, learn, grow into the amazing advocates and leaders and lawyers that you're going to be.

I'm also uncomfortable because it is my job to say: You are invited into this space. You are absolutely welcome in this space. In this space where people learn and, again, live. I really do, wholeheartedly welcome you. Because me [*sic*] and many people in this administration do absolutely believe in free speech. We believe that it is necessary. We believe that the way to address speech that feels abhorrent, that feels harmful, that literally denies the humanity of people, that one way to do that is with more speech and not less. And not to shut you down or censor you or censor the student group that invited you here. That is hard. That is uncomfortable. And that is a policy and a principle that I think is worthy of defending, even in this time. Even in this time. And again I still ask: Is the juice worth the squeeze?

DUNCAN: What does that mean? I don't understand…

STEINBACH: I mean is it worth the pain that this causes and the division that this causes? Do you have something so incredibly important to say about Twitter and guns and COVID that that is worth this impact on the division of these people who have sat next to each other for years, who are going through what is the battle of law school together, so that they can go out into the world and be advocates. And this is the division it's caused. When I say "Is the juice worth the squeeze?" That's what I'm asking. Is this worth it? And I hope so, and I'll stay for your remarks to see, because I do want to know your perspective. I am not, you know, in the business of wanting to either shut down speech, because I do know that if they come for this group today, they will come for the group that I am part of tomorrow.[12]

Even coming from a DEI administrator, these words—and the whole stunt in general—defy belief. Rather than doing her job and creating an environment where a federal judge could give the talk that he had been invited to give, Tirien Steinbach used her platform to give her own thoughts on the matter, repeatedly wondering aloud if the "juice" (a substantive lecture from a sitting federal judge) was worth the "squeeze" (a few upset law students who believed the world would end if they allowed the lecture to continue).

The answer, of course, is yes. At all times and in all places, *yes*.

Steinbach referred to "pain and suffering" that had been endured by this community for days leading up to the planned speech. What she failed to mention, of course, was that nearly all of the agitation had been caused by the protestors themselves, who seemed far more interested in Judge Duncan's talk than most of the rest of the campus. In the week before the speech, for instance, strange flyers began appearing on the walls of campus. Some of them were ordinary protest signs, listing Judge Duncan's judicial opinions that the students disagreed with—no different, really, from the digital list of complaints that Berkeley students had posted about me in the spring of 2007. But other flyers were not so ordinary. In one, dozens of copies of which were posted around campus, the protestors included the photographs of every member of Stanford's Federalist Society chapter they could find, then printed them with the students' names underneath. The headline of the flyer was "You Should Be Ashamed."[13]

Again, I hardly need to point out what would happen if a conservative student group printed up flyers with the names and photographs of the members of some left-leaning group—the Trans-Only Quidditch Team, for instance—and plastered those flyers all around campus.

There would be a line of civil rights attorneys a mile long outside Stanford's campus within minutes.

But Steinbach's prewritten address, condescendingly haranguing Judge Duncan, reveals the view prevalent at colleges when it comes to free speech on campus—and, more troublingly, free speech in general. In short, they believe that free speech is permissible only if that speech is not going to hurt the feelings of any protected class that has been deemed sufficiently "oppressed" by the woke neo-Marxists.

In recent years, this belief has led to some strange situations, and some very confusing "woke algebra." Take the case of Erika López Prater, an adjunct professor of art at Hamline University in St. Paul, Minnesota. During one of her lectures on the art of antiquity, she referred to several depictions of the Prophet Muhammad, which were once extremely common all over the world. While discussing one of these depictions, an image of the piece flashed behind her as part of a PowerPoint presentation. Several Muslim students—whose religion forbids depictions of the Prophet—complained to the school, and Professor López Prater was put on leave, then fired.

All it took was a few complaints, and the university caved.[14] That, sadly, has become the sensible thing to do according to the new rules of the woke. If the university administrators *hadn't* caved, they might have endured days of protests and boycotts—or even threats of physical violence—after which they might have just had to cave anyway.

So, rather than standing up for free speech, a university in the United States of America—a nation where freedom of religion is a founding principle—decided to enforce Islamic blasphemy laws instead.

There is no appeasing these people. No amount of contrition is ever enough. They hate not only the people whose views they don't agree with, they also hate anyone who is willing to act with some modicum of civility toward those people, as is clear from the events recounted below.

What Can We Do about It

The universities are not lost. But we have to fight back, with principle, vigor, and using all the tools we have, in order to reclaim them as havens for learning.

Remarkably, in the wake of the debacle at Stanford, the president of Stanford University and the dean of the Stanford Law School both issued Judge Duncan a written apology. They acknowledged that the students' conduct was unacceptable and contrary to their free speech policy. The reaction was fierce.[15]

The Stanford Law School dean, Jenny Martinez, was a classmate of mine at Harvard. She was a year behind me, and we were both on the Law Review together. I didn't know her terribly well, but she always seemed nice and friendly, and I assumed she must be reliably left of center. It was thus surprising (and encouraging) that she was willing to apologize and explicitly speak out against the shameful treatment of Judge Duncan.

Within hours, protestors gathered outside Dean Martinez's classroom, subjecting her to the same walk of shame that Judge Duncan had endured days earlier.[16] Like many people of Hispanic heritage before her, myself included, Dean Martinez sadly learned that being a "person of color" is not enough to keep the woke mob from knocking down your door if you dare to defend "fascist" principles such as free speech and open debate.

As this was occurring, a full recap of the incident appeared on the Washington Free Beacon, written by a reporter named Aaron Sibarium.[17] After that article went viral on Twitter, Sibarium planned a follow-up piece on the incident that would have referred to some of the protestors by name. Shortly thereafter, the Free Beacon was contacted by several protestors who demanded anonymity on the grounds that reporting on their actual identities might...of course, *cause harm*.[18] Amazingly, the people who had spent more than a week covering the walls of their university with Old West–style "WANTED" posters featuring the faces and names of conservative students didn't think it would be fair for a reporter even to refer to *them* by name.

In the aftermath, I wrote a letter to Dean Martinez and to Stanford's president, inquiring (1) whether the students who harassed the judge would be punished, and (2) whether the administrator who flouted the university's policy would be fired. Astonishingly, they responded to my inquiry in the affirmative.

I made clear that the students shouldn't be punished for engaging in legitimate protest. Had they protested outside, holding signs or leading chants, that would have been fully protected First Amendment activity. But the Supreme Court has explained that free speech does not create a "heckler's veto," a right to disrupt, shout down, and silence another speaker.[19] Moreover, these were *law* students. Had they been actual lawyers, and had they behaved the same way before Judge Duncan (or any other judge) in his courtroom—screaming, disrupting, and disgustingly saying they wished his daughters would be raped—they would have been held in contempt, put in handcuffs, and sent to jail.

Stanford responded to my letter by saying that the students would not be disciplined because their administrator had failed to enforce the school's free speech policy. But they announced mandatory free speech training for all their law students:

> In the next academic quarter, the law school will be holding mandatory educational programming for our entire law school student body on the topic of freedom of speech and the norms of the legal profession. A committee will be formed to seek feedback from faculty, students, and members of the legal community, including our alumni, and make further recommendations. And, we are making clear to our staff and students that the role of any administrators present

will be to ensure that university rules on disruption of events are followed. Staff will receive additional training to that effect. Students who violate these policies will be subject to sanctions. All staff will receive training so they understand clearly that such behavior is unacceptable....

Preventing or disrupting the effective carrying out of any event is both inappropriate conduct and a violation of university policy....

We must and will address with students the norms of the legal profession with regard to, for example, offering substantive criticism of legal arguments and positions rather than vulgar personal insults, and the potential consequences for their professional reputations of such speech. The oath a lawyer takes upon becoming a member of the bar in California requires one to swear or affirm that they "will strive to conduct" themselves "at all times with dignity, courtesy and integrity." Law students must be prepared to go out into a society that disagrees about many important issues and to act as effective advocates in that society. Learning to channel the passion of one's principles into reasoned, persuasive argument is an essential part of learning to be an effective advocate.

That wasn't everything I had asked for—the students were not disciplined for their reprehensible conduct—but it was a significant step in the right direction. And as for my inquiry whether Dean Steinbach would be disciplined or terminated, they responded concisely: "Associate Dean Tirien Steinbach *is currently on leave.* Generally speaking, the university does not comment publicly on pending personnel matters."

That was remarkable. It was one of the very few times a woke administrator has faced real consequences for silencing conservative speech. Time will tell whether the punishment will be permanent.[20]

Next, I wrote to the Texas State Bar, urging the bar to ask all graduates of Stanford Law School whether they had participated in harassing a federal judge, and to use their answers to that question in assessing "character and fitness" to practice law, an essential requirement of being a licensed lawyer. Specifically, I said, "I would ask that the Texas Board of Bar Examiners, in discharging their duties of assessing the character and fitness of prospective bar applicants, take particular care with students who have graduated from Stanford Law in class years 2023, 2024, or 2025. Specifically, I suggest that students graduating from those years be made to answer, in writing, whether they participated in the shameful harassment of Judge Duncan on March 9, 2023. I would leave it to the considered judgment of the Texas Supreme Court and the Texas Board of Bar Examiners what the proper remedy should be...."

Again, remarkably, the Texas Bar responded in the affirmative. Specifically, Texas Supreme Court chief justice Nathan Hecht—a brilliant conservative jurist, and a friend—wrote back,

> The Board has historically relied on law schools to report disciplinary matters that should be considered in determining an applicant's character and fitness for admission to the Texas bar. School reactions to recent violations of free-speech policies suggest that reliance is not justified. *The Board is planning to add questions to the bar application to inquire of applicants directly concerning incivility and violations of school policies.*
>
> Texas lawyers are expected to adhere to the Texas Lawyer's Creed, promising to "treat counsel, opposing parties, the Court, and members of the Court staff with courtesy and civility." The admission process should examine whether applicants can be expected [to] fulfill this promise. [Emphasis added.]

This was a major step forward. And we can hope that other state bars, particularly in red states like Florida, follow suit. Only when these student radicals face real and meaningful consequences for their egregious actions will their conduct change.

Likewise, in response to both this incident and a prior incident at Yale Law School where radicals shouted down and disrupted another speaker—not a judge, but a lawyer who had won a major religious liberty case before the Supreme Court and whom the activists therefore despised—Jim Ho, another judge on the Fifth Circuit, took another major step to defend free speech. Judge Ho is a dear friend of mine. Jim came to America as a one-year-old immigrant from Taiwan; he was a law clerk to Justice Clarence Thomas, succeeded me as solicitor general of Texas, was one of the top constitutional litigators in America, and was someone whom I aggressively (and successfully) urged President Trump to nominate to the Fifth Circuit.

In the wake of the incident involving the First Amendment lawyer at Yale, Judge Ho announced that he would no longer hire law clerks who had attended Yale Law School and matriculated after the students shouted down the speaker. And in the wake of the incident at Stanford, Judge Ho added Stanford to the list of schools from which he would no longer hire. Ironically, Judge Ho is himself a graduate of Stanford undergrad.

In this boycott of Yale and Stanford, Judge Ho has been joined by Eleventh Circuit judge Elizabeth Branch and at least twelve other federal judges (who have not been publicly identified).[21]

Now, for non-lawyers, it might be unclear why clerkships matter. But, for the graduates—especially of "elite" law schools—clerkships are immensely important. Each federal judge typically hires two to three law clerks, who then spend a year assisting the judge in researching and writing opinions, and top graduates compete vigorously to clerk for them. The top federal appeals court judges, in turn, regularly send their clerks to work the next year as Supreme Court clerks; each justice hires four, and the thirty-six clerks each year are considered the very pinnacle of law school graduates.

Clerkships carry with them enormous prestige, and law firms pay law clerks signing bonuses that can be in excess of $300,000. So, getting or not getting a clerkship is a big deal. And law schools compete with each other vigorously for how many top clerkships their graduates receive. The drop-off from the numbers of clerks from the top law schools can be steep: The year I clerked at the Supreme Court, there were eleven clerks from Yale and eight from Harvard, five from Chicago, three from Columbia, and two from Stanford. No other law school had more than a single clerk.

Judge Ho is already one of the most respected conservative judges in the country and, in time, may well become a major "feeder" judge, with many of his clerks going on to the Supreme Court. For Yale and Stanford clerks to be shut out gets the law schools' attention, and the attention of their future potential students.

As Judge Ho explained in a recent public address, "Some [students at Yale] have admitted to us that they disagreed with us at first—but now that they've seen how the administration is reacting, they get it. And now they're the ones urging us to keep it up—and not to pull back."[22]

And when the judges added Stanford to the list, Tim Rosenberger, the president of the Stanford Federalist Society, said that the judges are "showing real leadership in taking this step" and that he hoped more judges would follow their lead. But, he elaborated, "I'm certainly ready to work with our school to get pulled off the blacklist, and I think we have a lot of really good ideas for how to address the concerns these judges have."[23]

◆ ◆ ◆

It's not just at Stanford where students are hoping their school will pull back from woke policies and the censorship of conservative views. I believe that in every university in the United States, with very few exceptions, there are students who are still eager to hear opposing views, to welcome speakers who disagree with them, and to participate in the free exchange of ideas.

I've seen it live and in person.

For about four years I have hosted a podcast called *Verdict with Ted Cruz*, which is today on the iHeartRadio network. I launched the podcast on the first day of the first Trump impeachment. That night, at about one o'clock in the morning, after spending the entire day as a member of the "jury" hearing the House impeachment managers' case, I drove straight to a TV studio and recorded our first episode. We put it out in the morning, and recorded and published another one every night of the trial thereafter.

In a matter of weeks, our nascent podcast skyrocketed up the charts to become, for a time, the #1-ranked podcast in the world. I still do the podcast today—three times a week—and we have had over 60 million downloads. Every week we beat CNN for total listeners. (If you don't subscribe, you should!)

Every podcast is done alongside my co-host. Today, that's Ben Ferguson, the nationally syndicated radio host who has become a very dear friend. But for the first couple of years my co-host was Michael Knowles, another well-known conservative host who is likewise a very dear friend. Often, we'll have guests, including cabinet members, senators, House members, and other experts on topics of particular interest.

The purpose of the podcast is to take listeners behind the scenes, to explain what's really happening in politics, in law, in government, and in foreign policy. We try to pull back the curtain and explain what's really going on behind closed doors. Early on, my production team urged me to "dumb down" the content, but I pushed back hard. I didn't believe people wanted dumbed-down content. The analogy I drew was that, if you had some terrible disease, you wouldn't want the doctor to say you "had a boo boo." Instead, you'd want to know exactly what the hell was wrong. But you also wouldn't want it explained in arcane and technical jargon that only a medical doctor could understand. So I tried to do the same on the podcast. With the first Trump impeachment, I tried to explain, in depth but in understandable terms, what "impeachment" means, what "high crimes and misdemeanors" are, what "quid pro quo" is, what and where Ukraine is, what Burisma was, and a host of other questions that millions of people were struggling to understand.

As the podcast attracted more and more of a national following, I began to notice that the demographics of our listeners were markedly different from a typical Fox News viewer. Fox viewers tend to be older, many in their seventies or eighties. My podcast listeners, on the other hand, skew decidedly younger. Many of them are high school students or college students or young professionals. As I travel the country, I can almost always predict, as folks come up to me, that, say, a twenty-four-year-old man with a ponytail and multiple tattoos is overwhelmingly more likely to be a subscriber to *Verdict* than to be a regular viewer of Fox.

As that pattern of younger listeners began to be manifest (which, admittedly, was a major reason I launched the podcast), I decided to take *Verdict* on a national college tour. We went to the University of Wisconsin–Madison, Texas A&M, Catholic University, the University of Alabama, and Yale. At every venue, we had packed houses with enormous student interest.

Even at Yale.

When we arrived, I didn't know what to expect. It was just months after Yale law students had shamefully shouted down a conservative

Supreme Court lawyer, and I didn't know whether my reception would be the same. Michael Knowles, my co-host at the time, was a proud Yale graduate, even though his politics are very different from those of the current student body.

When we walked into the auditorium at Yale, we saw between six and seven hundred students gathered. About a third of them were politically left of center, something we discovered when I referred to Justice Ketanji Brown Jackson's recent confirmation and they cheered. I stopped and told them how glad I was that they were there; that, from their cheers, they were obviously across the political aisle from me, and I was particularly glad they had come to hear the discussion. Far too often, I explained, we don't talk to one another, and that has to change.

Most of the podcast was Q&A, for about ninety minutes. And, we told the students, our policy was "if you have a hostile question…come to the front of the line." There were numerous questions from the Left. One particularly acute exchange went as follows:

> STUDENT: I wanted to take a moment to celebrate our newest addition to the Supreme Court of the U.S., who I know we've already talked about, Justice Jackson. Since you're here tonight, though, in the name of fostering intellectual diversity and academic spaces, it would appear to me that you already recognize the importance of new perspectives. And as a young woman, seeing Justice Jackson on the Supreme Court is invigorating, truly. And on Tuesday, **it baffled me that you would ask such flagrantly racist questions to this exceedingly well qualified candidate.**
>
> Your colleagues in the GOP promised a respectful and dignified hearing for Justice Jackson, and to me, you did not uphold this. So today, **I wanted to create a space where you might be able to challenge your own thinking** as prudent

scholars often do. So I'm here to ask you, what are two nice comments you can give about recent nominee Justice Jackson's judicial experience, besides from 'she has an easy smile.'"

CRUZ: Well, let me start by thanking you for being here. And thank you for asking a substantive, important question. Thank you for engaging in a conversation. I think we all would be better off if we engaged in substantive conversations. There's a lot to praise about Judge Jackson. She is very, very bright. She is very, very accomplished. She is very talented. She has an impressive and inspiring personal story. I will say, sitting listening to her opening remarks where she described her personal story, she described her parents' journey—you had to be dead, not to be inspired by that journey.

And listen, I will say more broadly, if you look at the history of our country, if you look at the history of our country on race, it is absolutely inspiring to see an African-American woman serving on the Supreme Court.

I will also point out that **when it comes to issues of race, I think both the press and the modern Left are hypocritical on this question.** That **they only define someone as Black, or they only define someone as Hispanic, if they agree with them ideologically.** So, Clarence Thomas has been on the Court for decades. Clarence Thomas is a Black man. The Left hates him. They despise Clarence Thomas. And I'll tell you by the way, the treatment of Clarence Thomas on the left is markedly different than say, Antonin Scalia. Antonin Scalia was brilliant. He and Justice Thomas were every bit as conservative, and yet the vitriol that was heaped on Clarence Thomas—nasty, racist language from the Left.

There was one magazine cover that showed Clarence Thomas, as an Uncle Tom sitting at Scalia's feet, I think was racist and disgusting.

And listen, I will say this as an Hispanic man, Jorge Ramos went on television in Spanish and described me as a 'traitor to my race' for daring.... [laughter] Okay, look, that says something about the view of the Left that they're telling you: 'You have one way to view things and one way only. And if you don't, we'll demonize and attack you.'

So look, and by the way, in terms of having the first African-American woman on the Supreme Court, there was an opportunity for this to happen twenty years ago: there's a judge named Janice Rogers Brown, Janice Rogers Brown was a Supreme Court justice of the California Supreme Court. George W. Bush nominated Janice Rogers Brown to the D.C. Circuit....

The Democrats filibustered Judge Brown. That filibuster was led by a guy named Joe Biden. It also included people like Chuck Schumer, it included Pat Leahy, it included Dianne Feinstein; the reason they filibustered Judge Janice Rogers Brown is because she was a Black woman, but she was also conservative. And they did not want her to go to the Supreme Court. And they succeeded in filibustering her. They delayed her nomination for a couple of years until it finally went through. She finally went to the D.C. Circuit.

Now, everyone who was harrumphing in the media, that if you oppose an African-American woman who's a qualified judge, you're racist. Precisely zero of them thought it was racist for Democrats, including Joe Biden, to filibuster Janice Rogers Brown.

By the way, there was another nominee that Bush put forward, a guy named Miguel Estrada. Miguel is an incredibly qualified Supreme Court advocate. He was nominated [to] the D.C. Circuit as well, and the Democrats filibustered him. If you read the memos that were leaked from Ted Kennedy's lawyers, here's what Ted Kennedy's lawyers said about Miguel Estrada: **They said, We must stop him, quote, "because he is Hispanic." That's what Ted Kennedy's lawyers said in writing.**

Now, I'm going to suggest to you **if you oppose somebody *because of* their race, that is the definition of racist.** And look, I'll point out in your question, you said that my questioning of Judge Jackson was...you used the term "racist"?

Listen, racism is a horrific evil in this country. It is also an insult that the Left tosses around casually. I would welcome if you look at the questions I asked Judge Jackson. Every single question I asked her concerned her record, either her record as a judge sentencing defendants before her or her record writing academic materials and law reviews or her record giving speeches to law schools.

All of that is the job of the Senate in the advice and consent process. And so respectfully, I could not disagree more deeply when you say it is racist to examine a judge based on their record.

If the Democrats wanted to oppose Janice Rogers Brown because they oppose conservatives—you know, **do you think the Democrats were all sexist when they voted party line against Amy Coney Barrett? I'm willing to bet you don't. Because she's not a liberal woman.**

So you can't have it both ways, which is that when a Democratic nominee has a certain characteristic, anyone who opposes them is racist or sexist or what have you. But when a Republican nominee has those characteristics, it's

open season and you can go after them full force, and the
Left is righteous in doing so. The standard should be the
same. And I'm going to suggest what the standard should be,
is we should examine people based on their actual record.
And whether and to what extent that record demonstrates
they will defend the constitutional rights of all Americans.
I think that's what people care about. [Emphasis added.][24]

That was a real and direct and substantive exchange on racism:
something that very rarely happens any more on a college campus. And
throughout nearly ninety minutes, nobody screamed, nobody cursed
us out. Nobody stood up and hurled epithets or behaved as campus
radicals have elsewhere. Among the students were several who were
transgender; they did not protest or disrupt. They listened to the
conversation.

Afterwards, Michael and I went to grab drinks with a Jewish rabbi
who works on the Yale campus. He said, "Ted, tonight was important.
Tonight was the largest gathering of students I've seen at Yale have a
cordial, constructive, civil conversation about conservative ideas...in
twenty years."

Sadly, not a single faculty member and not a single administrator
attended.

But, as the gathered students at Yale demonstrated, there is still
a palpable hunger among young people for free speech, civility, and
reasonable discourse—and that is reason for hope.

CHAPTER TWO

"Malleable Clay":
K–12 Education

M arxism doesn't work.

Any college student with sense who reads enough world history will eventually reach this conclusion. Study for even a few minutes, and anyone can detect the rot at the core of Marx's central thesis.

This presents a problem for the Woke Totalitarians of today. If anyone can find out that your core ideas are built on a fraudulent, evil system just by reading, then even the most sophisticated propaganda campaign will not be enough to win hearts and minds.

Their solution?

Begin the indoctrination process before people can read.

In this, they are following in the footsteps of communists throughout history, who have understood the importance of beginning their revolutions with children. In my father's home country of Cuba, one of the first moves of Fidel Castro and his fellow revolutionaries was to dismantle the education system and rebuild it from the ground up, beginning almost immediately after they seized power in 1959. No longer would parents be the ones who taught their children values. The parents wouldn't even decide when and in what manner their children could leave the house and begin working. Every child in Cuba, according to Castro, now belonged to the revolution.

A few years earlier, while hiding out in the Sierra Maestra Mountains after his first failed attempt at a revolution, Castro had met a young doctor from Argentina named Che Guevara. Today, most people would recognize Che Guevara from the sketch of his face that adorns T-shirts and dorm room posters—the one that shows him looking skyward in a decaled hat and military uniform, usually accompanied by the phrase *Viva La Revolución*. At some point in the 1980s, for reasons that defy understanding, Che Guevara became a cult figure to young leftists who liked his clothes and his politics. Around that time, posters of him became some of the most popular items sold in college bookstores.

I still remember walking into a dorm room down the hall from mine in the late 1980s and seeing the man's smug face staring back at me. The fellow who lived there was active in left-wing politics at Princeton. I didn't know him very well, but I couldn't resist telling him how cool I thought the poster was.

"I see you're into murderous, torturing thugs," I said. "But when it comes to that stuff, Che's really an amateur. Why not throw up a poster of Adolf Hitler to go next to him? Maybe Chairman Mao or Stalin?"

He and I didn't speak much after that.

What I knew, of course—what most people whose relatives grew up in Cuba know—is that Che Guevara was a monster. According to a memoir written by his cousin, he enjoyed torturing small animals as a child.[1] When that no longer gave him the rush he was looking for, he moved on to people. In the late 1950s, when Fidel Castro and his fellow revolutionaries were still hiding in the mountains, Guevara often murdered people suspected of being disloyal to the revolution. He did so without giving these men a trial or allowing them to speak in their own defense. He would simply make the man in question kneel, say a few words, and then fire a single shot into the back of his head.

Writing about the experience in the mid-1960s, Guevara recalled the pleasure he got from murdering his fellow revolutionaries. "My nostrils dilate while savoring the acrid odor of gunpowder and blood," he wrote. "I'd like to confess, Papa, at that moment I discovered that I really like killing."[2]

Reading that quote, you might not guess that Che Guevara had strong views about early childhood education. But he did. According to him and Fidel Castro, getting the children while they were young was one of the most important goals of the revolution. Children were, in his words, "malleable clay with which the new man, without any of the previous defects, can be formed."[3]

By "defects," communists mean the things that get in the way of violent revolution—things like religion, traditional values, and a belief in the family as the basic structural unit of society. Castro and his allies believed that if children could be taught early enough to reject those things, they would become loyal and unquestioning soldiers in the revolution, willing to defend the principles of communism and Marxism forever.

The idea wasn't new. From the moment that Karl Marx and his disciples first began writing about their vision for the world in the mid-1800s, they dreamed of a society in which it was the state, not families, that would take care of educating children. Both Karl Marx and his partner Friedrich Engels viewed the nuclear family as a corrupting force on modern society—a "money relation" that should be supplanted by the state. In *The Communist Manifesto*, they stated plainly that the education of children, "from the moment they can get along without their mother's care," should be handled by the government rather than parents.[4]

This made sense, given that Karl Marx saw his own family mostly as an inconvenience. For years, he refused to provide for his wife or his six children by getting a job, choosing instead to write long books and articles full of turgid, barely readable prose for very little money. He relied on his parents and friends, mostly Engels, for what little income he had. According to most biographers, the Marx family lived in a constant state of squalor and poverty.

The man himself, as the journalist Paul Kengor put it in *The Devil and Karl Marx*, was "a slob." In 1849, less than a year after he published *The Communist Manifesto*, the Marx family was evicted for refusing to pay rent. In addition to the lack of payment, the landlord who kicked them out was revolted by Marx's "resistance to grooming," and appalled that he "drank too much, smoked too much, never exercised, and suffered from warts and boils from lack of washing. He stunk."[5]

Throughout Marx's life, while he was writing his books, his children suffered. Both his sons died from exposure, likely because of their father's refusal to pay for adequate medical care. Two of his daughters killed themselves by drinking poison. Late in life, he fathered a child out of wedlock with a maid he had hired to clean up around the house (for no money), and he refused to acknowledge that the child was his. Marx's wife, who often wrote that she wanted to end her life, died in misery soon afterward, and Engels ended up supporting Marx's daughter.

Again, this doesn't seem like the sort of person whose advice you would seek on *anything*, let alone something as important as the education of children. But Marxists are strange people. For years, disciples of their strange ideology have attempted to redesign education systems all over the world, always believing that *this* time, they'll manage not to screw everything up. Like Charlie Brown running toward the football that Lucy is propping up in the distance, these people always run at full speed toward their goals. They plan lessons, design curricula, and even build schools to further the cause of Marxism and bring about their worker's paradise.

Every time, they end up flat on their backs.

In 1917, after the Bolsheviks successfully revolted against the ruling classes in Russia, one of the first things the revolutionaries did was establish a school—where students were aggressively encouraged to snitch on their parents.

Almost exactly two years later, in 1919, communists in Hungary attempted to do something similar. It didn't go well. According to a biography of Georg Lukács, the education commissar of Hungary at the time, the whole thing quickly devolved into madness, as most Marxist ventures eventually do: "Special lectures were organized in schools and literature printed and distributed to 'instruct' children about free love, about the nature of sexual intercourse, about the archaic nature of bourgeois family codes, about the outdatedness of monogamy, and the irrelevance of religion, which deprives man of all pleasure. Children urged thus to reject and deride paternal authority and the authority of the church, and to ignore precepts of morality."[6]

Typically, you find very few mentions of things like mathematics, economics, or critical thinking in the curricula of these Marxist institutions. Those subjects take a back seat to "free love" and "the archaic nature of bourgeois family codes." Some communist schools may never get around to them at all. Of course, many of these Marxist education systems—and the regimes that attempted to implement them—didn't last very long. The Hungarian Soviet Republic, for instance, operated for only 133 days before parents found out what was going on and shut the whole thing down.

The rare exception, of course, is Cuba, where Fidel Castro and Che Guevara exerted brutal control over the entire country. In 1960, they established state-run preschools to teach children about Marxism. This was the year that my father returned to his native country to find that his home and his family had been devastated by the new Castro regime.

In his childhood home, he sat with my *abuela* and listened to stories about what she had been forced to endure as an elementary school teacher after the communists took over. She told him about the spies, the soldiers, and the constant sense that someone was watching her every move, making sure that every word she said was perfectly in line with the revolution. It was there, sitting at the kitchen table of the house he'd grown up in, that my father first heard the stories of the soldiers who had barged into his mother's classroom and told the young students to pray to Fidel Castro for candy—a story that affected me so deeply when I heard it as a child that it still comes readily to mind whenever I hear some left-wing activist extol the virtues of state-dictated education or other neo-Marxist principles. He also heard about how she had feigned insanity, kicking over chairs and foaming at the mouth, to avoid joining the revolution without being thrown in jail or shot.

When my father left Cuba for the last time in 1960, he was leaving behind a country that was about to be radically transformed. Most of that transformation would come about through education. Throughout the 1960s, as my grandmother endured the scorn of her neighbors (only some of whom believed she was truly insane, leaving her open to the incredibly dangerous charge of being a counter-revolutionary), Castro nationalized every educational institution in Cuba. The Communist Party established a children's auxiliary club and built boarding schools in the more rural areas of the country, where men only slightly younger than my father would be sent to learn revolutionary politics and agriculture. By the late 1960s, according to a recent history of Cuba, about 85 percent of high school students attended those boarding schools.

This total overhaul of the educational system was the first step in the grand plan of the leftist revolutionaries who had taken control of the country. Their mission, as Che Guevara put it in his most famous essay, "Man and Socialism in Cuba," was to do away with everything that had come before. "The new society in process of formation," he wrote, "has to compete very hard with the past."[7]

As my father got messages from old friends in Cuba during his first years in the United States, he learned just how hard Fidel and the revolutionaries were fighting against the past. The children who had been very small when he left were now being shipped off to state-run boarding schools in the countryside, and many people his own age were swept up in a literacy program that Che Guevara had helped to design. They were sent out to villages all over Cuba to teach young children and their mostly illiterate families how to read.

Even in this literacy program, revolutionary politics was paramount. The letter "F," according to the manuals, stood either for "Fidel" or for "fusil," which means rifle; the sample sentences all told the story of how Castro and his band of revolutionaries were going to save the country and reorient the economy toward communism.

Like all Marxists, the revolutionaries in the Castro regime knew that the best way to teach these backward, rotten principles was by sneaking them into supposedly objective lessons about reading, writing, and mathematics. Children, they knew, would be much more likely to absorb these principles if they were fed them at the same time that they were learning how to multiply numbers, tie their shoes, and find their way home from school. Ideas that seemed ridiculous to adults—such as the abolition of the family or the complete restructuring of the economy—would be more readily accepted by children, who had no better ideas to compare them to.

This was all part of a grand plan to get rid of everything that had come before. Tradition had to go, as did religion and all the old stories about Cuban history. There was nothing more dangerous to the revolutionaries, who wanted to bring about radical change in their society—change that was based on Marxism, which is rotten to its core—than veneration of the past.

"During the transition to this new future society," as the historian Ada Ferrer has written, "the past was not yet dead. And that made it deadly. For Guevara, the battle against the past occurred everywhere, even within individuals. To achieve communism, people had to defeat the past in themselves and adopt a whole 'new scale of values.' People had to be reborn, figuratively, as new men and new women."[8]

Reading these words today, it is difficult not to think of the various efforts we've seen on the American Left not only to rewrite our history but to annihilate it completely. In classrooms all over the United States, children are being taught to abhor our nation's past and to view our founders as evil racists who wanted nothing more than to enslave and torture anyone who wasn't White. Some are being taught a version of history authored by the "journalist" Nikole Hannah-Jones, whose 1619 Project has been compressed, rewritten, and dumbed down (a miraculous feat, considering the quality of the original product) specifically so that it can be used in K–12 classrooms.

According to this false version of history, our past is primarily one of genocide, rape, and murder; the United States was conceived not in 1776, when the founders signed the Declaration of Independence, but in 1619, when the first ship carrying African slaves arrived at Jamestown, Virginia. This version of our history claims, incorrectly, that the American Revolution was fought to preserve the institution of slavery. It teaches that America is irredeemably racist, and it says that the entire story of the United States of America can be told through one lens only—as a story of oppression—and that anyone who says otherwise is simply enacting White supremacy. Most important, it says that everything students have previously been taught about American history—everything their parents and grandparents believed about this country—is not only wrong, but racist.

In my last book, *Justice Corrupted*, I wrote about how this dangerous ideology ended up in classrooms all over the United States. I traced the ideology from its origins at Harvard Law School, where I saw up close how it was being developed, all the way through graduate schools of education at other major universities to secondary and primary school classrooms. Over a period of about three decades, beginning in the early 1990s, Critical Race Theory spread from these graduate schools of education to elementary schools, middle schools, and high schools in communities all across the country. By the time parents began looking over their children's shoulders during the Covid-19 lockdowns and seeing the utter nonsense that was being taught to them over Zoom, Critical Race Theory was already embedded in the curriculum.

To this day, most graduate schools of education still require all their students to take courses in which explicitly Marxist writings are on the syllabus. In September of 2022, RealClearEducation conducted an investigation into public universities in the state of Wisconsin and found that "virtually every primary- or early-education major must take at least one course focused on how to implement 'equity,' 'diversity,' and 'culturally relevant pedagogy'—buzzwords for radical identity politics—in their future K–12 classrooms."[9]

One of the syllabi the investigators studied instructed future teachers to "view the classroom with reference to 'interlocking systems of oppression, including…race, class, [and] gender,'"[10] and to plan lessons accordingly. There is every reason to suppose that this is not a phenomenon unique to Wisconsin. The virus of neo-Marxism—mutated with new strands of gender theory, Critical Race Theory, and other postmodernist babble—has spread from our nation's top universities to countless schools nationwide.

For the past few years, I've led a fight in the United States Senate to raise awareness about the horrible teachings contained within Critical Race Theory. I'm often met with objections from Democrats who insist, first of all, that Critical Race Theory is not being taught in schools. These people usually claim that *real* Critical Race Theory is nothing more than an obscure graduate-level set of ideas that isn't taught outside of a few university departments. Then, of course, often in the course of the same sentence, these same Democrats will insist that Critical Race Theory is vital, and that it *must* continue to be taught in elementary schools all over the country.

Whatever it's called, the ideas on race being taught in our schools are nonsensical and downright evil. That's why I've cheered on several efforts to ban CRT at the state and local levels, including in Florida and my home state of Texas.

But banning the racist and dishonest material might not be enough. Already, we've seen signs that the neo-Marxist Left's "war of position," in which they planned long ago to infiltrate every institution in this country, has proven quite successful. Every day, children graduate from public high schools in the United States spouting left-wing propaganda as if it is the complete, uncontroversial truth about the world.

Consider what happened to Vincent Lloyd, a Black professor from Philadelphia who had been a model leftist for most of his adult life. Since the early 1990s, Professor Lloyd has taught seminars about antiracism and the struggles of racial minorities in the United States. In many ways his early efforts—including work by Angela Davis, Ta-Nehisi Coates, and other prominent scholars who would later come to write the CRT syllabus—prefigured the "racial reckoning" that would enthrall the United States during the summer of 2020, during the Black Lives Matter riots in the wake of the death of George Floyd.

To Vincent Lloyd, Critical Race Theory was not a set of evil ideas, but a necessary framework for dealing with the institutional racism that he and his leftist colleagues believed was all around us in the United States.

One of his favorite jobs, as he wrote recently in a brilliant (and terrifying) piece for the new online magazine Compact, was teaching a seminar for gifted high school students. The last time Lloyd had taught the seminar, in 2014, the students had shown up eager to learn lessons about racism and oppression and how to combat them in modern society. As the six weeks of the seminar went by, he writes, "I could see the students forming bonds with each other and with me, and I could see their commitment to the course. They always showed up on time. They always did the work."[11]

But during the summer of 2022, things were different. Something about the students had changed. Whereas before Lloyd's students had been open to new ideas and eager to debate with their classmates, now they were much more close-minded and militant—a change Lloyd attributes to the sudden prominence of woke ideology after the "racial reckoning" that occurred in 2020.

The structure of the seminar was also markedly different. Now, rather than focusing on critical theory in general, the program would offer only "Critical Black Studies" and "Anti-Oppressive Studies" seminars. The former, according to the institute, would "seek to focus more specifically on the needs and interests of Black students."

It didn't take long for Professor Lloyd to realize that something was very wrong with the students. During the workshops he led on "race and the limits of the law," most of which would be focused on anti-Black racism, he noticed that the students were no longer interested in learning or discussing things with one another. Rather, they were interested in "crudely conveying certain dogmatic assertions, no matter what topic the workshops were ostensibly about."

In the piece for Compact, Lloyd lists those dogmatic assertions, almost all of which are staples of neo-Marxism and Critical Race Theory. In his words:

- Experiencing hardship conveys authority.
- There is no hierarchy of oppressions—except for anti-black oppression, which is in a class of its own.

- Trust black women.
- Prison is never the answer.
- Black people need black space.
- Allyship is usually performative.
- All non-black people, and many black people, are guilty of anti-blackness.
- There is no way out of anti-blackness.[12]

Almost immediately, the high school students Professor Lloyd had been tasked with educating began ganging up on their fellow students, particularly two Asian students who didn't always repeat the right bits of anti-racist dogma. Those two students were soon removed from the seminar. Before long, under the leadership of a college-aged teacher's assistant that Lloyd calls "Keisha," the students turned on him, believing that even he was not sufficiently radical.

This, as we've seen throughout history, is a common occurrence in revolutionary left-wing movements, particularly Marxist ones. Even the most revolutionary figure of today—the person who says all the right things and seems like he's got all the right ideas—can be shouted down and chased out of town by the new, more extreme revolutionaries of tomorrow.

As Professor Lloyd tells it, he walked into his seminar room four weeks into what was supposed to be a six-week seminar to find the students sitting unsmiling with pieces of paper in their hands. "Each student," he writes, "read from a prepared statement about how the seminar perpetuated anti-black violence in its content and form, how the black students had been harmed, how I was guilty of countless microaggressions, including through my body language, and how students didn't feel safe because I didn't immediately correct views that failed to treat anti-blackness as the cause of all the world's ills."[13]

On a first read, it's tempting to wonder where seventeen-year-olds would have learned such strange language, which sounds like something you'd hear in a graduate-level humanities seminar from hell. But we know exactly where they heard it.

This is the language that has infiltrated almost every middle and high school in America, where, from the time they're old enough to read, American children are taught that the country they live in is an evil place where even the kindliest, most mild-mannered professors are out to "perpetuate anti-Black violence" against minorities. It is no surprise that we are seeing the horrible effects of these ideas at elite programs first. The students who attend such seminars are, as Professor Lloyd points out in his piece, the top performers in their classes; they are the ones who've shown they can do the best job at taking what their high school teachers tell them and regurgitating it back to earn the highest grades.

Clearly, the mission that Cultural Marxists set for themselves in the late 1960s—to infiltrate the knowledge-making institutions of this country with left-wing ideas and change the culture in a major way—is far along the road to succeeding. Even today, when parents and politicians are more aware than ever that these ideas exist in our school system, the cultural revolutionaries manage to smuggle the ideas through anyway. Even in the face of legislation that makes Critical Race Theory illegal, and an all-out assault on the worst books and ideas by parents and independent media, these vicious ideas still dominate American education.

Anyone wondering how is obviously not familiar with the backhanded tactics of the modern Left. Proponents of Critical Race Theory, gender theory, and other neo-Marxist ideas will lie, obfuscate, and knowingly manipulate people to slip their ideas into our institutions. They are comfortable doing this because they believe they are on the side of the angels—though most of them don't believe in God or angels—and that their mission is righteous.

If you don't believe me, prepare to meet just one of the people who writes curricula for children in grade school.

Loopholes

"I'm a good salesman," says the man at the other end of the table. "But I'm also an *evil* salesman."

Like many victims of Project Veritas, the man has no idea that he is being recorded. He believes that the guy he's having dinner with is a potential romantic partner who shares his left-wing politics. He also believes, as many leftists do, that Critical Race Theory is integral to the education of children, and that it should be slipped into lessons about everything from politics and history to math, science, and economics. For the next two hours or so, he'll talk about how he designs curricula, sells them to school districts, and makes sure that that happens.

"They don't know...if you don't say the words 'Critical Race Theory,' you can technically teach it. People don't know what Critical Race Theory is."

Asked what's in these curricula, which the man sells to school districts for use in classrooms—often for enormous sums of money, which he claims goes "right into his account"—he says, "Everything. Banned books, stuff they don't want kids to see. All of it."[14]

In the state of Georgia, where these two men are having dinner, teaching Critical Race Theory is illegal—largely because of a bill passed by the state legislature in April of 2022, which made it illegal to teach children using materials that contained Marxist ideas such as Critical Race Theory. It was one of many similar bills that were passed around the same time.

Although the content of these bills varied, the aim of them all was pretty much identical: to ensure that students in elementary school would not have left-wing dogma shoved down their throats. Several of the bills explicitly stated that teachers could not include any material in their lesson plans that said one race was superior to another, or that some students bore hereditary guilt for the sins of their ancestors because of the color of their skin.

There was a time when you might have been surprised to learn that such bills were even up for debate in the United States, let alone that more than fifteen had passed in the span of a few months. I'm sure that the civil rights leaders of the 1960s, for instance, would have been surprised to learn that in the year 2023 teachers at public schools would still be so obsessed with race that it would become necessary for various state legislators to step in and tell them to teach something else *besides* aggressive advocacy for racial discrimination.

But the evidence of left-wing racism in our classrooms has become impossible to ignore. Every few days or so, it seems, we hear another story about radical neo-Marxist teachers in elementary schools, middle schools, and high schools across the country attempting to teach Critical Race Theory and other strange pieces of left-wing dogma to their students. Many of these stories came via the reporting of Christopher Rufo, a former documentary filmmaker who has set up a tip line where parents can send the ridiculous documents that come home with their children.

Each story is more shocking than the last. In a third-grade classroom in Cupertino, California, for instance, students were split into groups according to their race, then told to rank themselves according to how much "privilege" they had in society. Black students were placed at the bottom of this hierarchy, cast as eternal victims, and White students were placed at the top. During this lesson, the class learned that people with white skin had traditionally been oppressive to Black students, and that Black students would experience racism in society no matter what they tried to do.[15]

In Buffalo, New York, kindergarteners were made to watch a film in which the ghosts of murdered Black children spoke to them from beyond the grave to warn the children about the dangers that lurked around every street corner for people of color in the United States.[16]

Images from schools teaching lessons like these could be shared easily via social media. As parents were just beginning to learn the buzzwords and code phrases that accompany lessons in Critical Race Theory—things like "spirit murder" and "intersectionality"—they saw photographs of the classrooms where American children spent eight hours a day, five days a week. Many of these images came via the Twitter account Libs of TikTok, which exposed some of the more insane videos and images from leftists and shared them widely on social media. Parents saw rooms where rainbow flags hung above the blackboard beside giant "Black Lives Matter" banners, often without an American flag in sight.

In one video, a teacher with purple hair brags about how she tells her students to pledge allegiance to the Pride flag. Another says that he has been enjoying coming to work "in full drag" and watching the students whisper about his high heels and short miniskirts; the administrators at his school are apparently "just fine" and "very supportive" about his choice of attire.[17]

It seems these are the people Joe Biden was talking to in July of 2021 when he welcomed a crowd of left-wing educators to the White House and said that children are effectively property of the state. "You've heard me say it many times about children, but it's true," he said. "They're all our children. And the reason you are the teachers of the year is because you recognize that. They're not somebody else's children. They're like yours when they're in the classroom."[18]

Obviously, passing bills that ban racist texts from being taught in schools will not be enough. As long as people like the man who quietly slips Critical Race Theory into the curricula of our public schools are still employed, elements of the Left's neo-Marxist agenda will continue showing up in the textbooks, homework assignments, and even the *math* lessons that our children are given in school. Anyone who doubts the part about math, by the way, should familiarize themselves with the "K–12 Math Ethnic Studies Framework" that was introduced in Seattle Public Schools in February of 2019.

This framework, which comes in a handy chart with subject headings such as "Power and Oppression" and "History of Resistance and Liberation," includes these "learning targets":

- Analyze the ways in which ancient mathematical knowledge has been appropriated by Western culture.
- Identify how the development of mathematics has been erased from learning in school.
- Identify how math has been and continues to be used to oppress and marginalize people and communities of color.[19]

Reading through this document, it is tempting to be amazed at the extent to which supposedly graduate-school-level language is now completely normalized in public school systems all over this country.

Then, of course, there are the books that fill the shelves of our school libraries, only a percentage of which have begun coming to light in recent years. By now I'm sure you've seen some of the worst titles. We have *Gender Queer*, a book that gives children advice about masturbation and counsels them on how to tell their parents that they want to change genders—which, the book assures them, is a perfectly normal and even cool thing to do.[20] Other books that have been pulled from the shelves include *Lawn Boy*, which contains a graphic depiction of two ten-year-old boys having oral sex,[21] and a graphic novel that offers children this jaw-dropping advice: "A great place to research fantasies and kinks safely is on the internet. There are tons of people and communities out there who share your interests. . . ."[22]

Tellingly, if I had wanted to print excerpts from these books—which the Left assures us are perfectly normal and necessary to have in our kids' classrooms and school libraries—the book you're holding couldn't have been distributed to many bookstores across the country, particularly those with Christian leanings. So I decided it wasn't worth it.

Feel free to Google this nonsense, if you dare.

How to Fight Back

A few years ago, I walked into my daughter's bedroom and asked what she'd been learning about in school. She said she had been learning about Christopher Columbus...the "real" story.

I asked what she meant.

For the next few minutes, I heard about the crimes of Christopher Columbus in minute detail. Every murdered Native American, transmitted disease, and stolen acre of land seemed to be accounted for. I heard that Columbus, who claimed the land for himself because of his straight White privilege (or something like that), had not actually *discovered* anything at all but rather had landed on the shores of what would come to be known as America by accident. This "revelation," familiar to most adults in the United States, is something that American children encounter sooner or later in a textbook, believing that they're accessing some secret, hidden knowledge that the grown-ups don't want them to have.

When I was young, some kids found out about it by reading *A People's History of the United States* by the Marxist scholar Howard Zinn, a book that sold about a gazillion copies for its willingness to look at history from the vantage point of the oppressed rather than the figures we're accustomed to reading about. This book, as anyone who has cracked the cover will know, begins with an extremely unflattering account of Christopher Columbus and his "discovery" of America. It recounts how Columbus viewed the natives as little more than potential slaves, and reprints diary entries in which he spoke about his plans for conquest in language that makes the man seem like a maniac by modern standards.[23]

Sitting on my daughter's bed, I asked if she might be able to think of anything *good* that Christopher Columbus, or any explorers of his era, had done.

I observed to her, "We actually have a federal holiday, enacted into law, called Christopher Columbus Day." I continued, "Do we typically create federal holidays for racist and genocidal maniacs?"

What followed was a longer conversation. Now, I'm not vested in proving that Columbus was a saint; he was a man of his era, more than five centuries ago, and he certainly had his flaws. But he also had incredible courage and determination. He had the willingness to board a rickety wooden ship and to lead the *Niña*, the *Pinta*, and the *Santa Maria* off into the great beyond, at a time when many feared they would fall off the edge of the world.

Some time later, as our family was preparing for Thanksgiving dinner, my daughter and I began another conversation, about Pilgrims and Indians. She expressed her view, no doubt taught to her in school, that the Pilgrims were oppressors who brutalized and oppressed the Indians.

Again, I tried to press back gently. Did she suppose, I asked, that the violence was only from one side? The history of humanity has in many ways been a story of conquest, of one people conquering another. For millennia, wars have been waged, from Solomon to Alexander to Caesar to Genghis Khan to the Wars of the Roses. And inevitably the conquered have felt anger and resentment at their mistreatment. Did America's founding, and the Western settlement of our nation, come at the expense of Native Americans? Of course. Did the settlers carry out acts of brutality and oppression at times? Definitely. As has every other conquering nation in the history of the world. On every continent. In every era.

And were the Native Americans wholly innocent of violence? Of course not. From whence, I asked my daughter, did the verb "to scalp" come from?[24] In any war, there are tragic casualties on both sides.

I wanted her to see the connection between those two conversations. Those who vilify Christopher Columbus and those who decry the Pilgrims are both saying fundamentally the same thing. A simple thread connects them both, a question that reveals the premises that underlie the modern Left: Was the founding of America, the discovery and growth of the New World, a good thing or a bad thing?

America's founding, like the founding of any nation, had good chapters and bad chapters. It included acts of violence and brutality—like the founding of every other nation in history—but also acts of incredible grace and sacrifice and generosity. And America, *unlike* other nations, was founded on *ideals* that were pure and powerful and profound. No words are more important to our founding than these of Jefferson in the Declaration of Independence: "We hold these truths to be self-evident: that all men are created equal. That they are endowed by their Creator with certain unalienable rights. And that among these are life, liberty, and the pursuit of happiness." To be sure, our journey to realize that vision has been slow at times and imperfect. But it has been steady nonetheless. And over the course of two and a half centuries no nation in the history of our planet has lifted more out of poverty, has produced more prosperity, has liberated more captives, has defeated more tyrants, and has advanced more liberty than the United States of America.

Leftists hate that fact. And that's why they despise Columbus and Jefferson and Washington and, ultimately, America.

And so when their ideas are packaged up and sold to your children, press back. This is the first step toward making sure that our children are protected. Ask them what they're learning in school, talk to them about it, and see if you can gently correct the record.

Then, of course, there is the matter of speaking out publicly, which is not easy. It can often come with serious consequences.

When my grandmother feigned insanity to avoid teaching the principles of communism to her students, for instance, she knew that she would have to endure a stigma for the rest of her life. Some of her neighbors, she knew, would believe that she had lost her mind and could no longer care for herself. That was bad, but it was nothing compared to the neighbors who suspected, correctly, that she was faking the whole thing—the ones who knew that she harbored anti-revolutionary views. In Cuba in the early 1960s, that could sentence you to horrific torture and death. My *abuela* would sooner have walked straight into the path of Che Guevara's firing squad than say that she was against the revolution out loud.

Luckily, we live in the United States, where the penalty for defying the new woke totalitarians is not yet a firing squad or years in jail. For some people, it's a few days of being yelled at on Twitter. For others, it's possibly losing a job or having some friends send you concerned emails about how you should really "do the work" and get onboard with the revolution. To some, those consequences are endurable; to others, they're not.

If we want to defeat the woke takeover of our K–12 schools, we must fight back at home, fight back with other parents, fight back at school board meetings, fight back in our legislatures, and fight back in the public arena.

I've seen amazing things throughout this country, especially at political rallies where like-minded people have come together to fight for causes they believe in. I think most people would be surprised at how many friends and allies they can make by simply showing up at a rally or a school board meeting to protest what their children are being taught in schools. They would also be surprised at the extent to which they can come up with *better* things to teach when they put their heads together and discuss their values.

This is a good first step in taking our society back from the woke neo-Marxists who have captured it. Show up at meetings, make your voices heard, and see if you can make some friends along the way. That might sound quaint or naïve, but I've seen it happen.

When the parents of Loudoun County, Virginia, learned that Scott Smith, one of their own, had been arrested for disorderly conduct after expressing outrage over the sexual assault of his daughter by a boy wearing a dress in a school bathroom,[25] many of them were outraged. In some cases, they joined groups dedicated to ensuring that parents could have more control over what their children were learning. Within a few months, some of these groups—including Fight for Schools, which made national headlines—succeeded in getting several of the liberal school board members who had covered up the sexual assault removed from their posts; they also managed to sway many voters in Virginia toward Glenn Youngkin, who was then running for governor of Virginia on a parents' rights platform.[26]

Today, Glenn Youngkin—a friend and a man of integrity, for whom I campaigned vigorously all across Virginia—is one of the most important state-level voices in the fight against neo-Marxism, and he is in office for the simple reason that enough parents and other concerned citizens came together and decided that enough was enough.

Like I said, it can happen anywhere.

CHAPTER THREE

The Newsroom Revolution

"That's just not true, Senator."

It was January of 2016, and Jake Tapper was calling me a liar to my face. Jake and I had been sitting in the back of my campaign bus for about twenty minutes at that point, conducting an interview for CNN's *State of the Union* that would air that next Sunday.

I paused for a moment.

The disagreement, as best I can recall, had come in the middle of an otherwise fair and relatively pleasant interview about the upcoming presidential election, and it centered on a vicious terrorist attack that had occurred during the Obama administration. On November 5, 2009, Nidal Hasan, a major in the Army who had become radicalized, opened fire on his fellow soldiers at Fort Hood military base in Texas. As he shouted "Allahu Akbar!" ("God is great"), he murdered fourteen innocent souls, including a pregnant woman and her unborn child.[1]

Any reasonable person assessing what happened knew immediately that this was an act of radical Islamic terrorism.

But the Obama administration didn't acknowledge that obvious fact. In the weeks after the shooting, the Obama Department of Defense decided, instead, to classify the incident as a case of "workplace violence,"[2] thereby preventing the soldiers who had been injured or murdered from receiving the Purple Heart. This medal, which is given to soldiers who've been wounded or killed in combat, cannot be awarded for mere "workplace violence." The Obama White House was incredibly reluctant even to acknowledge that "radical Islamic terrorism" exists. (Indeed, a few years later, in 2012, the FBI bizarrely "purged" 876 documents from its own training materials to remove any references to "jihad" or "Islamic terrorism.")[3] But the result was a gross injustice for the soldiers who had been wounded or murdered at Fort Hood.

And one of my first legislative victories in the Senate had been to correct that injustice. In 2014, I introduced an amendment mandating that the Purple Heart be awarded to the victims of Hasan's terrorist attack. I was a member of the Senate Armed Services Committee, and the Obama Pentagon fought my amendment vigorously. At the time, Democrats had the majority in the Senate, but nevertheless I was able to garner bipartisan support for my amendment, and it passed into law through the Harry Reid Senate. Obama signed it, and, in 2015, I was privileged to be at Fort Hood and thank the victims and their families personally when the Army finally awarded the more than forty Purple Hearts that were long overdue.

The statutory language in my amendment made clear that the Purple Heart should be awarded if the perpetrator of the attack "was in communication with [a] foreign terrorist organization before the attack" and "the attack was inspired or motivated by the foreign terrorist organization." Which brings us back to Jake Tapper.

What I said on that interview was that Nidal Hasan (a self-identified "Soldier of Allah") had been in repeated email contact with the radical cleric Anwar al-Awlaki, that he had asked about the permissibility of waging jihad on his fellow soldiers, and that the Obama administration knew about those communications—they intercepted and read them in their entirety—but inexplicably did nothing to prevent Hasan from carrying out the attack.

That's when Jake interrupted and said I was just wrong. "That just didn't happen, Senator," he confidently asserted.

With the tape still rolling, I said, "Actually, Jake, it *is* true. And you're objectively wrong." Smiling, I continued, "The facts will back that up; as John Adams once said, 'facts are stubborn things.'"

After telling me once more that I was not telling the truth, Jake moved on to other questions. We spoke about the pressing issues facing the country at the time, including my disagreements with Senator Marco Rubio on immigration, a few tweets from the future president Trump, and then, if I'm remembering correctly, even *more* tweets from the future president Trump.

After about twenty minutes, the interview was over. Jake and the rest of the CNN crew headed out into the frigid Iowa air, and I took a seat in the middle of the bus with a Diet Dr. Pepper. My seven- and five-year-old daughters, Caroline and Catherine, played on the floor as I talked with my staff about the barrage of interviews and events we had in the day before us. Around us, the mood on the bus was collegial and loose, as usual. Campaigning is fun—relentless and exhausting, but also exhilarating—and our team had become a close-knit family. Even near-zero temperatures and the dour faces of liberal news crews couldn't dampen our spirits.

Then, about ten minutes after the end of the interview, I heard a knock on the door of the bus. Someone opened the door to find Jake

Tapper standing outside with one of his producers. Jake said he needed to speak with me, so I told him to come in and have a seat.

Right away, I could sense that something was off. Jake looked more serious than usual. So did the person he'd brought with him.

"So," he said, seeming to want to tread lightly. "I did some research about the Fort Hood shooting…the thing we talked about. It turns out you were right, and I was wrong."

I nodded, appreciating his honesty.

"Now, I know we negotiated with your team that the interview would be live-to-tape, but we're in a tough situation here. So, I wanted to offer you two options. The first is that we'll air the entire interview as it occurred, with my mistake in it. Then, I will go on air right afterward with a message admitting that you were right and I was wrong. The second—and this is the one I would prefer, obviously—is that we cut out that whole conversation about Fort Hood and air the segment that way."

Two feelings washed over me. The first was gratitude to my press secretary Cat Frazier, who'd negotiated the terms of the interview with the producers at *State of the Union*. On my instructions, she had told the producers—and all producers for major media outlets—that I would consent to interviews *only* if they were live (meaning the conversation would be broadcast as it occurred) or "live-to-tape," meaning the conversation would be recorded and then aired in full—with no editing whatsoever—at a later date. In other words, the news networks couldn't take footage from the interview, move it around, and cut into my sentences to alter the meaning of what I had said.

I had learned this lesson the hard way the week earlier, when I had been interviewed by Bob Schieffer, the veteran host of *Face the Nation*. Schieffer, who was thirty-four years my senior, was apparently astonished that a young pup like me was daring to fight back hard in the Senate, which is likely why his questions seemed to be dripping in condescension and hostility. In response, I laid out a detailed indictment of the myriad policy failures of the Obama administration. My criticism was effective, so much so that *Face the Nation* simply edited it out. We had done a pre-tape, and their production team presumably decided that substantive criticism of Obama was not to be tolerated. So they omitted it, and instead ran select portions of my interview interspersed with Schieffer sneering at my partial (and edited) answers. This type of conduct is not exclusive to *Face the Nation* or CNN; sadly, it happens to be a widespread practice in the industry.

From then on, I was careful to specify that if news networks were going to interview me on television, they would need to air the entirety of whatever I had to say—with no editing. If my team hadn't negotiated for this beforehand, Tapper and his producers would have been free to slice up the interview in any way they pleased. They could, if they really wanted to, have re-cut the interview so that *I* looked like the one who was wrong, then maybe worked in some CGI footage of Jake Tapper hitting me over the head with a mallet.

If I had been another candidate—or simply an American citizen whom CNN had stopped to interview on the street—the network would have been free to use the partial footage as they wished, slicing it up to fit whatever particular narrative suited them.

Maybe that's why the second feeling that came over me was a mild sense of vengeance. For decades, left-leaning networks like CNN had acted like the self-righteous hall monitors of American society, always ready to call out politicians and candidates—especially Republicans—for making any small slip-up. It didn't matter whether these errors were made in good faith or if the politician in question had corrected himself immediately afterward; the news media would descend like a pack of wild hyenas and run tape of the mistake (or "gaffe," as these things were commonly called) until every television-watching person in the United States had seen it.

Newspapers would print full articles about the single incident for months.

Now here I was with a chance to make an anchor go live on CNN and admit that he, too, was capable of screwing up—a fact that the network was usually able to hide because it had the final edit on most clips, not to mention full staffs of producers and fact-checkers looking after every word that was said on air.

I thought about it for a moment. Clearly, it would have been in my short-term interest to let Jake go on television and admit that he'd screwed up. In the early stages of a presidential campaign, scoring such a clear victory against CNN would have been quite popular among Republican voters. If I *really* wanted to spike the football, I could have taken the clip and tweeted it out with something snarky, drawing even more attention to the failures of CNN and helping my campaign even more.

But I didn't do that. Instead, I told Jake not to worry about recording his apology, nice as it would have been to see it air that Sunday. I said he could take option number two and cut out the argument we'd had, then air the full interview as if we'd never even mentioned the shooting at Ford Hood. To this day, no one has ever seen that portion of the clip, and I'm sure no one ever will.

You might be wondering why I did it that way. So did a few of my campaign staffers, who were on the bus when this conversation occurred. (I could practically hear them salivating when Jake mentioned that he might go on television and admit he'd gotten something wrong.)

I let Jake Tapper off the hook in part simply because I liked the guy. By the time I ran for president, we had known each other for two decades, having met during the election of 2000. I'd been a young lawyer working on the policy team for George W. Bush, and Jake had been a cub reporter covering the campaign trail for the left-wing website Salon.

We didn't agree on much—he was a Democrat partisan even then—but I could tell that Jake, unlike many of the bloggers and biased reporters he was coming up with, would be successful in the news business. He seemed to care about getting his facts straight, and he didn't usually allow ideology to drive the stories he wrote or the questions he asked. He at least aspired to objectivity, attempting to treat both Republicans and Democrats with at least some degree of rigor in his reporting. Also, in this instance, I respected that Jake was admitting he was wrong. In other words, he wasn't a Keith Olbermann type, who in my view often foamed at the mouth in his partisanship, or the Rachel Maddow type, who frequently came off as a deranged conspiracy theorist, and I felt that anyone who resisted the temptation to go in that direction should be rewarded for it.

Most important, though, we were at the beginning of what was going to be a long campaign. I wanted my relationships with media outlets to remain cordial. The left-wing press was overtly antagonistic, but I thought we'd be more effective in getting our message out if we treated them respectfully and kept the lines of communication open. At the time, CNN had not yet fully descended into what I consider to be unhinged partisanship, and it was an important outlet for reaching the voters (particularly, the data showed, independent or undecided voters).

For my first few years in the Senate, I went on CNN often, sometimes once a week. I'd even go on MSNBC with some regularity. When I would go on their shows, of course, I had no illusions that the anchors would give me the same fawning coverage or softball questions that they reserved for my Democrat colleagues, but there was a hope at least that you might have a reasonable chance to explain your views.

At the time, those outlets purported to follow at least some ground rules. The most important was that actual journalists, almost all of whom leaned hard left politically, were supposed to set aside those biases when they clocked in in the morning and began writing stories about politics. At the very least, they needed to *pretend* to do this. After 5:00 p.m., they were free to throw on their *I'm With Her* T-shirts or their pink fuzzy hats.

By the time I was sitting on my campaign bus with Jake Tapper, there had been a few clear signs that this model was breaking down. I'm not sure anyone could have claimed that the media was acting objectively when they widely disseminated the false report that an image published by former vice presidential candidate Sarah Palin's PAC had inspired the shooting of Gabby Giffords,[4] for instance, or that these organizations were unbiased when they gave days of breathless coverage to Occupy Wall Street protestors.[5]

But in the aftermath of those scandals, the institutions responsible needed to express remorse for deliberately misleading the public. When a journalist made a mistake, he or she needed to either resign or do a great deal of work to explain to readers how that error had come to be, and why it wasn't going to happen again. That's what Dan Rather did when he was forced to resign from CBS News in 2005 after being caught using fraudulent documents on *60 Minutes* to broadcast a false attack on George W. Bush.

In 2004, the *New York Times* did something similar when it was revealed that the newspaper had falsely claimed that Saddam Hussein had weapons of mass destruction. In that case, a reporter was forced to leave the paper, and editors at the *Times* conducted a full investigation to see how they had managed to get the story so wrong.[6]

But when Donald Trump began rising in the polls, this began to change. Toward the end of the 2016 general election, when most news organizations were giving Trump about a 2 percent chance of winning, the partisanship of the media wasn't yet fully unhinged (at least compared to what was coming). There were the usual hit pieces that would have been aimed at any Republican candidate. Donald Trump was called a fascist, which is a charge that liberal news outlets have levelled at every Republican since Ronald Reagan. In October of 2016, the *Boston Globe* ran a fake front page predicting the apocalyptic events that would befall everyone if he ever became president.[7] For a while, it seemed like this whole ordeal might conclude peacefully on Election Day, when Donald Trump was predicted to lose big.

Then he won.

For the previous few years, the bottom ranks of American newspapers and cable networks had been slowly filling up with young, woke staffers. These were people who had been educated in Critical Race Theory, postmodernism, and other neo-Marxist nonsense at our nation's top universities—Harvard, Yale, Stanford, and Columbia, among others. While at school, they had imbibed ideas about systemic racism and the alleged evils of American history. Some of them had gone straight into journalism from college, while others had stopped along the way at various graduate schools of journalism, where they sat in small classrooms and debated the new role of the journalist in a world where, they were assured, fascism was about to break out at any moment.

For the next few years, these young woke staffers sat at the bottom rungs of institutions such as the *New York Times*, CNN, and other news organizations that had been drifting further and further to the political left with each passing year. They wrote stories about the inherent racism of American society and occasionally conducted interviews with left-wing professors about similar topics. They pointed out why scenes in the latest installment of *The Justice League* were transphobic. They made "listicles" of all the times cats did funny things to other house pets, slowly building the case that this kind of nonsense belonged on the front pages of newspapers and the homepages of online news organizations.

Like all good neo-Marxists, they were biding their time, waiting for an opportunity to rise up and take control of the institutions that had hired them.

In November of 2016, as the American news business threw fits of hysterics over the new presidency of Donald J. Trump, they saw their moment.

American journalism has not been the same since.

Reporters and Revolutionaries

In August of 2019, the staff of the *New York Times* gathered for a town hall meeting at the newspaper's auditorium on Eighth Avenue in New York City.

The mood was tense, to say the least.

A few weeks earlier, Special Counsel Robert Mueller had released his long-awaited report on the Trump campaign's non-existent collusion with Russia, dashing the hopes of liberals all over the United States who had been assured repeatedly—often by reporters at the *Times*—that it was only a matter of time before President Trump was arrested, tried for treason, and shipped off to some prison colony in Siberia for his innumerable crimes.[8] Given just how wrong the *New York Times* had been about this massive story, and given the Pulitzer Prize they had won for their factually inaccurate reporting on it,[9] it would have made sense if the topic of the town hall meeting was how to do better in the future. At the very least, they might have issued a series of corrections.

For a few minutes, that's exactly the direction that Dean Baquet, who'd been the paper's executive editor for about four years at that point, tried to go in.

"We had a couple of significant missteps," he said. "This is a really hard story, newsrooms haven't confronted one like this since the 1960s. It got trickier after [it] went from being a story about whether the Trump campaign had colluded with Russia and obstruction of justice to being a more head-on story about the president's character. We built our newsroom to cover one story, and we did it truly well. Now we have to regroup, and shift resources and emphasis to take on a different story."[10]

As admissions of guilt go, this is not exactly impressive. But it's not like the executive editor of the *New York Times* was going to get up in front of his staff and say, *Well gang, we sure blew that one; someone go get all those prizes from the hallways and ship them back to the Pulitzer committee, stat.* Later in the meeting, Baquet would admit that the staff of his newspaper had been caught "a little tiny bit flat-footed" by the outcome of the Mueller investigation. He'd also say that the reaction of most readers of the *Times*, upon finding out that President Trump was not going to be sent to prison for collusion, was "Holy shit, Bob Mueller's not going to do it."

But the staffers who'd gathered in the hall that day didn't care that their newspaper had just blown one of the biggest stories of the twenty-first century. They didn't care that the newsgathering organization they worked for—the one that was still widely considered the "paper of record," to be studied by historians for decades to come—had fallen for a hoax that wouldn't have fooled Inspector Clouseau of *Pink Panther* fame. Evidently, none of them wanted to talk about how they might prevent their paper from basing another three years of coverage on something as flimsy as a lurid and fictional dossier, a few anonymous sources, and the word of a disgraced British spy working for the Hillary Clinton campaign.

They wanted to talk, as always, about racism.

As soon as Dean Baquet was done speaking, an unnamed staffer stepped up to a microphone and demanded, astoundingly, to know why the *New York Times* did not call President Trump a racist more often. Specifically, he or she (or they, or zim/zer) wanted to know why the paper did not explicitly use the word "racist" in headlines that described the president's actions and remarks.

Speaking with all the restraint he could muster, Baquet (who, it bears mentioning, happens to be a Black man) said that he believed that as a reporter, the best way to report what someone had said was... well, to *report what they had said*.

"You quote the remarks," said Baquet. "The most powerful journalism I have ever read, and that I've ever witnessed, was when writers actually just described what they heard and put them in some perspective. I just think that's more powerful."[11]

Twenty years earlier—even *three* years earlier—saying something like this to an audience full of journalists would not have been controversial. Everyone in the room, even the ones who were the most rabidly left-wing in their private lives, would have agreed (or at least pretended to agree) that straight-news reporters like the ones at the *New York Times* were not supposed to inject their own opinions into their stories, especially not when those stories were intended to give readers, and future historians, a fair and accurate summary of the day's events. Everyone in the room would have understood that journalists, no matter how impassioned their private political leanings, were not supposed to be activists. For most of the twentieth century, in fact, many of them would have refrained from being personal friends with anyone in politics, and perhaps even from *voting*, to avoid the appearance of any bias toward one side or the other.

During that time, when Dean Baquet and many editors of major newspapers were coming up in journalism, the American news business claimed that it strived for objectivity above all else. There had been a time, however, in the more distant past, when this hadn't been the case. In the 1800s, newspapers advocated explicitly for political parties, filling their front pages with overtly slanted and sensationalized news stories. Some, like the *New Orleans Daily Democrat*, even carried the names of these parties in their banners.

The type of reporting these papers did, which became known as "yellow journalism," was popular. But it left the American people without a place to go for a clear, unbiased account of the day's events. People had to rely on gossipy rags that sold for pennies on the street, or else look to the government for information, which would inevitably come with its own partisan slant, depending on the party in power. The choice was between sensationalized, slanted trash or government propaganda.

There's some debate about when exactly this changed. But most scholars of journalism agree that the shift began sometime in the early twentieth century. This is when the writer Walter Lippmann, who had, somewhat ironically, been heavily involved in writing government propaganda for the administration of President Woodrow Wilson, wrote an essay called "Liberty and the News." In that essay, published in 1920, Lippmann argued that the news business was giving people a sense that they were "being baffled and misled"; he lamented "the loss of contact with objective information," saying that writers and reporters were more likely to tell people what to think rather than giving them the honest truth. The news, in other words, was propaganda.

"Without protection against propaganda," he wrote, "without standards of evidence, without criteria of emphasis, the living substance of all popular decision is exposed to every prejudice and to infinite exploitation.... There can be no liberty for a community which lacks the information by which to detect lies."[12]

Gradually, over a period of a few decades, the job of a reporter became professionalized and even respectable. The *Washington Post*, *New York Times*, and many other newspapers employed enormous staffs whose job it was to collect facts, organize them, and deliver them to the American people in a manner that was accurate, sharp, and fair. That didn't mean that the news had to be boring, and it didn't mean that it had to be wishy-washy, either. It meant that reporters needed to find, or at least attempt to find, all sides of a given issue. They were supposed to follow the facts where they led—and it wasn't supposed to matter whether those facts were ugly, complicated, or inconvenient to the personal beliefs of the journalists.

Some of the best works of journalism ever published were written using exactly that method. If you go back and read through Bob Woodward and Carl Bernstein's coverage of the Watergate burglary and the cover-up that came after it, in the mid-1970s, you'll notice that there is very little emotionally charged language in their prose. Woodward and Bernstein did not call people "crooks" or "enemies of democracy," and they didn't write any more than they were able to uncover, one step at a time, through the use of documents and interviews. That process was often painful and deliberately slow, as they would write years later in their book *All the President's Men*, and it made many of their colleagues doubt that they had a real story at all.

But in the end, the reporting came together to tell an amazing tale of paranoia, corruption, and hubris on the part of President Richard Nixon and his band of crooked criminals—men whose various misdeeds I chronicled at length in the opening chapter of my last book, *Justice Corrupted*. One imagines that their reporting would not have been nearly as impactful, or as long-lasting, if it had been written in the style of today's revolutionary, activist journalists. "Racist Cuban Men Connected to President Richard Nixon, Who Is Also Racist, Break into Watergate Complex, a Building with Deep Ties to White Supremacy, Likely Trying to Steal a Videotape of Prostitutes Urinating on the President" doesn't quite have the same force as the calm, informative headlines that Woodward and Bernstein used in their reporting.[13]

Reflecting, years later at an event hosted by the White House Correspondents' Association, on the process of getting that story, Carl Bernstein used a phrase that great journalists of the past often employed when discussing their jobs. He urged the reporters in the room, many of whom were covering the Trump White House, to find and write "the best obtainable version of the truth." He talked about interviewing sources, painstakingly reviewing documents, and going back to those sources and documents dozens of times in the attempt to find the truth.[14]

As they listened, I'm sure many of the reporters in the audience were fantasizing in their heads about breaking the Trump-Russia collusion story wide open and earning similar acclaim for their work. By that time, many of the news outlets they worked for had even begun referring to the breaking non-story as "Russiagate," applying the standard suffix for all modern political scandals.

But there was a key difference. Whereas the Watergate scandal began with an actual crime—the break-in at the Watergate complex—that was eventually traced back to the president through careful reporting and analysis of documents, the "Russiagate" scandal moved in exactly the opposite direction. Liberal reporters who hated Donald Trump and had wanted to stop him from taking office (in part because of his mean tweets) looked around for anything they could find to prevent (and when that didn't work, to destroy) the Trump presidency, eventually settling on an obscure set of allegations that would later turn out to have been bought, paid for, and peddled to media outlets by the campaign of Hillary Clinton herself.

Every time these reporters hit a stumbling block or a brick wall in their pursuit of this fantastical theory, there was always another anonymous source to rely on or another set of unverified allegations to print. This type of "reporting" followed the example of Marxist forbear Lavrentiy Beria, Stalin's chief of the Soviet secret police, who joked about the ease with which he could indict his political enemies: "Show me the man and I'll show you the crime."

I'm sure that if any of these reporters ever had doubts about whether these stories were true or not, they were able to chase them away by convincing themselves that this was noble work—that Donald Trump, a *literal* fascist in their eyes, simply could not remain in power. This, of course, is the same excuse that Marxist revolutionaries throughout history have used to justify the monstrous crimes of the regimes they served. They have always believed that while their side might be doing very bad things, it was nothing compared to what came before.

Like the revolutionaries of the past, these new activist journalists—many of whom proudly count themselves among the #resistance, modeling themselves on antifascists in World War II—tolerated no opposition among their ranks. Speaking recently to Jeff Gerth, who wrote an excellent piece for the *Columbia Journalism Review* on the various missteps that the media made during the worst of the Russiagate scandal, the independent journalist Matt Taibbi described his experience.

Taibbi, who was a left-wing reporter for most of his life, wrote for *The Nation, Playboy, New York Press*, and *New York Sports Express*. He won a National Magazine Award for reporting he published in *Rolling Stone*. His work regularly drew comparisons to the gonzo journalism of writer Hunter S. Thompson, who had also covered politics for *Rolling Stone*. However, when Taibbi began writing stories raising doubts about the veracity of the Russiagate allegations against President Trump, left-wing media voices immediately denounced him. It didn't matter that he'd been "on the right team," so to speak, for so many years, or that he was a subject-matter expert on Russia, having lived there for most of his twenties.

"'It was a career-changing moment for me,' he said in an interview. The 'more neutral approach' to reporting 'went completely out the window once Trump got elected. Saying anything publicly about the story that did not align with the narrative—the repercussions were huge for any of us that did not go there. That is crazy.'"[15]

The journalists in the auditorium of the *New York Times* in 2019 were unwilling to allow the facts to shift their focus from their ideological commitments. Dean Baquet's answer on race was not good enough for them. The person who had asked the original question hounded him again when he tried to move on to something else, demanding that Baquet address the issue of why the *Times* didn't call President Trump a racist more explicitly.[16]

Suddenly, Dean Baquet, who had come up in the newsrooms of the late twentieth century, when objectivity was supposed to be the gold standard, found himself in the same position that countless professors, business executives, and politicians have been in over the past few years: standing in front of a room filled with angry, woke, (mostly) young neo-Marxists, all of whom want to shame and bully you into submission. If you say one wrong word during these interactions—if you even make a hand gesture that the crowd doesn't like—you'll find yourself trending on Twitter within seconds, and looking for a new job within minutes.

I'm sure Baquet knew better than anyone how carefully he'd have to tread for the next few minutes, which brought more and more questions on the same topic: race, power dynamics, and why the *New York Times* was not more concerned with calling out racism anywhere and everywhere it occurred.

In the middle of the meeting, one staffer rose to suggest that race should be part of *every single story* the *Times* published from then on. The full question is astounding:

> **Anonymous Staffer:** Hello, I have another question about racism. I'm wondering to what extent you think that the fact of racism and white supremacy being sort of the foundation of this country should play into our reporting. Just because it feels to me like it should be a starting point, you know? Like these conversations about what is racist, what isn't racist. I just feel like racism is in everything. It should be considered in our science reporting, in our culture reporting, in our

national reporting. And so, to me, it's less about the individual instances of racism, and sort of how we're thinking about racism and white supremacy as the foundation of all of the systems in the country.[17]

If nothing else, this long-winded, nonsensical question reveals just how deeply the principles of wokeness and neo-Marxism had already invaded the newsroom of the *New York Times* in the lead-up to the so-called "racial reckoning" that occurred during the summer of 2020. And how little journalistic standards mattered anymore at the *Times*; you could be a vapid Valley Girl with poor grammar, but you'd be celebrated if you virtue-signaled correctly (". . . the fact of racism and white supremacy being sort of the foundation of this country. . . . Just because it feels to me like. . . . Like these conversations about what is racist, what isn't racist. I just feel like racism is in everything.") It amply explains the coverage that came during and after the events of that summer, much of which might as well have appeared on the front page of the Communist Party USA's *Daily Worker*.

Near the end of his or her question, the staffer mentions how proud he or she feels that the *Times* would soon publish the 1619 Project, which would come out just a few weeks after the town hall meeting in 2019. In many ways the publication of this project, which is riddled with factual inaccuracies and gross and deliberate distortions of history, signaled a paradigm shift at the "paper of record," and in American journalism more generally. For years the new woke staffers had been at war with the old guard, and the old guard had been managing to hold them back to some degree. Every time there was a flare-up over some "microaggression" in a newsroom, the damage was mostly contained, and the story was confined to the media sections of other news outlets. Whenever journalists called out their employers on social media for being racist, as they often did, the top brass at those institutions would hold "listening sessions" and promise to "do better" in the future.[18]

But with the publication of the 1619 Project, the neo-Marxists began to claim victory over the real reporters who simply wanted to report the facts. And it was not enough, at least according to the staffers at the *Times*'s town hall meeting, to publish long propaganda pieces like the work of Nikole Hannah-Jones and other contributors to the 1619 Project. Antiracism had to be present in every story that the *Times* published, and in every section of the paper's coverage.

During the worst of the rioting burning through American cities in the summer of 2020, the *New York Post* published a piece by Charles Kesler, illustrated with a picture of a defaced statue of Thomas Jefferson, entitled "Call Them the 1619 Riots."[19]

"It would be an honor," Nikole Hannah-Jones replied on Twitter.[20]

A few months later, when my colleague Tom Cotton wrote an op-ed urging President Trump to "send in the troops" to restore order to American cities,[21] the young staffers at the *New York Times* were incensed. Over a period of a few days, they conducted a smear campaign against Senator Cotton on Twitter, posting the identical message, "Running this puts Black NYTimes staff in danger."

And their hysteria had its intended effect: the *Times*'s editorial page editor, James Bennet, was immediately forced to step down. Of course, Bennet was a partisan Democrat (indeed, his brother currently serves as a Democratic senator from Colorado). His punishable offense was even *acknowledging* that any contrary view existed. Bennet prostrated himself before an all-staff virtual meeting and apologized for publishing the op-ed—under what kind of pressure, I can only imagine. According to publisher A. G. Sulzberger, the "tone" of the op-ed was "needlessly harsh," and as a result, "both of us concluded that James would not be able to lead the team through the next leg of change that is required."[22]

Mind you, nobody thought Bennet agreed with Senator Cotton. Indeed, nobody on earth thought that *anybody* at the *Times* agreed with Cotton that we should be more vigorous in stopping the Antifa and Black Lives Matter rioting and looting. But because he dared to publish an op-ed—that he vigorously disagreed with—*from a sitting U.S. senator*, Bennet was effectively forced out of his job. He resigned in June of 2020.[23]

This incident gave the nation a rare look not only into the nasty internal politics of the *New York Times*, but also into the extremely far-left political views of the reporters who work there. In a sane world, the stories about left-wing rioters running rampant through cities, attempting to burn down federal buildings, and causing millions of dollars of damage to property would have been the story of the decade; there would have been correspondents on the ground covering these riots with a sustained critical eye, counting up all the damage done and doing long narrative exposés on just how these rioters had been spurred to violence by their ideas. Had the mobs been right-wing groups engaging in some kind of anti-immigration protests, you can bet that the coverage would have gone in that direction. But the rioters shared the politics of most *New York Times* reporters, so that didn't happen.

Back at the newsroom, this complete incuriosity about the world was beginning to grate on journalists who actually wanted to do…well, *journalism*. One of them was Bari Weiss, a relatively young left-wing editorial writer who was not completely woke or insane. She had been hired by the *Times* shortly after the 2020 election, ostensibly to help address the lack of ideological diversity at the paper. At first glance, it seemed that she was a perfect fit. Although she did write about issues such as the censorship of conservatives on social media platforms and the various ways that Jewish people were discriminated against by the Left, she also shared a great deal of the *Times*'s supposedly liberal values. For starters, she was an openly gay woman who had voted for

Barack Obama twice. She was also a sharp writer and a deep thinker who believed in developing stories carefully and following them wherever they led.

But the mob hated her. To the new neo-Marxist woke contingent at the *Times*, Bari Weiss might as well have been Adolf Hitler. When she tweeted a picture of an Asian figure skater in 2018 with the caption "Immigrants: they get the job done" (a terrific line from the musical *Hamilton*), the internal message boards of the *New York Times* lit up as if she'd committed some kind of hate crime. It turned out the figure skater, unbeknownst to Weiss, had been born not in a foreign country but in California, although her parents had immigrated from China some decades earlier. The young woke staffers were "offended" and "disgusted" by the tweet, or at least they were performing disgust and offense to please their fellow revolutionaries.[24]

According to the laws of woke, whoever is most offended, or can claim the greatest oppression, gains the most status; the incentive, therefore, is to take offense at everything and never give anyone—especially not conservatives—the benefit of the doubt. After a few more months of passive-aggressive (and sometimes plain-old aggressive) jabs from the leftist staffers in her office, Bari Weiss made the decision to leave the *New York Times*, once the most respected institution in American journalism. Her resignation letter, addressed to the paper's publisher, A. G. Sulzberger, and still available on her website, is a remarkable document—one that should be assigned and discussed at every journalism school in the country. I would encourage readers to look it up and read the whole thing.

A relevant sample:

...the lessons that ought to have followed the election [of Donald Trump in 2016]—lessons about the importance of understanding other Americans, the necessity of resisting tribalism, and the centrality of the free exchange of ideas to a democratic society—have not been learned. Instead, a new consensus has emerged in the press, but perhaps especially at this paper: that truth isn't a process of collective discovery, but an orthodoxy already known to an enlightened few whose job is to inform everyone else.

Twitter is not on the masthead of The New York Times. But Twitter has become its ultimate editor. As the ethics and mores of that platform have become those of the paper, the paper itself has increasingly become a kind of performance space. Stories are chosen and told in a way to satisfy the narrowest of audiences, rather than to allow a curious public to read about the world and then draw their own conclusions. I was always taught that journalists were charged with writing the first rough draft of history. Now, history itself is one more ephemeral thing molded to fit the needs of a predetermined narrative.[25]

I couldn't have said it better myself. What Bari Weiss puts her finger on is the tendency of all revolutions—especially Marxist ones—to insist on complete agreement at all times. When you're dealing with a woke, neo-Marxist movement, the truth is whatever the revolutionaries need it to be at that very moment. This is why, when communists come to power in a given society, independent newspapers are usually among the first institutions to fall. It happened in the Soviet Union, and it certainly happened in Cuba. The revolutionaries knew that if people were able to find objective truth, their regime could not last.

What's most troubling about the woke revolution in the United States, of course, is that the revolution began, and is being perpetuated by, the institutions of American journalism themselves. The calls (for censorship, race obsession, and total adherence to the woke narrative) are coming from inside the house.

At first glance, it may seem a little excessive to spend so much time on the internal politics of the *New York Times* in a book about Cultural Marxism. It may seem like a foregone conclusion that the people who work there are hopelessly woke and unbelievably biased in selecting their stories. I'm sure many people think that they have been for decades.

But like it or not, for decades the *Times* has been considered the gold standard as far as newsgathering institutions go. If there is one journalistic institution that *should* be equipped to deliver straight, unbiased news to the American people, it's this one. The paper has millions of dollars, access to the best journalists in the world, and a brand that most people in the country recognize and trust. It's been that way for nearly a century now. Moreover, virtually every journalist and every editor in America reads the *Times*; its stories drive print, television, and radio stories in markets across the nation, large and small. As the writer Gay Talese put it in his book-length biography of the paper, *The Kingdom and the Power*, Americans have viewed the institution for years as "necessary proof of the world's existence, a barometer of its pressure, an assessor of its sanity. If the world did indeed still exist…it would be duly recorded each day in *The Times*."[26]

This is the point.

From the outside, it would seem that the *New York Times* should have more institutional safeguards against being corrupted in this way than any other organization in history. The stages that a story must go through before publication—each one intended to make sure that the facts within that story are accurate, fair, and unbiased—are numerous, and they are not present at most journalistic institutions in the United States. This raises a question. If this much bias from woke neo-Marxists has been allowed to take over at the *New York Times*, once considered the gold standard of American information-gathering, what the hell is going on at other places that *don't* have the resources, manpower, and institutional prestige that the paper of record does?

As Geoffrey Chaucer memorably put it in his prologue to *The Canterbury Tales*, "If gold rust, what shall iron do?"

The answer, as many of us who've been following the news business for the past few years know, is that the institutions we once trusted to bring us information will continue to rust and corrode until very little is left of them. The news organizations that were once called "mainstream" will drift further and further toward the radical left—selecting their stories and writing them to please an increasingly radicalized audience of woke neo-Marxists—and ultimately die out when they realize there is no more room to their left.

If you need proof, look around.

The State of the Union

Today, the landscape of American journalism is grim. Even the outlets that enjoyed a brief sugar high during the Trump presidency, largely by publishing countless stories warning their loyal readers that fascism was coming at any moment, are now seeing a marked decline in revenue. This is especially true at CNN, which (hilariously) attempted to launch a streaming service called CNN+ in 2022, believing for some reason that viewers who barely watch the network for free would suddenly want to pay $9.99 a month for the privilege.

The fact that the service lasted less than thirty days and aired only a handful of shows speaks to the absolute unwillingness of people to pay for anything with the toxic letters "CNN" attached to it.

It's no surprise that trust in the mainstream media has hit an all-time low. The most recent figures indicate that only 7 percent of Americans have "a great deal" of trust in the mainstream media.[27] In November of 2022 a Canadian foundation hosted a debate on the proposition that we should trust the mainstream media. Arguing for the motion were Malcolm Gladwell and Michelle Goldberg, figures from the *New Yorker* and the *New York Times*, respectively. Arguing against it were the author and commentator Douglas Murray, for whose excellent work I have great respect, and Matt Taibbi, whom I had the pleasure of meeting just before he testified before Congress about the Twitter Files.

At the beginning of the debate, the audience was split along relatively even lines: 52 percent believed that the mainstream media should, in most instances, be trusted, while 48 percent believed that it usually shouldn't be. With every minute that the debate went on, that balance shifted steadily. For about one hour, Murray and Taibbi provided countless examples of stories that the mainstream media had bungled, citing precise quotes, dates, and headlines. They covered the Hunter Biden laptop story, which was deliberately buried by virtually every "mainstream" news outlet in the country because it would be damaging to Joe Biden, as well as various stories about Covid that later turned out to have been completely false.

"I grew up in the press. My father was a reporter. My stepmother was a reporter. My godparents were reporters. Every adult I knew growing up seemed to be in media," said Matt Taibbi, according to a summary of the event in *National Review*. "I love the news business. It's in my bones. But I mourn for it. It's destroyed itself."

When the debate was over, the audience was polled again. After hearing the arguments from both sides, the balance had shifted completely. More than a third of the audience (39 percent) had changed their views and now supported the motion that the mainstream media should not be trusted. It was the single largest swing in the history of the Munk Debates, which have been running for many years.[28]

Sadly, the responsibility that journalists once felt to get a story right and to admit their errors—the very sense that made Jake Tapper come back onto my campaign bus, apologize, and try to keep the record correct as recently as 2016—is falling quickly away, replaced by an unabashed left-wing activism that would have been unthinkable in past decades. In the war between the Nikole Hannah-Jones faction of American journalism, whose adherents appear to believe that reporting is simply a means to achieve their neo-Marxist political goals, and the old guard, who were trained to believe that the news business exists to inform the American people about the world around them, the neo-Marxists are winning.

Like all good revolutionaries, they are "pulverizing" the past, either forcing their older, more sane colleagues to adopt their views, or shaming them into submission with baseless accusations of racism, sexism, or transphobia.

It's working.

Rather than attempting to return to some notion of fairness and objectivity in their reporting, these organizations are leaning even harder into their left-wing activism. In January of 2023, a longtime editor at the *Washington Post* named Leonard Downie published a long, supposedly well-researched piece in the back pages of the paper titled, "Newsrooms That Move beyond 'Objectivity' Can Build Trust."

In this piece, written in prose that is stilted and confusing enough to make Karl Marx himself proud, Downie—who, as he notes, was an editor at the *Post* back when the paper was publishing its famous Watergate coverage—recites his new woke talking points perfectly. Reading through the piece, one gets the impression of an eighteenth-century French nobleman trying desperately to talk his way out of being guillotined as the revolutionaries begin gathering outside his door—by declaring his loyalty to the revolution.

The very notion of objectivity, Downie writes, "was dictated over decades by male editors in predominantly White newsrooms and reinforced their own view of the world. [Today's reporters] believe that pursuing objectivity can lead to false balance or misleading 'bothside-sism' in covering stories about race, the treatment of women, LGBTQ+ rights, income inequality, climate change and many other subjects. And, in today's diversifying newsrooms, they feel it negates many of their own identities, life experiences and cultural contexts, keeping them from pursuing truth in their work."

For the rest of the piece, Downie quotes more than seventy-five people who work in newsrooms, most of whom are on board with this strange neo-Marxist way of looking at the job of a "journalist." They speak throughout of the imperative to center "lived experience" over facts, and the apparently urgent need to call many more things racist much more often.[29]

How anyone could read the modern corporate media for even one day and come to the conclusion that they don't call things racist enough is beyond my understanding. I also wonder what these people mean when they say lived experience—are they comparing it to dreamed experience? What they really mean, of course, is that their own emotions and feelings—and especially their own ideological dogma—should be elevated above actual facts, quotes, evidence, data, or reality to the contrary.

One editor at the *Los Angeles Times* said that he was trying to make sure that journalists felt safe engaging in activism, noting that the leadership of that newsroom was "trying to create an environment in which we don't police our journalists too much. Our young people want to be participants in the world." Another editor said plainly: "Objectivity has got to go."[30]

For a long time, journalists attempted to hide their passion for left-wing activism. Now, they are utterly brazen in their partisan ideological bias and their willingness to actively deceive the public to advance their agenda.

That's because they don't think they're doing anything wrong.

How to Fight Back

Of course, there are reasons for hope. There always are.

Individual citizens can speak up and hold the media accountable for its misrepresentations. As we saw with the army of "pajama bloggers" who took down Dan Rather,[31] sunshine can be a powerful tool against lies. Likewise, the voices of countless Americans mocking CNN for its "fiery but mostly peaceful protests" chyron, as their reporter stood before a massive burning building, had a profound effect. As did the millions online who mercilessly mocked the NBC reporter who claimed that the NASCAR audience chanting "F*** Joe Biden" was yelling "Let's go Brandon!"[32]

Moreover, in the past few years alone, several new media organizations have sprung up to offer alternatives to the biased, left-wing mainstream media. Some are outspoken about their conservative leanings, while others attempt to go at the news in a more objective manner. Bari Weiss, admirably, has started a media venture called The Free Press, which aims to give an unbiased look at current events.

The Daily Wire has built an entire media empire, routinely breaking stories that the corporate media ignores. In the aftermath of the Scott Smith incident in Loudoun County, it wasn't reporters at our nation's "premier" media institutions who got to the root of the story. It was an excellent investigative reporter named Luke Rosiak, who did weeks' worth of on-the-ground reporting—what Woodward and Bernstein became famous for—to reveal the massive cover-up in the Loudoun County school system. To this day, his reporting on the subject serves as the most accurate account in all of journalism of left-wing corruption at the local level.

Likewise, conservative viewpoints can often be found on outlets like Red State, *National Review*, The Daily Caller, The Daily Wire, Breitbart, Town Hall, the *Washington Examiner, Washington Times, New York*

Post, and New York Sun, not to mention Fox News, Newsmax, OANN, and most of talk radio.

We need more right-of-center media outlets. Or just outlets that report actual *facts*, rather than left-wing dogma. Conservatives and libertarians with real resources need to invest seriously in (1) starting new media outlets, (2) growing the reach of existing reasonable outlets, and, critically, (3) buying major branded corporate media outlets. In 2013 Jeff Bezos, the left-wing billionaire, bought the *Washington Post* for $250 million. That's a lot of money, to be sure, but nobody thinks Bezos bought the *Post* because he believed in the long-term profitability of print media. Rather, in my estimation, he wanted to control the commanding heights of political discourse.

There are countless conservative business leaders today who could have afforded the purchase price of the *Post*, but most no doubt took a narrow cost-benefit analysis and concluded that a slightly higher profit margin could be found in manufacturing widgets in Tennessee. But if we do not retake journalism from the neo-Marxists who have captured it—if we allow the media to remain overt propagandists—American capitalism cannot survive much longer. Not just the *Post*; those who care about free speech and vibrant democracy should buy newspapers in major cities across America, along with major networks like ABC, NBC, CBS, or CNN. And not just English-language media, but Spanish as well.

Buying these institutions could dramatically—and instantaneously—transform the media landscape, as we saw in 2022 when Elon Musk invested $44 billion and purchased Twitter. And then shocked the tech world by releasing what would be called "the Twitter Files," which took a deep, often horrifying look at the extent to which left-wing neo-Marxists had taken over not just American journalism, but Big Tech as well. The corporate media largely ignored the Twitter

Files because reporting on the story—one of the greatest scandals of modern times—conflicted with their own political agenda. But the right-of-center outlets provided at least some coverage for the shocking revelations.

The leftists' takeover of Big Tech has been perhaps their most sinister achievement—so that the events that occurred behind the curtain at Twitter, Facebook, YouTube, Google, and other platforms merit a much longer discussion.

Which begins now.

CHAPTER FOUR

Big Tech

For as long as we've been a nation, there have been "open secrets" in Washington, D.C. I'm sure most people are aware, for instance, that Speaker of the House Nancy Pelosi, who often gets inside briefings on the American economy and what's about to happen to it, has an uncanny ability to pick stocks that substantially beat the market.[1] Likewise, many have noticed that several top members of the Democratic Party were...let's just say *more friendly than necessary* with noted pedophile Jeffrey Epstein.[2]

Around the end of President Obama's first term, when Twitter and Facebook were just beginning to become the de facto platforms for sharing information and conducting political discussions online, we began hearing about another open secret. In this case, it was about the tendency of Big Tech platforms like Twitter, Facebook, YouTube, and Google to "shadow ban" conservative content. The allegation was that the employees at these tech companies—who, as everyone knew, were almost exclusively on the left—were intentionally limiting the reach of conservative figures online.

With each passing day, these allegations became more and more plausible. A simple Google search about a hot topic would yield results from uniformly left-wing publications, typically relegating more conservative content to the eighth or ninth page of the search results—which, in terms of the internet, might as well be Siberia. Numerous conservative figures who used Twitter as their primary means of communication reported that their "engagement," meaning the number of people who could see and share their posts, would suddenly plummet with no explanation. One day the posts that a conservative person made would be getting millions, even tens of millions of views; the next day, those numbers would be in the thousands or even hundreds. The same thing also happened on YouTube, the video-streaming service that Google acquired in 2006, as users who posted conservative content regularly saw their reach stifled, and at times were even notified that their accounts had been "de-monetized" or that their videos could no longer be shared.[3]

From the beginning, I saw the danger of allowing this to continue. In part, that was because I had seen first-hand the power of social media networks like Facebook and Twitter during my first campaign for Senate in 2012. During that campaign, we would routinely organize rallies and generate grassroots momentum relying heavily on Facebook. At times, I'd participate in livestreamed question-and-answer sessions, allowing me to speak with people all around Texas who weren't able to come out and ask me questions in person.

Although I still preferred to do the bulk of my campaigning face-to-face—and still do—the internet allowed me and my campaign to do amazing things. For starters, it brought together conservatives from all over the state and the nation who had the same ideas and frustrations but didn't know it—or at least didn't know that there were other people who felt the same way. If you look through the early Tea Party message boards, for example, you'll often see messages from new Facebook users who are overjoyed at having found a community of people who'd been stepped on, ignored, and otherwise marginalized by the political status quo.

Together, these people formed a movement that sent shock waves through the nation, issuing a stunning rebuke to the Obama administration and the left-wing policies they were pushing down everyone's throats. Their support helped send me to Congress in 2012—as well as several other candidates, both then and two years earlier, who campaigned against the Washington establishment, including my friends Mike Lee of Utah and Rand Paul of Kentucky. Although we came from different backgrounds and represented different constituencies, these other new lawmakers and I came together with the common purpose of pushing back against the massive overreach of the Obama administration.

To most of the corporate media, we were partisan bomb throwers who loved chaos and attention. As one headline in *GQ* put it in a profile of me, I was nothing but a "Wacko Bird from Texas" who wanted to impose my will on the nation's capital.[4]

But that was Washington. Back home, the people had our backs. And thanks to the advent of social media, the people had more of a voice than ever.

It was around the time that the Washington establishment, particularly the long-established media institutions, realized that they didn't have as much power as they once did. As these people soon found out, the average Texan was not apt to begin his or her day by reading the latest long-form profile in the *Washington Post* or the *New Republic*, long considered two of the most important publications in American politics. (During the Clinton administration, the *New Republic* was only half-jokingly referred to as "the in-flight magazine of Air Force

One.") Increasingly, though, the average Texans *did* begin their day by opening Facebook or Twitter and scrolling through their feeds. So did the average Iowan, the average North Dakotan, and millions of people from states all over the country.

On their social media feeds, people found posts and speeches that often came straight from the source, delivered without the mediation of partisan journalists or political pundits. At the time, posts were largely organized chronologically, meaning that when users logged onto Twitter or opened the app on their smartphones, they would see each post from everyone they were following in order, without anyone deliberately pulling the strings or putting a thumb on the scale. Suddenly I was able to deliver a speech or a more subdued address right from my office and send it out to the hundreds of thousands (and later millions) of people who were following me on social media.

This meant a deeper and more immediate connection with my constituents, which was good. It also meant that I could spend less time in television studios rubbing shoulders with the Washington elite, which was even better.

I can still recall vividly, for instance, the thousands of supportive messages that came my way during my Obamacare filibuster. At the time, in 2013, it was my first year in the Senate, and I spoke for over twenty-one hours nonstop on the Senate floor to try to stop Obamacare from being implemented. While the corporate media attempted to paint me and my colleagues as lunatics and attention-seeking cretins, the people watching C-SPAN or Fox or live feeds of our speeches knew why we were fighting so hard to draw attention to the issue. At the time, my daughters were just three and five, and I tried to read them a bedtime story every night I was home. So when evening fell, I decided to read them *Green Eggs and Ham* from the Senate floor so they could watch on TV. To this day, one of my favorite pictures ever is of both girls in their pajamas watching in amazement as Daddy read Dr. Seuss to them on national television.

The prolonged filibuster galvanized public pressure on Congress to do everything possible to stop Obamacare from stripping millions of Americans of the healthcare plans they liked—recall that Obama's cynical "if you like your healthcare plan you can keep your healthcare plan" pledge was named (even left-wing) PolitiFact's "Lie of the Year" in December of 2013[5]—and causing tens of millions to face skyrocketing healthcare premiums. Many Republicans were furious that I led that filibuster; while they were happy to campaign on stopping Obamacare, they didn't want to actually use the leverage we had to stop it.

During that fight we coined the hashtag #MakeDCListen, which went viral. So much so that, in the midst of the filibuster, I decided to make history by reading actual tweets on the Senate floor for the first time:

> We will not go quietly into this disaster called Obamacare. Make it cover everyone or no one. #MakeDCListen
>
> #MakeDCListen Because we the people are onto you and will not stand for tyranny. Hoo-rah!
>
> #MakeDCListen Because it makes entry-level jobs disappear for young Americans.
>
> #MakeDCListen Because I want to keep my own doctor.

Ultimately, House Republicans listened to the overwhelming pressure from their constituents and stood together to fund the entirety of the federal government but defund Obamacare. Unfortunately, Senate Republicans proved more insulated from the will of the people, and Senate GOP leadership chose to side with Obama and the Democrats and totally undercut Republican unity and resolve. What resulted was a sixteen-day government shutdown—forced by Obama's refusal to negotiate or compromise—culminating in a complete surrender from Republican leadership.

Social media was the vehicle for transmitting millions of voices to #MakeDCListen, and it was the beginning of a growing movement. In the years that followed, my aggregate follower count grew to over ten million, and I daily receive encouragement online, along with a lot of sentiments...let's say, *less than* supportive. Scrolling through Twitter or Facebook over my years in the Senate, I learned that there were people in the country who hated my guts. Like, *a lot*. It was as if the small group of students who had made a Facebook group to protest my commencement address at UC Berkeley back in 2007 had switched platforms, found one another, and invited a few hundred thousand of their angriest, most liberal friends to do the same.

When the haters were funny, I laughed along. Once, when a deranged lunatic threatened to murder both me and my father and to blow up the sun if we didn't pay him $3 million, one fellow tweeted, "I don't care what they do to Cruz...but this blowing up the sun thing sounds serious!" I cracked up, and sent the tweet to my team for them to laugh at as well.

Likewise, when angry liberals created a meme with a picture of me along with the caption "This man ate my son," I retweeted it, simply observing, "He was delicious."

Few things de-fang the angry woke mob more than laughing at them, not taking their antics remotely seriously. And as long as you have reach online, doing so is incredibly potent.

Nasty messages like this are part of being in public life. You're especially liable to get them if you habitually stomp across some of the most fraught political minefields in American politics, as I've always been fond of doing. One does not speak openly about topics such as race, history, and LGBTQ issues these days without inviting some measure of scorn from the most unhinged corners of the internet.

But I've never minded the online hate. The truth is that I see wading into contentious political issues as a major part of my job. I do it, at least in part, on behalf of people all over this country who are too afraid to say what they really mean, who fear (quite reasonably) that speaking out might lead to the loss of their livelihoods. Unlike most people, I am elected by the people, and I have a large platform to make myself clear on every issue; even when my words are taken out of context by people who'd like to see me sent back to Texas to live out my days in what they assume would be miserable anonymity, people can always check the record for themselves.

In the beginning, this is what made social media sites like Twitter so game-changing. People could type their words into Twitter via their computers or smartphones, and those words would go out to all of their followers without mediation or intervention. Like-minded people could find each other through hashtags or the app's search function, and communities could form across state lines, coasts, and even oceans. It's no surprise that in March of 2012, the then general manager of Twitter said the company belonged to "the free speech wing of the free speech party."[6] This freedom to say what you wanted to say, without fear that your words would be censored or altered by a bunch of green-haired engineers sitting in an office somewhere, was a large part of what drew people to Twitter in the first place. It's what allowed for such honest, frank conversations to occur on the platform, and why Twitter soon became the de facto "public square," where ideas could be shared and arguments about those ideas could proceed without any online hall monitors stepping in to shut things down.

Slowly, almost imperceptibly, that began to change. It was around 2015, shortly after I announced my run for the presidency, that I began to notice that a few of the conservative-leaning accounts I'd once followed were no longer showing up on my feed quite as often as they used to. Shortly thereafter, I began hearing stories from friends that their numbers—meaning the number of followers they had, or the number of people who could see each of their posts online—would often decrease sharply for no reason.

At first, this seemed to be limited to a few accounts. But the same story came up again and again. By the time my campaign had ended, this apparent tendency of tech platforms to censor people with conservative views had become impossible to ignore. In 2018, when numerous people went public with allegations that they were being "shadow banned" in this way by Twitter, the company roundly denied it.[7] They seemed to believe that the allegations, which could not be proven without access to the secret algorithms and internal records of Twitter (which, of course, they were hell-bent not to reveal), would go away as long as the company's representatives kept issuing blanket denials.

That's what they did in February of 2019, when I asked flat-out during a hearing of the Committee on Commerce, Science, and Transportation whether Big Tech companies such as Twitter and Facebook, as a matter of policy, censored the posts of conservative users. "Both this committee," I said,

> and the Judiciary Committee on which I also sit have repeatedly asked tech companies [for] even basic, bare bones data in terms of how many speakers on their social media platform are they silencing and to what extent are they engaging in shadow banning. And shadow banning, by its nature, has been reported to be a process where a particular speaker is silenced but that speaker doesn't know it because they send out a tweet, they send out a post, they appear to be communicating and yet the tech platform does not allow those—including those who have affirmatively opted in and chosen to hear that speaker—simply doesn't allow them to hear that speaker and those words, that speech goes into the ether.... And what is deeply frustrating is they have never once, to my knowledge, answered the question: Are they doing it? To what extent is it widespread? To what extent

is it politically targeted? How do they assess who they will silence? That is a degree of power handed to a handful of tech billionaires in California to monitor and police and put not just a thumb but all five fingers, a fist, and their foot on the scales of political discourse.[8]

The witnesses offered no concrete answers to the question but said, in so many words, that they were not aware of any explicit shadow-banning policies at these companies.

This is more or less the same stance that Twitter had taken publicly in July of 2018, when the company said, "We do not shadow ban....And we certainly don't shadow ban based on political viewpoints or ideology."[9]

Still, given how many caveats were also worked into their statement—including descriptions of how Twitter "ranks" certain tweets via a complex algorithm—it was clear to most Americans that Twitter was no longer the "free speech wing of the free speech party." It was clear, at least to those of us who'd been paying attention, that this company, along with Facebook and Google, routinely censored and shut down speech that the leaders of these companies deemed unacceptable.

And it was clear, given the makeup of these companies, which posts—and, by extension, which *people*—were "unacceptable."[10]

This became even clearer during the four years that President Trump was in the White House—years that must have felt like centuries for the far-left tech workers of Silicon Valley, with all the "hate speech" they claimed was flying all over the place. With each day that passed they made fewer and fewer attempts to hide their outright liberal bias. Writing in a tweet in 2017, for instance, a man named Yoel Roth, who had served in various content-moderation roles at Twitter since joining the company as an intern in 2014, claimed that there were "ACTUAL NAZIS IN THE WHITE HOUSE."[11]

(The capital letters, as I'm sure you already guessed, are his.)

In the years to come, of course, it would be revealed that Roth had a checkered past of his own that he probably didn't want to come to light. As his future (and very temporary) boss Elon Musk would point out, Roth wrote a thesis at the University of Pennsylvania that seemed to recommend the use of "adult internet services"—meaning gay dating apps—by minors. In fact, he wrote that Grindr and other "hookup apps" might possibly be viewed as "loci for queer youth culture," and that rather than "trying to drive out teenagers entirely, service providers should instead focus on crafting safety strategies that can accommodate a wide variety of use cases for platforms like Grindr."[12]

The more people looked into the inner workings of Twitter, the more they realized that it was run almost entirely by people who shared the politics of Yoel Roth. In fact, some of them made Roth look positively right-wing by comparison.

All the while, of course, the leadership of Twitter continued to insist that having such a rabidly left-wing staff had no effect on the content moderation policies at the company. Even when people pointed out public information, such as the fact that more than 99 percent of political donations from Twitter employees in the 2022 midterm elections went to Democrats,[13] they adhered to this line.

It was literally impossible to believe.

By the time we started hearing rumors of a new virus that had originated in Wuhan, China, spreading to countries all over the world, Twitter's problem of censorship had gotten worse than ever.

Repeatedly, though, cries from the public about the importance of free speech fell on deaf ears, at least where Big Tech companies were concerned. Big Tech's defenders pointed out, usually with some glee and sense of superiority, that Twitter and Facebook were private companies, and that the First Amendment to the United States Constitution applies only to censorship from the government.[14]

In this, they were generally correct. It is true that the First Amendment to the Constitution, ratified in 1791, was at first intended to apply only to the federal government. In fact, its scope was even narrower than most people realize. The text of this amendment reads, "*Congress* shall make no law…abridging the freedom of speech" [emphasis added]. In the years since, courts have held that this prohibition applies not only to Congress but to the entire executive branch and (after the ratification of the Fourteenth Amendment) to state and local governments as well.

But the First Amendment does not apply to private companies. Unless…unless, as the Supreme Court has repeatedly held, the private company is acting as an instrument of the government. And that's exactly what Big Tech began to do.

In June of 2021, emails between Dr. Fauci and Facebook CEO Mark Zuckerberg became public. In one of them, Zuckerberg explicitly offered for Facebook to help "make sure people can get authoritative information from reliable sources." The details of that offer were (conveniently) redacted, but it was widely speculated that Facebook was offering to actively suppress so-called Covid "misinformation," including, presumably, claims that Covid-19 originated in a Chinese government lab. Sadly, it appears that Zuckerberg was more than happy to play the role of official censor for the Deep State.[15]

Never mind that, even at that early date, the evidence that Covid had likely escaped from a Chinese lab was overwhelming; in fact, the evidence that it had been engineered in that lab through gain-of-function research was considerable. That inference was contrary to the narrative that Fauci and others in government wanted to disseminate, and so they were more than willing to use Big Tech (with the energetic complicity of the corporate media) to silence any and all who dared question the official story.

Interestingly, at the time, I was aggressively pushing out the actual facts about Covid. In March and April of 2020, I devoted four full podcast episodes of *Verdict with Ted Cruz* to painstakingly laying out the evidence that the virus had escaped from a Chinese government lab.[16] And Big Tech, for whatever reason, did not block or try to stifle the reach of my podcast (at least as far as we know).

Today, *even the Biden administration* has been forced to admit that it is extremely likely that Covid came from a Chinese lab;[17] but in 2020, if you tried to post that on Facebook, your voice could be silenced.[18] (Much more on this in Chapter Nine.)

Likewise, there were numerous high-profile cases of medical experts being banned from Twitter for going against the regime. In the early months of 2020, when President Trump was still in the White House, these decisions appeared to come mostly from within the tech companies themselves, but all too often in direct coordination with career bureaucrats at the CDC.[19] Given the frosty relationship that existed between the Trump White House and social media companies at the time, it makes sense that there wasn't much contact with political leadership, while the Deep State was more than willing to push its own agenda.

For example, the conservative activist Charlie Kirk was shadow banned for years due to his beliefs—so much so, in fact, that he scheduled a meeting with Twitter CEO Jack Dorsey in 2018 to demand answers. During that meeting, as Kirk would later reveal, Jack Dorsey insisted that nothing shady was going on with his account. But for the next few years, his follower count remained stagnant and his reach seemed to stall. It wasn't until Elon Musk took over that Kirk noticed his follower count growing in a way that seemed to accurately reflect his activity on the platform.[20] The same thing happened to Dan Bongino, who—thanks to the Twitter Files—is now aware that he was slapped with a "search blacklist," meaning that few users could find him by searching his name or Twitter handle.[21]

Still, these stories were usually buried in the mainstream media. Those who brought them up were told that they were buying into some kind of conspiracy theory.

Then, almost as soon as Joe Biden became the presumptive Democratic nominee for president, the Democratic censorship machine kicked into overdrive. Evidently, the young woke staffers at Twitter communicated early and often with the young woke staffers on the Biden campaign—some of whom, we know, had come up in the same schools and went to the same cocktail parties (and did the same drugs and slept with the same men, women, or both). Throughout the fall of 2020, as we now know thanks to the bombshell release of the Twitter Files, Twitter was practically the PR team for the Biden campaign, censoring posts and removing whatever content might make it less likely that Biden would become president of the United States.[22]

It's no surprise that Twitter worked so hard to make sure that Joe Biden and his band of Cultural Marxists ended up winning the White House in 2020. These people shared beliefs about nearly everything, especially when it came to censorship and the danger that "free speech" could pose to the world. At the very least, they probably assumed that the hot rhetoric and threats of investigations that had been coming from the Trump White House—and Republicans in Congress, myself included—would stop once Biden took office. On the first point, at least, they would turn out to be exactly right. The second, not so much.

That is why, during the most heated months of the election, the woke staffers of Twitter worked so hard to please their overlords on the Biden campaign. They would do almost anything to stop people from attempting to look "under the hood," so to speak, and figure out how the censorship machine of Silicon Valley was really working. They were able to do this, of course, because they knew that Jack Dorsey, their CEO, shared the same leftist politics that they did—something anyone could tell just by looking at the man's strange facial hair, bloodshot eyes, and penchant for flowing robes and sandals.[23] They never thought that anyone else would take over. Certainly not a "free speech absolutist" who would make exposing the company's secrets one of his first orders of business.

Consider this email that was sent from one Twitter staffer to another on October 24, 2020, less than two weeks after the world had begun hearing about a mysterious laptop belonging to Hunter Biden, Joe Biden's troublesome (and troubled) youngest son.

"More to review from the Biden team," said one staffer, whose name is redacted even now. Below this person's note is a list of five supposedly "offensive" tweets, which presumably related to the Hunter Biden scandal in some way. Of course, there's no way to check.

Shortly after the email came in, someone at Twitter removed those tweets. Three hours after the request came through, that person responded with, "handled these."[24]

It sure looks like they were taking orders from the Biden campaign: the "Biden team" says jump, the Twitter staffers ask how high. No doubt they believed they would never get caught.

Clearly, Twitter had come a long way from the open, free-speech-first platform that set the world on fire in the early decades of the twenty-first century. Looking at the sordid details of how it handled the Hunter Biden laptop story, and at how it made key decisions about other matters relating to free speech, reveals that Twitter—like other Big Tech companies, especially Google[25]—was overrun by the same woke neo-Marxists who have taken over our universities, elementary schools, businesses, and countless other institutions.

But when it comes to Big Tech, the damage to our democracy has been far more severe. It has led not only to the indoctrination of countless American young people, but to the corruption of our public square and the rigging of our elections. Today, the very means by which most Americans get their news and interact with one another have been twisted and poisoned by partisan actors who believe it is their duty to spread radical leftist ideas far and wide, and to suppress any ideas that might compete with them, often under the cover of algorithms and other formulas that are too complicated for the average American to understand.

So before we move on to the details of the Hunter Biden laptop scandal, Covid, and other controversies that have dominated the headlines in recent years, it's important that we understand just *how* woke these companies really are, and how things got so bad in the first place.

However bad you think it is, it's worse.

Literal Nazis in the White House

On the morning after election night of 2016, the entire city of San Francisco fell silent.

This silence, which would soon be interrupted by constant cries of *"Racism!"* and *"Russia did it!,"* was particularly pronounced in the southern part of the city, commonly known as Silicon Valley. There, in the headquarters of several of our nation's top tech companies, particularly Facebook, Twitter, and Google, the mood was somber and intense.

Several employees, according to eyewitness accounts published later, were openly weeping; others made grand speeches to their friends about extremism, racism, and the future of democracy.[26] No one seemed able to believe that Donald J. Trump, a man who had risen to prominence in significant part through the provocative and near-constant use of his Twitter account, had managed to become president of the United States, largely by using social media to circumvent the mainstream media and take his message straight to the people.

One of the first orders of business that day, according to the journalist Allum Bokhari, was gathering in all-hands meetings, at which the higher-ups delivered impassioned addresses to their employees.

At the headquarters of Google, which sits on Amphitheatre Parkway in Mountain View, California, CEO Sundar Pichai expressed open hatred for Donald Trump and everything he stood for. At one point, when a Google employee asked whether anything positive had come from the election, Pichai laughed, along with the hundreds of other employees in the room, seeming to suggest that it was ridiculous to think that anything good could possibly come from a Trump presidency.

As Bokhari, who spent a great deal of time early in his career at Breitbart News exposing the liberal bias of Big Tech, wrote, this was "shocking." He noted that in his home country of Britain, if the head of a supposedly politically neutral organization such as the BBC had come out with such negative statements about a political candidate—let alone one who was now president—that person would "quickly be given a one-way ticket out of the company."

"Google," he continued, ". . . may not be a quasi-state-run organization like the BBC (indeed, Google is far more powerful), but it regularly makes similar public commitments to neutrality—its CEO has even done so under oath, before Congress. What's more, with its dominance over search results, online news aggregation, and smartphone operating systems, Google's capacity to influence democratic elections goes far beyond that of any other company. The only entities that come close to its potential influence are other Silicon Valley giants, such as Facebook and Twitter."[27]

Reading Bokhari's book *#DELETED*, which was released in September of 2020 and contains this anecdote in its first chapter, we can see just how soon after Donald Trump's election it was that the Cultural Marxists at Big Tech companies—who, of course, blamed the new president's election on sexism, racism, xenophobia, and the patriarchy, everything they were taught to smash during their years in our nation's left-wing universities—sprang into action.

One small group of employees at Facebook, according to a BuzzFeed article published shortly after the election, got together to rewrite code in a way that would suppress "fake news." Another group drew up an entirely serious plan to move the company's headquarters to Canada.[28] Others, according to Bokhari, "discussed ways to change their groups' purchasing decisions to boycott small businesses whose owners supported Republicans."[29]

Over at Twitter, the bar for what was considered "hate speech" came *way* down. Suddenly, hate speech was anything that might, even in some indirect way, lead someone somewhere to think that Donald Trump was *not* an actual Nazi—which presumably nearly every employee at Twitter did. That meant that any conservative influencer or person who interacted with conservative accounts was now liable to be de-amplified, shadow banned, or shut down simply for their political opinions, and that they would have no recourse for getting their accounts reinstated once the ban took effect.

Again, if they complained, these people would be swiftly reminded that Twitter was a private company, which could ban anyone at any time, and for any reason. In the same breath, though, Big Tech's defenders would claim that Twitter did *not*, under any circumstances, single out people with certain political beliefs for de-amplification or censorship. Besides, they'd say (with no acknowledgment of the irony or inconsistency), no one has a right *not* to be shadow banned online—if Twitter doesn't like your ideas, it's perfectly fine for them to turn down the dial, so to speak, just slightly on who gets to *see* those ideas, thereby allowing other, more enlightened ones to be seen instead.[30]

As one liberal academic put it in an article for *Wired* magazine, "Politicians and pundits howling about censorship and miscasting content moderation as the demise of free speech online" need to be reminded "that free *speech* does not mean free *reach*."[31]

This seems to suggest that when shadow banning and censorship *did* occur at Twitter in the pre–Elon Musk era—and, again, they assured us they were not happening—it was mostly a failure to amplify conservative voices, not a deliberate attempt to *silence* those voices. This is a key difference. Whereas the former is a passive activity, not unlike running a business (say, a monster truck racetrack or, alternatively, a nail salon) that happens to attract customers primarily of a particular gender or race, the latter is active discrimination; it would be like opening a store and refusing to serve customers of certain races or genders.

But we learned from Bari Weiss's reporting in the second installment of the Twitter Files that the company routinely put people on "blacklists," telling the algorithm not to boost or even display their tweets. This is what happened to Jay Bhattacharya, a professor at Stanford University who awoke one morning in 2020 to find that his follower count, as well as his engagement numbers, had declined sharply after he posted several (true) facts about the inefficacy of lockdowns.

As Bari Weiss—who, it must be said, seems to be doing just fine after her resignation from the *New York Times*—showed in her reporting, which relied on thousands of documents that were uncovered after Elon Musk acquired Twitter in October of 2022, this is unequivocally "shadow banning," something that the heads of Twitter have repeatedly denied doing—often right to my face during congressional hearings on the matter.

They just used a different name for it.

"What many people call 'shadow banning,'" according to one of Weiss's sources, "[Twitter] employees call 'Visibility Filtering,' or 'VF.'" It was used by employees at Twitter to "block searches of individual users; to limit the scope of a particular tweet's discoverability; to block select users' posts from ever appearing on the 'trending' page; and from inclusion in hashtag searches. All without users' knowledge."

The team that was in charge of deciding whom to block and censor, according to Weiss, handled "up to 200 'cases' a day."[32]

When people who had been banned or noticed their engagement suddenly taking a nosedive complained, they would usually be met with some jargon from Twitter about how they had violated Twitter's policies against "hateful conduct" or "misinformation."[33]

Of course, the accusations of "hateful" speech and "misinformation" only seemed to flow in one direction, which was left to right. The left-leaning staffers at Twitter would accuse just about everyone on the right of violating Twitter's terms of service, place secret restrictions on their accounts using complex algorithms, and then pretend they had no idea what was going on when people began asking questions.[34]

This double standard produced some interesting results.

Consider the case of Sarah Jeong, who was hired to become a member of the *New York Times* editorial board in August of 2018. Shortly thereafter it was discovered that a few years earlier, in 2014, Jeong had made multiple blatantly racist comments using her Twitter account. In one of the messages she had said, gleefully, "White people have stopped breeding. You'll all go extinct soon. This was my plan all along." In another, she had asked, "Are white people genetically predisposed to burn faster in the sun, thus logically being only fit to live underground like groveling goblins?"

Sadly, there were more. In another, Jeong had said "oh man it's kind of sick how much joy I get out of being cruel to old white men." These tweets had been public for years. But it was only when the *New York Times* hired Jeong to write about social media and technology—a job that surely would have required them to scroll through her Twitter account, at the very least to see if she'd called an entire race *groveling goblins*—that people began to dig through the various racist things she'd said and repost them on Twitter.[35]

It will not surprise you that Twitter did not ban Sarah Jeong for hate speech either when she first posted the messages or when they resurfaced in August of 2018. They didn't take down the posts, either.[36] Of course, one can easily guess what would have happened if Jeong (or anyone else) had expressed a racist desire to make *African-Americans* "stop breeding," or said that she got great joy from "being cruel to" old *Mexican* men. And if she had said any of these things about trans people, she might still be in federal prison as we speak.

In response to the online uproar, Jeong broke out the Cultural Marxist playbook, claiming that it wasn't *she* who'd been racist, but *everyone else*. As an Asian woman, she said—using language that would later be picked up by the *New York Times* in its defense of hiring her, a decision the paper would stand by, employing Jeong for a year until she stepped down for unrelated reasons in 2019—that she had sent these tweets not to be racist, but to "mimic the language" of the people who often harassed her online for being an Asian woman.[37]

The whole thing, you see, was supposed to be funny.

I'm sure you understand. For Marxists, vicious racism is acceptable and even "funny" as long as it is directed at the "oppressors." For them, it's a real knee-slapper to say the wrong class or the wrong race should "stop breeding" or that they're "groveling goblins."

I'm sure that one brings the house down at cocktail parties thrown by the *New York Times*. But in the real world, it's just plain racist. But from her comments, Jeong would appear to believe—like other well-known (and well-paid)[38] neo-racists, Ibram X. Kendi and Robin DiAngelo among them[39]—that everything in life is about power, and that the modern world is a struggle of powerful people (White men) against non-powerful people (everyone else). This is an explicitly Marxist worldview, shared by left-wing activists and Democratic politicians everywhere. The fact that the people at Twitter seemed to agree—something they demonstrated by not banning Jeong for "hateful conduct"—is just another example of how the platform embraced neo-Marxism.

Of course, there are far more extreme examples. Consider that at this very moment Twitter has yet to deactivate the account of Ayatollah Ali Khamenei, the "Supreme" Ayatollah of Iran. This is a man who regularly calls for the overthrow of what he calls "the usurping Zionist regime"—meaning Jews—and who often refers to the United States as "deceitful, untrustworthy, and backstabbing," among other things.[40] He routinely leads mobs chanting "Death to America" and "Death to Israel," and he has also expressed support for the *fatwa* issued by his predecessor, Ruhollah Khomeini, against the writer Salman Rushdie for his novel *The Satanic Verses*—a *fatwa* that was, tragically, partially carried out in upstate New York when a deranged young man stabbed Rushdie several times, taking out his eye and leading to several other serious injuries.[41]

That, apparently, does not meet the standard of "hateful conduct" or "misinformation" that Twitter used to decide who got to tweet and who did not. The things that *did* get taken down as misinformation, you'll notice, were not actual threats of violence or seriously offensive views—the Taliban, for instance, was still allowed to tweet as much as it wants.[42] Rather, the things that were commonly labelled "misinformation" by Twitter were the kinds of things that were apt to offend a very specific kind of affluent, probably White, liberal living in a major city in the United States. That means no inconvenient facts about Covid, election security, or the sterilization of children.[43]

But it wasn't until the election of 2020, when the liberals at Twitter, Facebook, and Google began believing that the "literal Nazi" in the White House might soon go away, that one concern began overriding everything else. Now, "misinformation" would be defined as anything that could potentially be harmful to Joe Biden's electoral prospects.

This, as we now know, is what made them censor a story in the *New York Post*, initially published on October 14, 2020, that went into great detail about some of Hunter Biden's overseas business deals, many of which involved his father and other members of the Biden family.[44] It would have been clear to anyone working at Twitter around this time, when the presidential race was still very much up in the air, that having the *Post*'s story go into wide circulation would have been very bad for Joe Biden. "Hunter Biden," according to the story,

> introduced his father, then-Vice President Joe Biden, to a top executive at a Ukrainian energy firm less than a year before the elder Biden pressured government officials in Ukraine into firing a prosecutor who was investigating the company, according to emails obtained by The Post.
>
> The never-before-revealed meeting is mentioned in a message of appreciation that Vadym Pozharskyi, an adviser to the board of Burisma, allegedly sent Hunter Biden on April 17, 2015, about a year after Hunter joined the Burisma board at a reported salary of up to $50,000 a month.
>
> "Dear Hunter, thank you for inviting me to DC and giving an opportunity to meet your father and spent [sic] some time together. It's realty [sic] an honor and pleasure," the email reads.[45]

And on it goes from there. As we now know from Matt Taibbi's excellent reporting in the first installment of the Twitter Files, employees at Twitter immediately flagged this story as possible misinformation. They removed links to it, stopped it from being shared, and even blocked its transmission via direct message, a tool, Taibbi points out, "hitherto reserved for extreme cases, e.g. child pornography."[46]

Internally, everyone likely knew exactly why they had done this. Obviously, it was because having the story come out would have been bad for Joe Biden and the Democrats.

Explaining that to the outside world, however, would prove much more difficult. To do so, Twitter initially said that the post violated its "hacked materials policy," a justification that even some employees of the company had trouble believing. One employee, writing a few days after White House press secretary Kayleigh McEnany had her account locked for simply *talking about* the story, said he was "struggling to understand the policy basis for marking [the story] as unsafe." He added that "the best explainability argument for this externally would be that we're waiting to understand if this story is the result of hacked materials. We'll face hard questions on this if we don't have some kind of solid reasoning for marking the links unsafe."

If you look through the screenshots of these emails included in the Twitter Files, you'll notice that at this point, the Twitter folks began including the words "PRIVILEGED AND CONFIDENTIAL," written in bold and all caps, in the subject lines of their emails— something they hadn't done with the initial communications about the story.[47] As a lawyer, I can tell you that this is something you do when you know that whatever you're about to say would *definitely* get you into legal trouble if it were to be read aloud in a courtroom (or released to the public).

What these employees failed to consider, of course, was that it was Twitter the company, not its employees, which owned the privilege, meaning that if a new owner ever took over the company—say, a tech billionaire with strong views on free speech and censorship—he could publish the emails in full, thereby waiving any privilege entirely. That is why we are now aware of just how hard employees at Twitter worked to conceal the Hunter Biden laptop story from the public, at least until the election could happen and put Joe Biden in the White House. We know how many complaints they ignored from the Trump campaign about this deliberately censorious practice, and how aware they all were that what they were doing was wrong.

Reclaiming Control

Just a few years ago, those of us who complained that we were being censored online were often called conspiracy theorists. Social media companies claimed that they were unbiased purveyors of information who were not beholden to one political party over another. They claimed that they were neutral when it came to politics, and that they didn't censor anyone for their political beliefs.

Today, these companies censor more than ever. But they no longer pretend that they're neutral.

Take, for instance, the treatment that the conservative commentator Matt Walsh received for saying on YouTube that the transgender influencer Dylan Mulvaney—a biological male who rose to prominence in early 2023 for dressing like a prepubescent girl—is a man. A few days after Walsh posted the video in which this claim appeared, YouTube demonetized his account.

According to YouTube, referring to this person who had said, among other things, that we should "normalize the bulge" (referring to the intact male genitals that often jutted out from the bottoms of the small women's swimsuits he wore), as a "man" was now an example of "hate speech."[48]

There are few better ways for a tech platform to announce to the world that it is firmly on the side of the Cultural Marxists.

Clearly, leftists have the same attitude toward social media that they have toward entertainment, namely that it exists for *them* and no one else. As soon as conservatives begin to use these platforms—or, God forbid, to use them *effectively*—the Left needs to step in and find a way to re-stack the deck against conservatives.

There was a moment in the early 2010s, which happened to coincide with my first years in the Senate, when the playing field *was* almost completely level, at least when it came to social media. There were very few tech company employees looking to censor people online, and the definition of what constituted "hate speech" was the familiar one that most ordinary people could agree on. It's no surprise that during those years we saw a resurgence of conservatism in the United States unlike anything we'd witnessed since the early 1980s—a resurgence that brought me and many others to Congress and ended with the election of a president who, fittingly, rose to office in significant part because of how transformationally he had been able to use his Twitter account.

Then those on the left who had written the algorithms and set up the companies in the first place decided to strike back. They demonetized our accounts, limited our reach, and threw the label of "hate speech" at anything we said that they happened to disagree with. For a while, we could only guess at the extent to which these far-left tech workers had their fingers on the scales at Facebook, Twitter, YouTube, and Google. We got a small peek behind the curtain with the release of the Twitter Files, which showed the world just how blatant and one-sided the censorship regime was.

But that was just one company. Now, it's time to find out what's happening with the rest of them.

How to Fight Back

On February 13, 2023, I sent a letter to numerous social media companies, including Meta (Facebook), Google, Twitter, and TikTok, launching an oversight investigation into their use of algorithms to shape the "news feeds" of users, many of whom are now children. I'm the ranking member on the Senate Commerce Committee, which has jurisdiction over all of Big Tech. My intention was to ensure that this investigation went far beyond a simple look into political bias—which, by now, we all know is happening—to also consider the full panoply of disastrous consequences that might come from allowing one group of like-minded people to control and curate all the information in the world.

On TikTok, for instance, a platform that is engineered to be as addictive as possible—not to mention that it is owned by companies controlled by the Chinese Communist Party—the algorithm often shows content that has been demonstrated to promote eating disorders and self-harm to young girls.[49] There are also "influencers" on TikTok, as well as on Instagram, from whom young teenagers who are feeling bad about themselves (as they all do from time to time) can learn that the answer to their problems is not going outside and making some friends, but changing their gender.[50]

According to reports from young people who were sucked into the transgender movement as teenagers, large numbers of them first found the community on TikTok and Instagram. They were encouraged by others on the platforms to explore wearing clothes for the opposite gender and even hormone therapy and permanent surgery.[51]

Taking on Big Tech will not be easy. I believe we need a five-prong strategy. *First*, we need vigorous oversight, from Congress and, ideally, from an administration with the courage to rein in the tech abuses. That's what I'm trying to drive in the Senate Commerce Committee.

Second, we should aggressively enforce our antitrust laws. By any measure, the giant tech companies are larger and have more market power than Standard Oil when it was broken up by the federal government; they're bigger than AT&T was when it was broken up. And it has long been integral to our antitrust laws that monopolies cannot abuse their monopoly power, as Big Tech is doing right now.

Third, we should vigorously enforce our consumer protection laws, which prohibit fraud. The basic promise of social media is: if you choose to follow someone, you'll see what they say; and if they choose to follow you, they'll see what you say. Big Tech violates that promise daily.

Fourth, we should use "Section 230" immunity to incentivize Big Tech to end censorship. Section 230 of the Communications Decency Act of 2006 gives Big Tech a special immunity from liability—basically a government subsidy—that nobody else enjoys. It was passed at a time when the internet was in its infancy and Congress wanted to encourage this nascent technology. But at that time Congress believed that tech would be a "neutral public forum," that is, that it would not censor or silence speakers based on political ideology. Today, that premise has been completely disproven. So we should amend Section 230 to apply *only* if a platform is, in fact, neutral. If not, the company should be fully liable for anything on its platform, just like everyone else.

And *fifth*, others in business—like Elon Musk—should make the investment in free speech by creating new platforms or purchasing existing platforms.

During the Trump administration, the president wanted to get tough on Big Tech. And I met with over a dozen senior officials, in the White House and at the DOJ, the FTC, and the FCC, urging them to do so. But the administration's approach lacked focus and was overly siloed. The next Republican administration (because no Democrat will do it) must bring serious creativity and a laser focus to using all the tools of government to ending Big Tech censorship. And I intend to do everything humanly possible to make that happen.

CHAPTER FIVE

Mr. Marx Goes to Washington

When I became a senator, I knew that I was going to be reading a fair amount of legislation. I also expected to read briefing books, data on government programs, and the writings of judges and political appointees whose nominations I would be considering for confirmation as part of my job.

What I didn't know was all the *other* reading the job would entail.

In the spring of 2022, for instance, I ended up sitting in my office thumbing through the latest editions of neo-racist propaganda for children, most memorably the book *Antiracist Baby* by Ibram X. Kendi. Other titles were similarly absurd. I'm sure that anyone who happened to pass by and see me sitting there with my boots on my desk making my way slowly through this woke slush pile from hell would have been surprised. Surely, they'd say, you could just look up the summaries online, or maybe assign some poor congressional intern the task of wading through this interminable nonsense?

Maybe. But for as long as I've been in government, and even when I was a lawyer in private practice, I've always found it's better to examine the original sources yourself. My apartment in Washington, D.C., is filled with books and stacks of papers; so are several rooms of my home back in Texas. Most of these are books that I've enjoyed throughout my life—from biographies to history to economics to literature—while others are things that I've read to prepare for oral arguments, debates, congressional hearings, and even campaign stops over the years. I'm sure that somewhere on my shelves, you'd find things that would surprise you. Compendiums of Critical Race Theory, for instance, and several books authored by Karl Marx, cited in the pages of this book.

In recent years, I have also spent many hours sitting in the basement of the Capitol at a small table in the Senate's sensitive compartmented information facility, the only place I am permitted to read most classified government documents. (Unlike some former senators from Delaware, I don't think you can just take these things home on the plane with you and peruse them at your leisure in the garage by your Corvette.)[1] Sitting in the SCIF, as it's called, I've read documents about everything from foreign intelligence to nuclear preparedness to cyber-vulnerabilities to FBI background files on Supreme Court nominees, all while a military aide watches from a desk out front and makes sure I don't stuff anything into my briefcase (or in my pants, as Clinton national security advisor Sandy Berger was convicted of doing with classified documents).[2] On the walls are posters that look like they could have come from World War II, bombarding anyone who enters the SCIF with messages like *Only YOU Can Stop a Leak*.

I should confess that fairly early in my Senate career I eagerly rushed down to the congressional SCIF looking for whatever information the government had about UFOs. I went in with every expectation that I would find at least one document about little green men, flying saucers, or secret experiments conducted out in the deserts of Nevada. It gives me no pleasure to report that I walked out of the SCIF that night *extremely* disappointed.

Of course, most of my reading doesn't have to happen inside a secret facility. Most of it doesn't deal with things like UFOs or secret intelligence operations our military is conducting overseas (though some of it does). Most of my reading, rather, consists of news reports, books, and widely available technical documents. Some of it isn't reading at all, but rather watching YouTube videos and reading Twitter threads about every subject imaginable. With some regularity, I have to master materials in all these media to prepare for confirmation hearings.

In the first six months of 2023, exactly three non-judicial Biden nominees were defeated in the Senate. *All three* were before the Senate Commerce Committee, where I'm the ranking member (the senior Republican).

The first was Gigi Sohn, a left-wing activist whom Biden had nominated to the Federal Communications Commission. She hated Fox News, in particular; some of her notable prior comments included these remarks:

"I believe that Fox News has had the most negative impact on our democracy. It's state-sponsored propaganda, with few if any opposing viewpoints."[3]

"I agree that scrutiny of big tech is essential, as is scrutiny of big telecom, cable & media. And trust me, the latter have played their own role in destroying democracy & electing autocrats. Like, say, Fox News?"[4]

She had also liked and retweeted other leftists labeling Donald Trump a "White supremacist" and calling for defunding the police.[5]

Most astonishingly, she had spent years supporting and fundraising for Fight for the Future, a group that erected billboards across the country accusing multiple senators on the Commerce Committee of being "corrupt." They had called Roger Wicker and Marsha Blackburn (both Republicans) corrupt, but also numerous Democrats. So I asked Ms. Sohn if she agreed with the group that Arizona Democrat Kyrsten Sinema was corrupt. She said "no."

I asked her if she agreed that Montana Democrat Jon Tester was corrupt. She said "no."

I asked her if she agreed that Michigan Democrat Gary Peters was corrupt. She said "no."

At this point, Maria Cantwell, the Washington State Democrat who's chair of the committee, asked, somewhat jokingly, "Am I next?" And I laughed, "As it so happens, you are!"

Just a few months earlier this same group, supported by Sohn, had sent a letter to Chuck Schumer demanding that he fire Cantwell as chair of the Commerce Committee—because we had not yet confirmed Gigi Sohn.

As I observed, it was the first time I had seen a nominee so extreme that she had attacked half of the committee charged with confirming her, including her own party.

I also noted ruefully that I was a little offended that this left-wing group hadn't attacked *me*. "What do I have to do to attract their ire?" I asked.[6] I'm glad to say they heard me; shortly thereafter they put out a tweet trying to crowdfund a billboard attacking me, which featured the website tedcruzhatesfreespeech.com. Well, it turns out the group wasn't particularly competent...they didn't actually own that website.

So I bought it.

And I encouraged folks to support the billboard and go to the website that had been set up to attack me—which now automatically redirects to my campaign fundraising page on tedcruz.org![7]

Needless to say, having a left-wing radical like Sohn as the deciding vote on the Federal Communications Commission—with massive power over television, radio, telephones, and the internet—would have been profoundly dangerous. But, thankfully, exposing her extreme record was enough to defeat the nomination.[8]

The second non-judicial Biden nominee to be defeated was Phil Washington, whom Biden had nominated to become the administrator of the Federal Aviation Administration (FAA), which issues and enforces standards on manufacturing, operating, and maintaining aircraft in the United States. As you might imagine, this is an important job. The administrator is required to oversee thousands of planes and pilots and to do everything possible to ensure the safety of the roughly two million Americans who fly every day.

As presidential appointments go, this one is typically nonpartisan. If you look at past heads of the FAA, they have typically been apolitical experts in aviation. Most of them have either served in the military or worked as a commercial pilot, or both. At a minimum, the people who have held this position at the top of the FAA have typically spent decades working in aviation.

In the age of Joe Biden, whose every move seems to be dictated by the woke neo-Marxists who surround him, congressional oversight has become immensely important. It has never been more vital to ensure that the people who staff our federal government are competent, clearheaded, and free of left-wing ideological extremism. That's not to say that Joe Biden isn't free to nominate anyone he wishes to fill federal positions, of course, or that those nominees can't assume those positions if the Senate confirms them. But it is my job to make sure that if these people are extreme or unqualified—which, when the Biden administration is involved in the nomination process, is not an uncommon occurrence—the American people know about it.

By all appearances, Phil Washington was a decent man who had served honorably in the military for twenty-four years. The problem was that he didn't know a damn thing about airplanes.

So, at his hearing, I asked him about his experience.

"Have you ever flown a plane?"

"No, I have never flown a plane."

"So, you weren't a military pilot or a commercial airline pilot?"

"No, Senator."

"Have you ever worked for an airline?"

"No, Senator."

"Have you ever worked as an air traffic controller?"

"No, Senator."

"You ever worked for a company that manufactures airplanes?"

"No, Senator."

"You ever worked for a company that fixes airplanes?"

"No, Senator."

Washington's lone claim to "aviation" experience was that he had spent the previous twenty months as the CEO of the Denver airport, which basically meant he was in charge of the parking and restaurants and stores—essentially, running a giant shopping mall. But I gave him a chance to explain whether any of that related to aviation safety:

"You're in charge of coffee shops and clothing stores and newsstands. You're not in charge of the pilots, are you?"

"No, Senator."

"You're not in charge of the airplane mechanics, are you?"

"No, Senator."

"You're not in charge of the air traffic controllers, are you?"

"No, Senator."

At that point, it was clear to every observer that Phil Washington had precisely *zero* experience in aviation safety. But perhaps he was a quick study. Maybe he had learned about it in his free time. So I asked him about the worst air disasters in the past decade, the two recent crashes of Boeing 737 Maxes—one on Lion Air in 2018 and the other on Ethiopian Airlines in 2019—that together had resulted in the loss of 346 lives. At the time of those crashes, I was the chairman of the aviation subcommittee of Commerce, so I spent quite a bit of time meeting with experts and learning about the technical details of both crashes. I was one of the first to call for grounding every 737 Max (something the FAA did shortly thereafter) until we could be confident it wouldn't happen again, and I had played a leading role at a subsequent hearing cross-examining the CEO of Boeing for the shockingly poor corporate behavior that precipitated the crashes. The CEO resigned shortly thereafter.

In short, the crashes were caused because a new system Boeing had installed, called the MCAS system, automatically steered the nose of the plane down, repeatedly, in response to erroneous signals from what are called the angle of attack (AOA) sensors that incorrectly indicated the plane nose was rising at too steep an angle. Each plane has two AOA sensors, but on at least one of the planes a bird strike had sheared one of the sensors off the plane, and the MCAS system responded to false data. Inexperienced pilots didn't know how to respond, and the plane tragically steered itself down directly into the ground.[9]

I asked Washington about the specifics of the crashes:

"OK. The MCAS system is responsible for the crashes at issue. What happens when you get a different reading from two different sensors?"

"Can you repeat that question, Senator?"

"What happens when you get a different reading from two different angle of attack sensors?"

"Well, I think human reaction needs to take over if that occurs."

"So why did that not happen on the Lion Air and Ethiopian Air flights?"

"Well, Senator—I'm not a pilot. I don't know if I can answer that particular question...."

"Mr. Washington, I believe you. But, at the end of the day, that's the fundamental problem. For this administration to nominate someone as

FAA administrator who can't answer the question why were 346 people killed in horrific crashes that resulted in the 737 Max being grounded for a long time is striking. By the way, Administrator Dickson [under Trump], after the FAA recertified the 737 Max, *he went and flew it personally.*"[10]

At the end of the questioning, nobody in the room believed Phil Washington had the experience necessary to be the administrator of the FAA. And that was enough to defeat his nomination.[11]

The third nominee to be defeated was Ann Carlson, whom Biden had nominated to run the National Highway Traffic Safety Administration (NHTSA). The NHTSA, like the FAA, is an agency with critical safety responsibilities. And once again, Biden had nominated someone with no actual *experience* with highway safety. Instead, Carlson was a law professor at UCLA and an environmental extremist. As the Shirley Shapiro Professor of Environmental Law at UCLA and a faculty affiliate of the Emmett Institute on Climate Change and the Environment, she had helped a for-profit law firm specializing in "climate change lawsuits" sue numerous energy companies.[12] As one of her UCLA colleagues said, Carlson was "the perfect person for the job" because she would "play an important role in crafting automobile-efficiency standards that are central to the country's efforts to address climate change."[13]

All of that qualified Carlson to be a card-carrying Green New Deal zealot, but none of it related to automobile safety. (Which does actually matter!) But it seems that the Biden White House didn't care. Presumably they wanted an activist running the agency, someone who could use its authority to wage ideological war on internal combustion engines. Thankfully, Carlson's record as an environmental extremist was undeniable, and I think Senate Democrats were a little shell-shocked from the defeat of Sohn and Washington. My team and I were able to build such strong opposition to Carlson among energy producers and farm and agricultural groups that it became clear she wouldn't have the votes to get through, and so the White House pulled her nomination *before her hearing.*

This pattern exists across the government. Over the past three years I've seen the Biden administration repeatedly nominate people for key positions who were manifestly unqualified to serve. In some cases, these people have been confirmed over my strident objections, as was the case with Judge (now Justice) Ketanji Brown Jackson. A vast percentage of the time, these people were nominated because they were "diverse"—meaning that they belonged to some supposed "victim" group that the Biden administration believed was underrepresented in the federal government—or because they were willing to follow orders from woke neo-Marxists in the White House.

Usually, both.

As president, Joe Biden has not prioritized expertise or competency when nominating people to fill his administration. Ideology and political activism appear to be much more important in the selection process. Anyone who doubts this need only consider the resumes of Pete Buttigieg, who heads the massive Transportation Department despite only ever having been the mayor of a small town, and of Rachel Levine, who seems to have been given control of a major portion of the Department of Health and Human Services solely because Levine is a "transgender woman."

There was a time, for instance, when the Biden administration was pushing a candidate to become comptroller of the currency (a position within the Treasury Department) who, as recently as 2019, had expressed openly *Marxist* views. And when I say "Marxist," I don't mean simply that this woman, whose name is Saule Omarova, believed in high taxes and the transfer of wealth. I mean she studied Marxism in the Soviet Union at Moscow State University, she wrote her undergraduate thesis on "Karl Marx's Economic Analysis and the Theory of Revolution in *The Capital*"[14] while studying on the Lenin Personal Academic Scholarship,[15] and—while at Cornell Law School—she was a member of a Facebook group called "Marxist Analysis and Policy."[16]

That group does not even try to hide its mission. This is the description on the Facebook page: "This Marxist group is a platform for analysis, policy and polemics from the perspectives of a diverse range of Socialist and anti-capitalist views.... We are against exploitation, inequality, racial discrimination and ecological destruction at the core of Capitalist social relations. The working class has the potential and the ability to change Capitalism and in the process change itself. Only working people, by their own efforts, can free themselves from Capitalism. We stand for the self emancipation of the working class and Socialism."[17]

Now, I have been sounding the alarm about Joe Biden and the neo-Marxists who surround him for over a hundred pages now, but even for them, this seems a little too on the nose. As my good friend John Kennedy memorably said to Omarova at her confirmation hearing, "I don't know whether to call you Professor or Comrade."[18]

Thankfully, last year the Senate defeated her nomination. Being unqualified to lead an agency is one thing, but believing that the entire economy that the agency you want to work in regulates amounts to "exploitation, inequality, racial discrimination, and ecological destruction" is ridiculous. It'd be like giving the Joker a job as the Gotham City police commissioner.

As Biden continues to fill the government with Marxists—mostly Cultural Marxists, but on occasion some old-school economic Marxists—it becomes clearer and clearer just how seriously this administration is attempting to transform the federal government, and by extension American society. Since day one, they've been quite clear about this goal, at least to those of us who've learned to read their long, buzzword-laden documents.

Take a look.

The Cost of "Equity"

From their first days in the White House, the folks in the Biden administration appear to have been governing according to the principles of Cultural Marxism. Hardly a day goes by when they don't speak about "equity" and "antiracism" as if they are the highest goals of the American government. Most of the executive orders the president has signed and the key legislation his administration has tried to pass includes provisions about race, gender, and past oppression that would completely reorient the goals of the federal government.

Take Executive Order 13985, for instance, one of the first that Joe Biden signed when he took office.[19] It reads like some unholy conflation of Karl Marx, Ibram X. Kendi, and a freshman at Wesleyan University using ChatGPT to write a C-grade essay on racism.

According to this executive order—which Biden somehow squeezed in between one initiative to shut down our oil industry and another to eliminate gas stoves—"entrenched disparities in our laws and public policies, and in our public and private institutions, have often denied...equal opportunity to individuals and communities. Our country faces converging economic, health, and climate crises that have exposed and exacerbated inequities, while a historic movement for justice has highlighted the unbearable human costs of systemic racism."[20]

This language, which might at first seem unintentionally vague and sloppy, is in fact *intended* to be vague. It is written to hide the fact that "equity," as the word is used by the modern Democratic Party, has nothing to do with equality of *opportunity*. It has nothing to do with making sure that everyone, regardless of race or gender, is treated *equally* under the law.

And of course there is absolutely no need to sign an executive order to *that* effect. Under federal law, it is *already illegal* to treat people differently based on their race, gender, or religion. I would encourage anyone who doubts this to read the full text of the Civil Rights Act of 1964, which was passed into law over the strident objection and filibuster of Southern Democrats. (When the Left demagogues on race, one very inconvenient fact for them is that a much higher percentage of Republican senators supported the Civil Rights Act than did Democratic senators.)

What the Biden administration wants to do, instead, is promote equality of *outcome*, ensuring that the United States government—and, eventually, all schools, businesses, universities, and other institutions—replaces the goal of fairness with "equity," a term that is nearly impossible to define and even harder to implement.

As I've pointed out before, the word "equity" itself is a rather insidious piece of political propaganda. You almost have to admire how easily left-wing activists have been able to insert it into public life and government documents without anyone so much as batting an eyelash. To those who haven't immersed themselves in the strange, borderline incomprehensible literature on which this concept is based, I'm sure the word looks just like "equality" and seems to mean the same thing. I suspect that when most people heard President Biden read the summary of Executive Order 13985, they didn't think twice about the strange new word that was now the number-one priority of the federal government.

It's worth pausing for a moment to consider the true meaning—and, more important, the implications—of making "equity" the central guiding principle of our federal government. It does *not* mean "equality," as President Biden's executive order suggests.

Here, for the uninitiated, is an explanation of the difference between the two words from the Milken Institute School of Public Health at George Washington University, which is fairly representative of the average leftist's view on the matter:

> While the terms equity and equality may sound similar, the implementation of one versus the other can lead to dramatically different outcomes for marginalized people.
>
> Equality means each individual or group of people is given the same resources or opportunities. Equity recognizes that each person has different circumstances and allocates the exact resources and opportunities needed to reach an equal outcome.[21]

In other words, the federal government cannot stop until all outcomes are equal. Presumably, that means that all institutions must have equal representation, and that all groups in society—however you choose to define those groups, whether along racial, ethnic, or sexual lines—must have the same outcomes across the board. If someone conducts a study and finds that Nicaraguan people who identify as transgender, say, make an average of three dollars less per year than non-Nicaraguan, non-transgender citizens, equity has not been achieved.

And if that outcome has not been achieved, it is probably because someone, at some point in the past, rigged the system against trans Nicaraguans out of racism and transphobia. It's not because we live in a nation of more than 300 million human beings and some of those human beings will—because of disparate abilities and disparate effort—achieve more or less than other human beings. In the eyes of the neo-Marxist Biden administration, everything can be explained by racism. As Ibram X. Kendi himself has put it, "As an anti-racist, when I see racial disparities, I see racism."[22]

Although it may not be evident on a first read, this executive order—along with many other documents published by the Biden White House—is an explicitly neo-Marxist document. Rather than drawing economic battle lines the way Karl Marx and his first disciples did, it reframes the debate along the lines of race, gender, and sexuality. Anyone who has ever been discriminated against or "marginalized" is now part of the revolutionary class, and the solution is to ensure mandated "equity" for all people.

If you're wondering just how radical this idea is—and how much of a change it represents from government policies of the past—consider that even Senator Bernie Sanders, once the most woke, far-left extremist in the United States Senate, doesn't quite know what to make of it. Asked about the difference between "equity" and "equality" on a recent episode of *Real Time with Bill Maher*, Senator Sanders reacted to the question with the kind of confused look he usually reserves for people who ask about the three different expensive homes he owns.

"I don't know the answer to that," he said.

A few minutes later, after Bill Maher patiently explained the difference between the two concepts, Senator Sanders admitted that he believed "equality" was a better goal than equity.[23]

By the time Senator Sanders got this question, of course, it was already too late. The tentacles of the federal government had already glommed on to nearly every institution in the United States, attempting to reorient them toward the strange new goal of equity.

This took several bizarre forms. In the realm of transportation, for instance, Secretary Pete Buttigieg seems to have made it his principal crusade to fix the unbearable "racism" of our nation's roads and bridges. Speaking in July of 2022, as airline flights were being cancelled at record levels and the price of gas was nearing all-time highs—problems that you might think fall under the purview of the secretary of transportation—Buttigieg instead spoke at length about how "there is racism physically built into some of our highways."[24]

As proof for this odd claim, Buttigieg said that in the early twentieth century "an underpass was constructed such that a bus carrying mostly black and Puerto Rican kids to a beach...in New York was...designed too low for it to pass by, that that obviously reflects racism that went into those design choices."[25]

To anyone familiar with political history, the remark set off alarm bells. Secretary Buttigieg's source was *The Power Broker*, a thousand-page biography of city planner Robert Moses that was published in 1974. (This book by Robert Caro, along with his four-volume biography of President Lyndon Johnson, is almost required reading in political circles.) It tells the story of how Robert Moses, a progressive Democrat who was never elected to public office, was able to work the levers of civic power and redesign much of New York City and Long Island according to his will.

The book is an excellent achievement of biography. But it is also, as Vincent J. Cannato has pointed out in *City Journal*, "deeply flawed."[26] In its pages, you'll find a portrait of Robert Moses that contains very little nuance, despite the book being longer than anything Leo Tolstoy ever published. Caro seems to have decided relatively early in the reporting process that his subject was racist—which, given the time he lived in, might well be true—and to have shaped and framed all the available evidence to make this point.

Sometimes this zeal to construct a narrative made him get things wrong, and the "racist overpass" anecdote is one example. According to several historians, including one at Columbia University whose students spend months every year trying to prove that anecdotes from the book are correct, it's just "not true." As even the fact-checker at the *Washington Post* had to acknowledge, initially coming out in defense of Buttigieg's claim,[27] the evidence is that the low height of these overpasses was "due to cost."[28]

Now I know that it may seem strange to linger for so long over a mildly stupid claim that Pete Buttigieg made more than a year ago. I'm sure that in the months since he has made remarks that would make the one about racist roads look like the solution to a complex differential equation.

But I think it's important to note just how reductive and idiotic the modern Left's view of history—and the present—has become. The fact that these people, who have been so indoctrinated with the black-and-white, good-and-evil worldview of Cultural Marxism that they probably don't even recognize it, can look at something as innocuous as a concrete highway and see evidence of racism means that there is virtually nowhere they *won't* be able to find racism (or sexism, or transphobia).

Below, by the way, is a list of things recently labelled "racist." Presumably the Biden administration believes we should address all of them through government action in order to bring about perfect "equity." (Each item on this list comes from a real article or book, links to which can be found in the endnotes section of this book.)

- Car accidents[29]
- Math[30]
- Hiking[31]
- Television[32]
- Being nice to other people[33]
- Beer[34]
- Disaster preparedness[35]
- Latin and Greek[36]
- Classical music[37]
- The Sun[38]

If the people pushing this nonsense were all professors in humanities departments, that would be one thing. But they're not. The people who decide how the federal government will spend trillions of dollars are fully on board with these ridiculous ideas. The reason Pete Buttigieg went on his rant about racist highways in the first place was to gin up support for a billion-dollar project to make the highways *less* racist.[39]

When the federal government completely reorients itself to pursue a nonsensical, inherently Marxist goal like "equity," these are the kinds of programs we'll have—programs that spend trillions of dollars, make wealthy White liberals feel good about themselves, and bring zero results. And when the federal government's view of history is so flattened and stripped of nuance and dissent that even something as innocuous as a highway overpass can be racist, there is no limit to what it can spend these trillions of dollars on.

Of course, when it comes to the modern Left, a few trillion dollars in wasted money is the *best-case* scenario. As we've seen repeatedly over the past few years, the pursuit of "equity" at all costs can lead us to much darker outcomes than debt.

Consider, for instance, the various proclamations that the Biden administration has issued in defense of "gender-affirming care" for children. Again, this phrase doesn't sound terribly offensive when you first encounter it. Much like "equity," "gender-affirming" sounds like a perfectly reasonable policy goal to most Americans. Why would anyone want to stop children from getting "healthcare" that "affirms" something as important as their gender?

But like "equity," the phrase "gender-affirming care" masks a terrible reality. That reality, sadly, is that over the past decade, largely thanks to the spread of Critical Theory and the advent of social media, an astounding number of young people have fallen under a grave misapprehension about the nature of sex and gender. According to this idea—which is now enthusiastically supported by some of the top medical associations in the country—children who prefer to wear clothing that is more typically worn by the opposite gender, or who play with toys that don't seem to align with their biological sex, must be trapped in the wrong body.

It's difficult to know exactly where this bizarre notion came from. But its effects are clear. According to a study published in, of all places, the *New York Times*, the number of children identifying as transgender in this country has nearly *doubled* since 2017.[40]

To most people, this is a troubling trend that should be treated with extreme caution. As we've seen over the past few years, once a child is launched down the path of trying to change his or her gender, the road back can be immensely difficult, even impossible.

But to the Biden administration, this sharp rise in children who identify as trans is good news. This is an administration, after all, that has decided to base its every policy objective on the principle that there are millions of people in special "victim groups" being oppressed in the United States every day. The more people who claim to belong to such "victim groups," even if those groups are brand-new and growing at alarmingly fast rates, the more this warped view of the world makes sense.

So it's no surprise that the Department of Health and Human Services under Joe Biden, which is led by a "transgender woman" named Rachel Levine, has repeatedly passed guidance that encourages children who are struggling with their gender identity to go through dangerous and often irreversible procedures to "affirm" their gender.[41]

Of course, it's worth pausing for a moment to consider what this word "affirm" actually entails. What the Biden administration is *really* saying when they use this word is that any child who feels that he or she has been "born in the wrong body" should first be referred to a gender clinic, where a doctor will do a cursory evaluation and then prescribe off-label drugs to stop the onset of puberty. Once that's done, the child will be offered a course of "top surgery" and "bottom surgery," depending on which direction the sex change is going in.

Even these are sanitized terms for what is really going on. "Top surgery" is a medically unnecessary double mastectomy that renders a girl who has it unable ever to breastfeed. Anyone who wants a vivid—and accurate—description of "bottom surgery" needs only to visit the website of *Teen Vogue* (of all places), which recently published an explanatory article, complete with videos, about the procedure. According to a blurb beneath the video (and with apologies to the fainthearted), it shows how "the scrotum [of a patient] is opened in order to remove the testicles, and how the tip of the penis is severed in order to fashion a clitoris. The remaining scrotum sack and shaft of the penis (the long part) are then repositioned to create the vagina's labia and vaginal canal."

When the procedure is done in reverse, the details are even more gruesome. They can also be found in the same video, published by *Teen Vogue* and marketed to young women who are confused about their sexuality.[42]

As the journalist Abigail Shrier has written in her excellent book *Irreversible Damage*—which transgender activists succeeded, for a time, in getting pulled from the shelves of some bookstores—the transgender craze has historical analogues. "The Salem witch trials," known for public hysteria and demands for absolute conformity, are "[close] to the mark. So are the nervous disorders of the eighteenth century and the neurasthenia epidemic of the nineteenth century. Anorexia nervosa, repressed memory, bulimia, and the cutting contagion in the twentieth.... Three decades ago, [teen girls] might have hankered for liposuction while their physical forms wasted away. Two decades ago, today's trans-identified teens might have 'discovered' a repressed memory of childhood trauma. Today's diagnostic craze isn't demonic possession—it's 'gender dysphoria.' And its 'cure' is not exorcism, laxatives, or purging. It's testosterone and 'top surgery.'"[43]

The key difference between these past crazes and the current one, of course, is that the United States government never encouraged young girls to, for example, become anorexic. But today, the government—which has been overtaken by neo-Marxists who, having run out of victim groups to defend, are driven to invent new ones every day—is encouraging the propagation of a serious mental disorder, and of "care" that "affirms" that disorder, all so these folks can make themselves feel good about defending "LGBTQIA+ youth."

In order to do so, they need to ignore mountains of evidence. They must ignore, for instance, the fact that a high proportion of transgender children eventually grow out of their gender dysphoria: "For decades, follow-up studies of transgender kids have shown that a substantial majority—anywhere from 65 to 94 percent—eventually ceased to identify as transgender."[44] They must ignore the fact that hundreds of people who've undergone sex-change surgeries have now come to deeply regret the decision, often speaking of the decision to transition as "the worst thing that's ever happened to" them.[45]

And yet anyone who brings up these valid objections is labelled a bigot or a transphobe. The person objecting is told that more than 80 percent of young people who identify as trans have reported suicidal thoughts; failing to give in to their every delusion is therefore a form of genocide.[46] Oddly enough, trans activists never stop to wonder whether the extremely high rates of mental illness among so-called "transgender youth" are simply due to the fact that gender dysphoria, the condition that defines trangenderism, was itself recognized as a mental disorder, until recent years when that definition was sanitized and erased.[47]

Again, this might not be so bad if the problem were simply a social one. But the government is now involved, and it's getting much worse, including at the state level. The California State Assembly has passed a bill that would take custody and visitation rights from parents who don't "affirm" a child's gender.[48] A new law in Washington State allows shelters to take in "transgender minors"—children—without notifying their parents, effectively permitting state-sanctioned kidnapping when parents don't go along with the new dictates of the Left.[49]

This law, and the many others like it that will surely be up for debate in state houses all over the country, reveals the most sinister thing about Cultural Marxism: that beneath all the nice talk about "equity" and "antiracism," it is about power. No matter how well-intentioned or innocuous it might sound, every policy we've heard about from the Biden White House—the banning of gas stoves, the teaching of Critical Race Theory in schools, and the promotion of drag shows for children—is really about killing our past traditions and disbanding the family, and doing so by force if necessary.

When Joe Biden says that providing "gender-affirming care" is the best way to show our children love, understand what that means. It means that, in the name of their extreme ideology, the Cultural Marxists now want children under the age of sixteen years old subjected to life-altering drugs and permanent sterilization. Teenaged girls are having double mastectomies.[50] And this is now a *multi-billion*-dollar business at clinics and hospitals nationwide.[51]

My view is simple: No child has the maturity to make the serious, life-altering decision to be sterilized or permanently mutilated. And any adult who does that to a child is engaged in child abuse.

Anyone who doesn't believe that the nice, liberal administration of Joe Biden will act with extreme violence toward anyone who stands in its way should, at the very least, spend a few minutes considering the career and recent actions of Attorney General Merrick Garland, who has effectively become the "enforcer" for the Biden administration.

Double Standards

On March 1, 2023, just a few hours after I had completed my questioning of Phil Washington, I walked down the hall to the hearing room of the Senate Judiciary Committee, where some of my colleagues had begun questioning Attorney General Merrick Garland.

By that date, I had already questioned the man many times. During his confirmation hearing in February of 2021, I had expressed concerns—concerns that would, unfortunately, be vindicated by his conduct in office—that he would use his position as attorney general to attack the political enemies of the Biden administration, turning what was supposed to be a non-partisan department into a de facto weapon of the state. In the twenty-four months since that hearing, which ended in Merrick Garland's being confirmed by a vote of 70 to 30, he had brought many of my worst fears to life, in some cases surpassing anything that I could have dreamed up.

I'm sure that if I had suggested during his confirmation hearing, for instance, that Merrick Garland would soon be sending the FBI after parents who'd showed up at school board meetings to protest the teaching of Critical Race Theory in their kids' classrooms, that would have been dismissed as impossible. If I had suggested that he would do so in response to a memo from the National School Boards Association (NSBA) that labelled these parents "domestic terror" threats and suggested going after them using the Patriot Act, that would have been deemed absurd.

But that's exactly what happened on October 4, 2021, when Merrick Garland sent a memo warning of "an increase in harassment, intimidation and threats of violence against school board members."[52]

During my questioning of Merrick Garland in October of 2021, we had had a tense exchange about the circumstances surrounding his crackdown on parents. I pointed out that none of the incidents cited in the footnotes of the NSBA's initial memo had involved any actual incidents of violence or intimidation. One of them, in fact, was an incident involving a man named Scott Smith, who was tackled by police when he spoke a little too loudly at a school board meeting in Loudoun County, Virginia.

As many people soon found out, Smith's daughter had been sexually assaulted in school by a boy wearing a skirt—a boy who had only been in the girls' bathroom with Smith's daughter because the school had a policy, no doubt in accordance with the Biden administration's guidance that allowed students to use the bathroom that best aligned with their chosen gender identity.[53] After the assault, the school had transferred him to another school, where months later he sexually assaulted *another* young girl. (He is now, finally, a convicted sex offender.)[54] It's no wonder that Scott Smith felt the need to speak up at the school board meeting, during which several school administrators claimed that the assault never happened and anyone who expressed concerns about the school district's transgender bathroom policies was either bigoted or delusional. Any father would have done the same thing.

Garland's targeting of parents like Scott Smith is part of a pattern. Sadly, Merrick Garland has become the most political attorney general in our nation's history. He has repeatedly been willing to use the machinery of the Department of Justice to target and persecute Biden's political enemies.

Take, to give another example, Mark Houck, who was awakened in the early hours of the morning on September 23, 2022, by a full team of FBI agents with body armor and rifles, who pointed their guns at Houck and his wife—all in full view of his seven children.[55]

His crime, according to the Department of Justice, involved a small altercation that Houck had been in more than a year earlier, during which he had shoved someone.

Under normal circumstances, of course, a shove wouldn't have resulted in an early-morning FBI raid. But the circumstances, in the view of Merrick Garland and the Biden DOJ, were not normal. That was because the altercation that Houck had been in took place on the sidewalk in front of an abortion clinic, where Houck had been leading a peaceful pro-life protest. By all accounts, this was something he did often, always remaining quiet and calm while he made his points and read from scripture.

That afternoon, however, a stranger had begun screaming at Houck and taunting his son, who was standing nearby. According to testimony that Houck would give later, the man had yelled racial slurs at Houck's son and told the twelve-year-old boy, "Your dad's a fag."

Understandably upset, Houck shoved the man out of the way. As any father might have done.

The man fell backward, injured his finger, and later filed charges.[56]

Ordinarily, this wouldn't be the kind of case that draws the attention of the FBI or the Department of Justice. If the altercation had taken place on almost any other sidewalk in the United States, it probably wouldn't have reached a courtroom. Indeed, the radical left-wing prosecutor Larry Krasner refused to bring a case against Houck, sensing that such a case would likely be impossible to win.

Then Merrick Garland stepped in.

At some point, the Biden DOJ under Merrick Garland decided that Houck should be prosecuted under the "Freedom of Access to Clinic Entrances Act," which was passed during the Clinton administration to prohibit "violent, threatening, damaging, and obstructive conduct intended to injure, intimidate, or interfere with the right to seek, obtain, or provide reproductive health services."[57]

These were bogus charges, which is why Mark Houck was acquitted on January 30, 2023, and is considering suing the Biden DOJ for prosecutorial misconduct.[58]

But the charges weren't meant to stick. They were meant to serve as a warning to other sidewalk counselors and people who participate in similar activities outside abortion clinics.

Around the same time as Mark Houck was arrested, we saw dozens of violent attacks on crisis pregnancy centers across the country by violent left-wing groups. In July of 2022, these terrorists firebombed a clinic in Nashville and scrawled "JANE'S REVENGE" on the side in spray paint. Similar attacks had occurred in many cities.[59]

But it appears as if the Department of Justice did almost nothing. In the months after these attacks occurred, there was virtually no evidence of any movement by the DOJ on finding these violent criminals, investigating them, or prosecuting them.[60]

The double standard was obvious.

When I questioned Garland about the obvious disparity between the DOJ's treatment of these two sets of events, asking him to explain why a sidewalk counselor like Mark Houck had his home raided by federal agents armed with rifles and a battering ram while left-wing terrorists were free to keep firebombing as they pleased, he said that I was wrong.

"It is a priority of the department," he said, "to prosecute and investigate and find the people who are doing those firebombings. *But they are doing it at night* and in secret...and we have found two, or one group, which we did prosecute."

"You found one," I said, "how many have there been?"

"There have been a lot. And if you have any information specifically as to who those people are, we would be glad to have that."[61]

As more than a few people noticed during this hearing, Attorney General Garland seemed to have come up with a new policy for the Biden Department of Justice. Apparently, they don't prosecute violent crimes anymore if they happen *at night*. It's too hard to find the perpetrators. Under Attorney General Merrick Garland, the DOJ will now only go after criminals who have the good sense to do their bombings, assaults, and vandalism in the light of day—especially if their victims are conservative Republicans.

Which brings us to the main point, obvious to careful observers for almost three years now. The Department of Justice under Merrick Garland has repeatedly failed to prosecute the crimes of left-wing groups like Jane's Revenge, apparently because Merrick Garland and Joe Biden, not to mention the rest of his crew in the White House, *don't care* about those crimes. Instead, it seems that they are sympathetic to the violent criminals who commit these acts because they have the same political beliefs.

This, keep in mind, is coming from the same DOJ that decided to devote thousands of man hours—the "most wide-ranging investigation in [the DOJ's] history," according to Garland[62] (*more "wide ranging" than the investigation into 9/11*, the worst terrorist attack in our nation's history)—to the prosecution of virtually everyone present at or around the Capitol Building on January 6, 2021, including a student from the University of Kentucky who was sentenced to *a month in prison* though she was convicted of nothing more serious than "entering and remaining in a restricted building."[63] It's the same DOJ that, despite Mark Houck's offer to turn himself in voluntarily, decided it would be better to send dozens of FBI agents to his home with guns, shields, and a battering ram, where they could terrorize the man's children and show his neighbors what would happen if *they* decided to go against the Biden White House on a core issue like abortion.

When I asked Garland whether he had personally approved that raid, he dodged responsibility, claiming that the FBI had decided to conduct the raid on its own. Of course, the FBI *reports* to the Department of Justice, which is under the control of the attorney general, so I asked him if he would like to apologize to Mrs. Houck and her seven children, who were woken up early in the morning to the sight of armed men screaming with guns.

He said no.

Keep in mind that apologizing would have cost him nothing. At the very least, he could have expressed sympathy for the children who were forced to endure the traumatic experience of an FBI raid before breakfast. But he didn't, because he and other Biden administration officials undoubtedly believe that Mark Houck—and, by extension, his family—are on the wrong side of history. And apparently Houck's pro-life beliefs make it okay (in their minds) to send federal agents with guns to his home and traumatize his children, if only because it should discourage more people from speaking out against the government in the future.

This, you might notice, is where Marxist movements always lead. A single set of ideas comes down from the top, and anyone who dissents even slightly must be taken out or silenced by the state. Already we've seen how the Biden administration has done this through social media censorship, public shaming, and even the use of heavy weaponry.

But these are far from the only means that the government has to enforce its neo-Marxist ideas.

CHAPTER SIX

The Long March Reaches the Boardroom

In the spring of 2018 I welcomed a group of senior executives from Bank of America to my office in Washington, D.C.

They weren't happy, and neither was I.

A few months earlier, in the wake of the horrific mass shooting that took place in Parkland, Florida, on February 14, 2018, killing seventeen students and staff members at Marjory Stoneman Douglas High School, these executives had issued an edict stating that Bank of America would no longer do business with companies that manufactured "assault-style" weapons.[1]

This statement had come as a surprise to hunters, sportsmen, and hobbyists all over the country. It also deeply concerned the many small business owners who sold weapons to those folks for self-defense. These people weren't sure precisely what Bank of America meant by "assault-style weapons," a term without a precise definition. They didn't know when the announced policy would take effect—or what restrictions Bank of America might try to impose on its customers next.

Around the same time, customers of the financial giant Citigroup had learned that their bank would no longer do business with anyone who sold handguns to people under the age of twenty-one, something that was perfectly legal under federal law and most state laws at the time.[2] This announcement, like Bank of America's, had come out of nowhere, and there was no telling when new announcements might come.

When I first saw these edicts, I was furious. During my years traveling around Texas, I had met many small business owners who sold firearms, and I suspected that a fair number of them had money with Citigroup or Bank of America. Even if they didn't work with these institutions through their businesses, I was sure that many of them had college funds, checking accounts, or personal investments with either or both banks.

Suddenly these people had good reason to fear that they would no longer have a bank because of the way they had chosen to make a living—which, I must stress again, was perfectly legal. Not to mention expressly protected in the Constitution.

Like most mass shootings, the one that occurred at Marjory Stoneman Douglas High School in Florida would not have been solved by the policies that Bank of America and Citigroup had announced. Tragically, once again it was a case of a sick young man slipping through the cracks of the system and then deciding to inflict horrific pain on his classmates and teachers in the worst way that he could.

There have been too damn many of these shootings. I've been there, on the ground, repeatedly, in the aftermath of these terrible crimes. In Santa Fe. And Uvalde. And Sutherland Springs. And El Paso. And Dallas. And Midland-Odessa. I've wept with grieving family members and consoled shattered law enforcement. And I emphatically agree with the constant refrain afterwards: we must do something.

But the something we do should actually *stop* these crimes. That's why, repeatedly, I have introduced legislation to prevent mass murders. To target felons and fugitives and those with serious mental illness, to prevent them from acquiring guns, and to lock them up when they try to buy guns illegally. At every stage, Senate Democrats have voted against or even filibustered my efforts to prosecute gun criminals and get them off the street.[3]

And for schools in particular, we must do more. So I have introduced legislation to enhance school safety, to *double* the number of police officers in schools, and to provide $15 billion for mental health counselors in schools to help troubled and alienated young men before they commit an unspeakable crime. Again, Senate Democrats have repeatedly blocked and voted against my legislation to improve school safety.

Their preferred political outcome—disarming law-abiding citizens— consistently *does not work*. Across the nation, the jurisdictions with the strictest gun control laws routinely have among the highest crime rates and murder rates.[4] The data are compelling, but apparently the Democrats' objective is to achieve their political goals rather than actually solving the problem.

Judging by their conduct, Democrats have zero interest in going after actual gun criminals and stopping them from committing horrible crimes (indeed, they support Soros prosecutors who let murderers go out on the streets *after* they have committed vicious murders). Instead, their only interest is a political objective: to restrict the law-abiding citizens' right to keep and bear arms.

And, of course, it was precisely those political objectives of Democrats that the banks were trying to achieve—by coercion. And so, in May of 2018, I wrote letters to both CEOs to hold them to account for their blatant disregard for the rights of their customers, among other things:

Recently, your banks announced decisions to try to use your market power to restrict your customers' lawful gun sales and gun purchases beyond what federal and state laws require. At Citigroup, customers are now required to exceed the three-day waiting period for background checks, to refuse firearm sales to adults under the age of 21, and to refuse to carry certain magazines that federal law allows. Customers who do not comply will have to "transition their business away from Citi." Bank of America, likewise, plans to stop lending to companies that manufacture certain semi-automatic long guns.

No doubt these new policies were designed to placate liberal activists, earn favor with Democratic officeholders, and garner Citigroup and Bank of America media praise. Indeed, they track several pieces of legislation that my Democrat colleagues have already offered. But they are not welcome in Texas.

The citizens of Texas—including your millions of customers in Texas—appear to have a stronger commitment to protecting our constitutional liberties than do your boardrooms. Texans value Liberty and our God-given right to protect ourselves and our families too much to allow giant banks to dictate our rights, including our right to keep and bear arms.

The Bill of Rights should not be subject to corporate pressure or financial coercion. This is especially true given that less than 10 years ago, both of your institutions asked the public for a bailout. At the time, you both asserted it was in the public interest to do so.[5]

I went on to compare these efforts to Operation Choke Point, a similarly abusive initiative undertaken by the Obama administration that sought to cut off banking resources and put pressure on lawful gun sellers. I also asked for specific data on how these companies had come to write and issue these edicts.

Specifically, I wanted to know whether they had been pressured to do so by any Democratic politicians.

A few days later, the leadership team at Bank of America contacted my office to set up a meeting.

The executives arrived at the Russell Building of the Senate, where I have my office, in a small group. They carried briefcases and notepads, hoping to plead their case and address my questions so that I would stop attacking them so relentlessly in public.

I had no plans to stop doing that. But as usual, I was happy to listen and consider their arguments.

As it turned out, they didn't have many.

As soon as these executives sat down in my office, I asked the woman who had authored the policy what kind of guns she envisioned banning when she wrote it.

"Assault weapons," she answered promptly, using the preferred term of Democratic politicians and anti-gun activists everywhere.

I asked her politely, "Tell me, what is an assault weapon?"

"Well," she said, struggling. "Um, a machine gun?"

And there it was.

For the next few minutes, I explained to her that assault weapons are not, in fact, machine guns. Machine guns, as anyone who bothers to do a cursory Google search on the subject will learn, are fully automatic weapons. The user pulls the trigger once, and multiple bullets come out. These guns are extremely dangerous, and they are designed to inflict maximum damage. That's why the United States military uses them. It's also why it has been functionally illegal for civilians to own or sell these guns in the United States for more than eighty years.

"Absent very specific special licenses," I said, "it is *already* illegal for either of us to go out and buy a machine gun. When lawmakers use the term 'assault weapon,' they are not referring to machine guns."

By this point, I could see the eyes of everyone else in the room looking down to the floor. I could tell that for some reason, it had never occurred to these people that before trying to ban something, they should try to learn what, exactly, that thing was.

So I thought I'd let them know.

"Assault weapons, according to every law that has tried to define them, are not defined by their firing mechanisms. They're not defined by their lethality either. They are instead defined by cosmetic features. For example, having a collapsible stock can make something an assault weapon. Having a pistol grip on a rifle can make something an assault weapon. Having *two* pistol grips on a rifle can make something an assault weapon. **The term is meaningless when it comes to the law, and it includes hundreds of types of guns that ordinary hunters and sportsmen use every day.**"

I let them know that if you looked at Senator Dianne Feinstein's most recent assault weapons ban, which had come to a vote in the Senate in 2013, more than two thousand guns were described as "assault weapons" simply because of cosmetic features that had absolutely nothing to do with their lethality. Most deer rifles, for instance, have firing mechanisms that are functionally identical to the so-called "assault weapons" specified in the Democratic legislation.

Looking toward the ceiling, I adopted a slightly more playful tone.

"You know," I said. "It would be great if there were some entity in America that could handle things like this. An institution that could perhaps study public policy issues, examine the evidence, look to the data, consider the constitutional issues, and hear from experts on a wide range of issues. This entity could even maybe be constructed in such a way so that the people could have a say in its membership, so that it might have legitimacy in the eyes of the public. It would actually represent Americans."

The executives shifted uncomfortably and exchanged knowing glances. Clearly, they knew where this was going.

"Wait a second! There *is* an institution like that. It's called the United States Congress, and it's designed to resolve questions just like this one. And instead of letting that body do its work—instead of respecting democracy—you're sitting here and telling me that you just tried to ban something without even knowing what the hell it is."

From there, the meeting proceeded in the manner that I had expected. I upbraided the executives for abusing their financial power to try to usurp the job that the American people had elected me and 534 of my colleagues in Congress to do—and for doing so in an utterly half-assed manner, with blatant disregard for the constitutional rights of their customers. Then they took turns imploring me to "do something" to combat the problem of gun violence in this country, apparently defining the word "something" as *anything and everything that Dianne Feinstein and the Democrats say.* We did not, it should go without saying, make much substantive progress.

To this day, I don't know whether these banks coordinated with Democratic politicians to write their policies. I don't expect I'll ever get a straight answer on that point.

But I was reminded of something quite valuable that day—namely, that Democrats, whose capacity for shamelessness never ceases to astound me, were no longer willing to play by the rules of democracy. Those rules, many of which are unwritten, essentially say that when you lose a political debate in the legislature—when one of your bills is defeated, for instance, or a nominee you supported does not get confirmed—it is incumbent upon you to go back to your office, figure out why, and come up with better ideas so that you can win next time. Or persuade the voters that you were right, and win the next election.

This is how democracy works. It's how we arrive at compromises and write the laws that govern a nation of more than 300 million people, all of whom come from vastly different circumstances and walks of life. When we try to take shortcuts through that process, the results are disastrous.

But Democrats, who have benefited immensely from the long, slow march of neo-Marxists through the institutions of this country, seem to have decided that the short-term victories are worth abandoning the democratic process. They have effectively turned the Fortune 500 companies—many of which are staffed, and even led, by people with extreme left-wing views already—into their personal political enforcers. For the past few years, whenever Democrats lose at the ballot box or fail to get their way in Congress, many of the major corporations of this country have stepped up and tried to implement radical, Marxist change anyway, often against the will of the American people.

For a long time, they continued to do this because they did not pay a serious price for undermining the will of the American people. During the worst of my fight with Citigroup and Bank of America, for instance, many commentators assumed that there would be a widespread backlash among the customers of these two institutions, and there was, to some extent.

But it wasn't enough. The banks were simply too powerful to feel the pain in any serious way. And any pain they did feel was, according to the new woke executives, worth it.

They knew that anything was better than being attacked by the woke mob.

According to a recent report about Citigroup in the *Wall Street Journal*, the fight over the bank's gun control policy helped Citigroup executives "develop a process for when to weigh in on hot-button issues such as abortion or racial equity.... And the financial hit to the bank was minimal."

In interviews, the *Journal* reported, executives had said "they would do it all over again."[6]

In fact, over the course of the approximately five years since I met with executives from Bank of America in my office, several companies *have* done it all over again. Which led to yet another closed-door meeting in my Senate office. This one was also quite tense.

It occurred in the spring of 2021, just after the state of Texas had passed a law that was intended to secure the integrity of our elections. This law, known as Senate Bill 7, enhanced protections for voter integrity so that Texans could have greater confidence in our electoral processes. It was passed largely to address the serious concerns that many Americans had raised about our voting systems after the election of 2020, including widespread allegations that it was rife with fraud and errors.

And Texas was not the only state to act. Around the same time, the state of Georgia had passed similar legislation to ensure that its elections were safe, secure, and transparent. Senate Bill 7, which passed both houses of the Texas State Legislature on May 30, 2021, ensured, among other things, that the use of mail-in ballots would go back to pre-pandemic levels. It also imposed penalties on counties that failed to adequately purge their voter rolls of dead or fraudulent voters and otherwise keep track of their books to prevent fraud.[7]

Democrats had fought hard to stop this bill from becoming law. But they had failed.

Once again, the Democrats had lost in the legislatures—which is supposed to be where it counts. They had also lost on the facts. Despite several efforts by President Biden and the Democrats to falsely label the voting laws in Texas and Georgia as "Jim Crow 2.0," the Democrats were disappointed to find that most Americans were broadly supportive of protecting the integrity of our electoral processes.

But then, predictably, a small number of woke people put enough pressure on the major corporations of this nation to force them into action. A few weeks after Georgia passed its own election integrity law, Coca-Cola (which is headquartered in Atlanta) released a statement condemning the entire state.[8] Not to be outdone, Major League Baseball announced that it would move the All-Star Game, which was scheduled to be held in Atlanta, to Denver, Colorado.[9] (They did this, by the way, despite the fact that nearly 50 percent of the people in Atlanta are Black, compared to just 9 percent of people in Denver. Thus, MLB denied African-American small businesses in Atlanta tens of millions of dollars in revenue, moving those profits over instead to one of the whitest cities in America.[10] So much for "equity," I guess.)

In Texas, there were similar woke statements from multiple corporations, nearly all of which were written in suspiciously similar language. They asserted that this bill, which was written to ensure that all citizens of Texas would have a right to vote in elections that were truly free and fair, would somehow "erect barriers" to "diversity, equity, and inclusion."

Shortly after reading these statements—which, I was infuriated to see, implied strongly that all the Republicans in the state legislature, as well as the governor and the lieutenant governor, were racists—I invited the CEO of one of the companies that had written and released a statement to come to my office.

This CEO, whom we'll call "Bob" for the purposes of this story, showed up in Washington a few weeks later.

Asking most of the staff to leave and closing the door to my office so that Bob and I could speak candidly, I asked him (politely at first) why his company had released such an absurd statement.

Before he could answer, I asked him which provisions of Senate Bill 7 did he and his company believe were racist. Were there multiple offending sections?

"Just point to one, Bob," I said. "Tell me which page, or which *line*, of this bill you think is racist, and we can go over it together."

He paused.

"Well," he said. "It's the whole thing, really. I was told—"

"Just give me a page number. Or a section number."

Bob paused, looking slightly worried.

Then it clicked.

"You haven't read it, have you?" I asked him.

He shrugged.

"Bob, you haven't read a single page of this bill?"

"No," he said, sighing.

"Can you name even a single provision of the bill?"

"Um, well, the drop box stuff . . . and the voter ID stuff. . . ." (Texas law had long limited the use of drop boxes, and voter ID likewise had long been Texas law.)

I replied, "Bob, every time the Democrats come after your company, proposing new taxes or regulations that would hammer your profitability, you're immediately on the phone to me and others asking for help, and yet you're more than willing to baselessly condemn the Republican governor, lieutenant governor, and the state legislature all as bigots. What the hell is wrong with you?"

"It's just the way things are! A bunch of African-American employees came to me and said the bill was racist, and that they were really upset, and so I approved the statement . . . but it was never intended to be political! We weren't trying to take a side."

Sadly, he was right. By the time "Bob" and I sat down in my office for our vigorous discussion about Senate Bill 7, this vicious cycle had become extremely, distressingly familiar. The leaders of a major company would begin to feel pressure—whether from social media campaigns by external activist groups or, increasingly, from the internal ranks of its own staff—and in a panic they'd do whatever they had to do to avoid getting cancelled, shamed, or fired for going against the new woke orthodoxy.

It hadn't taken long for the executive suite to learn which issues would lead to freak-outs and boycotts from the staff, and then to preemptively address those issues with statements, tweets, or grand gestures like what the MLB and Coca-Cola had done in Georgia. When ordinary Americans complained that these companies were acting in a way that was completely contrary to their values, the companies in question usually ignored them. It wasn't long before people began asking *why* such large companies, which had always attempted to appeal to as many potential customers as possible, had suddenly become so enamored of radical, left-wing politics.

The answer, as usual, could be found by following the money.

ESG and the Big Three

When major American corporations release statements expressing their newfound woke beliefs, they are almost always appealing to a particular audience. Given that these statements usually come out on Twitter and are reported widely in the news, many people make the mistake of assuming that this audience is the American people.

That is incorrect.

In recent years, the *real* audience for the statements and actions of publicly traded corporations—which is how just about every company whose name you know can be classified—has been three massive investment firms: BlackRock, State Street, and Vanguard.[11] Unlike most American companies, which do a great deal of PR to gain as much market share as possible, these investment firms, known as the "Big Three" on Wall Street, are not household names. Most Americans don't think about them until it's time to check up on their 401(k) plans or start college funds for their children.

But lately, that is beginning to change. This is because whenever we hear a story about a major corporation doing something woke and idiotic, we'll hear soon afterward that it did so at the behest of one of the "Big Three": BlackRock, State Street, and Vanguard.

Although most Americans don't think very much about these firms or what they do, their influence is massive. As of 2022, these three firms manage just over $20 trillion in assets, an amount that rivals the entire gross domestic product of the United States. That money is invested in all kinds of American companies, from Coca-Cola and Citigroup to Bank of America to United Airlines to Apple. But unlike those companies, the "Big Three" didn't get their money by inventing things, selling things, or offering great services.

They got it because we, the American people, gave it to them to invest.

At the most basic level, the "Big Three" provide a simple service. They take money from ordinary Americans, usually in the form of 401(k) plans or mutual funds, and then they decide how to invest that money so that customers will get the highest possible return on investment. (At least in theory. As we shall see.) The idea is that their customers—meaning us, the people whose money they are managing—can go about their lives without having to constantly keep an eye on the stock market. That way we don't have to research every stock that's in our 401(k)s and buy the ones we think are going to make a profit. Much like lawyers or accountants, these investment fund managers provide subject-area expertise and guidance for people who don't have the time or the inclination to acquire that expertise themselves.

For a long time, politics didn't factor into this equation, at least not in any major way. The employees at these investment funds simply studied companies, decided which ones stood the best chance of making money, and then invested the hard-earned money of their customers with those companies. It mattered little what kind of culture these companies had or whether the CEOs of these companies were Republicans, Democrats, or independents. As long as the executives at the companies weren't sexually harassing people in the office or clubbing baby seals to make their products, investors could reasonably assume that there was money to be made, both for the investment firms and for their customers (who, again, were mostly ordinary Americans looking to get good returns on their investment accounts).

Then, slowly, that began to change.

People first noticed that something was slightly off in January of 2018, when Larry Fink, the CEO of the investment firm BlackRock (by far the largest of the "Big Three," with more than $9 trillion under management),[12] wrote a letter to the CEOs of the companies in which BlackRock was invested outlining a "new vision" for what the investment firm wanted to see going forward.

"Without a sense of purpose," he wrote, "no company, either public or private, can achieve its full potential. It will ultimately lose the license to operate from key stakeholders. It will succumb to short-term pressures to distribute earnings, and, in the process, sacrifice investments in employee development, innovation, and capital expenditures that are necessary for long-term growth. It will remain exposed to activist campaigns that articulate a clearer goal, even if that goal serves only the shortest and narrowest of objectives."

The solution, according to Fink, was to consider factors that went beyond simple profit and loss. Going forward, companies should anticipate the demands of left-wing activists and create corporate policy accordingly.

As he explained, "Where activists do offer valuable ideas—which is more often than some detractors suggest—we encourage companies to begin discussions early, to engage with shareholders like BlackRock, and to bring other critical stakeholders to the table."[13]

Around that time, Fink began to promote a new movement known as ESG, which stands for "environmental, social, and governance."[14] According to this method of investing and running companies,

BlackRock would no longer take only profit and loss into account; it would, rather, consider a wide range of factors when deciding how to invest the hard-earned money of Americans. Consideration of what impact a given company might have on the climate, for instance, or how friendly a given company was likely to be toward the transgender community, would now be important.[15]

There were antecedents for this approach. There has never been a time when investment funds weren't worried about investing in companies that sold bad things, or companies that made things that would soon become obsolete or frowned-upon by society. That's why they pulled money out of South Africa (which at the time still imposed the racist apartheid system) in the 1980s; it's the reason they have avoided putting money into (even legal) marijuana companies for years.

But ESG was something new. Rather than simply avoiding putting money into companies that make bad products, the "Big Three" investment firms began using their voices and votes as shareholders to change the values of the companies that they did invest in, almost always to align with woke values.

They were able to do this because when BlackRock puts money into a company—Coca-Cola, for instance—BlackRock becomes a shareholder in Coca-Cola. This means that BlackRock is able to cast votes on what the company should and should not do and to exert massive influence on the companies it has invested in. Unlike ordinary people who invest in companies such as Coca-Cola, or even some smaller investment funds, the "Big Three" make massive purchases, giving them the ability to exert influence on the CEOs of these companies as they see fit. They wield a lot of power when it comes to executive compensation packages, the size of bonuses, and who can get reelected or reappointed to corporate boards.

Not only are they investing in mutual funds; the Big Three also manage trillions in "index" funds, which invest in every single company in a given category (for example, the S&P 500). Index funds are very convenient for investors, because they allow the investor to diversify risk, invest in equities across a broad sector, and minimize administrative costs. But they also ensure that the Big Three are massive shareholders in almost every significant company traded on Wall Street.

As of 2019, it was reported that the Big Three control an average of about 25 percent of the voting shares of all companies listed on the S&P 500 index,[16] meaning as a practical matter that these companies cannot make a move unless BlackRock, State Street, and Vanguard say it's okay.

This is a major problem.

For one thing, funds that embrace ESG principles significantly underperform those that seek profit alone. According to a recent study in the *Harvard Business Review*, "*none* of the high sustainability funds" measured in the year 2022 "outperformed *any* of the [non-ESG] funds" [emphasis added].[17] Another study, conducted by professors from Columbia University and the London School of Economics, revealed similar shortcomings in ESG funds.[18] Anyone interested in the details of just *how* poorly these funds do can find key data at consumersresearch.org. Consumers' Research is a group that has made tremendous strides in keeping track of and cataloguing businesses that go woke and lose money.

But the Big Three have found ways around this.

As the former biotech entrepreneur (and current candidate to be the Republican nominee for president) Vivek Ramaswamy has pointed out in his excellent book *Capitalist Punishment*, ESG investing typically comes in two forms. One of them is "greenwashing," whereby investment funds take the money given to them by their customers and invest it in ventures that are virtuous in the eyes of the Left:[19] sustainable energy companies, vegan dog treat conglomerates, or maybe manufacturers of plant-based sandals.

By now, it has been well-documented that these funds consistently make less money than traditional investment funds. In fact, most customers *know* that they won't get the same returns when they invest with funds that openly advertise themselves as being primarily focused on ESG. Presumably some investors—and the executives of the companies they invest in—are willing to take the financial hit because they want to get approving nods when they go to the country club at night. (Or, as is frequently the case, the ESG virtue signaling is designed to distract the press from reporting on other bad conduct by the firm, such as utilizing child labor in China or Africa for their products.)

An even more insidious form that ESG takes is what Ramaswamy calls "green-smuggling." This is when the investment firms take the money of customers who have *not* opted into the many "social responsibility funds" that these firms offer and nevertheless use their money (without their permission) to further those same left-wing political goals.[20]

When most Americans invest money with BlackRock, State Street, or Vanguard, they are doing so because they believe that these firms know what they're doing with money. They believe that the people who work at these firms will research companies, decide which ones stand the best chance of providing high returns, and then invest the money accordingly. They believe, in short, that the Big Three and other major investment funds care only about making them as much money as humanly possible. After all, the customers are depending on the investment companies so they'll be able to send their kids to college, and to retire comfortably.

What they *haven't* bought into is a bunch of woke business leaders sitting around and deciding that they'll use the money of their clients—money that has been entrusted to them because their customers want to keep it safe and make it grow—to further progressive political goals, which, as we've seen, usually comes at the expense of maximizing profits.

But this is exactly what has been happening.

In 2018, for instance, just a month after Larry Fink gave his speech announcing that ESG was now effectively the law of the land in corporate America, the country was rocked to its core by the Parkland shooting. Almost immediately, as Vivek Ramaswamy tells the story, the "Big Three," BlackRock in particular, started looking for ways to enforce the political preferences of the radical-left Great Reset crowd—who believe that citizens' owning firearms is unacceptable, in part because it might prevent the government from imposing its will on the people—on the entire country.

"They met with gun retailers and manufacturers," Ramaswamy explains, "and pressured them to sell fewer guns by either getting out of the gun business altogether (as Kroger chose to) or voluntarily raising the age limit for gun purchases from eighteen to twenty-one."[21]

But, as he points out, there was a catch. "BlackRock couldn't use its dedicated social responsibility funds to lobby gun sellers and makers because those funds had to divest from gun manufacturers and therefore didn't have a shareholder's voice or vote anymore. So BlackRock leveraged the massive weight of all the billions in its *non-ESG* funds to convince gun sellers not to sell guns. It used its supposedly profit-focused funds to advance social goals that had nothing to do with profit. The millions of investors in those funds, many of them gun owners, had never signed up for that; they just wanted diversification and profit. BlackRock's companywide commitment to ESG made it smuggle social activism into *all* its funds."[22]

It's no coincidence, of course, that in 2018 BlackRock owned over 300 million shares of Bank of America, giving it a nearly 4 percent stake in the company. I wonder whether the pressure campaign being waged by BlackRock—and Vanguard, which owned more than 7 percent of Bank of America's shares in 2018—was a significant part of the reason that executives from the company ended up in my office in the spring of that year, defending a gun control policy that they didn't seem to understand.

Apparently the executives at Bank of America were just doing what is required of them—now that ESG investing is the norm in corporate America. They reacted to the news of the day by pushing policies that Democrats had been trying and failing to get through Congress for decades, knowing that it was the only way to appease the leaders of the massive investment funds that owned their stock and kept the money coming in.

Over time, it became clear that the pressure wasn't just coming from the likes of BlackRock, State Street, and Vanguard. While these institutions certainly wielded the most power and influence over the Fortune 500, they were far from the only groups pressuring our major corporations to go woke to win acclaim from the radical Left. One of the most active, it turned out, was the Human Rights Campaign (HRC), a left-wing group described by the *New York Post* as "the largest LGBTQ+ political lobbying group in the world."[23]

It should come as no surprise that the HRC has received funding from the Open Society Foundations run by George Soros,[24] the same man who has been waging a quiet campaign to elect radical-left district attorneys in cities all over the United States in an attempt to "remake the justice system" of this country. The goal appears to be the same with the HRC: to circumvent the legislative and judicial processes of the United States in order to push a left-wing agenda that the majority of the American people would not support if it ever came to a vote.

Rather than pressuring companies directly in the way that some major investment firms do, the HRC hides behind seemingly altruistic motives. Every year, the group publishes a "Corporate Equality Index," issuing every company in the United States a "CEI score." On its face, this score is supposed to be a measure of how accommodating these companies are to women, gay people, and other sexual minorities who might want to work there. At a first glance, that might sound harmless, or even beneficial.

But that's not how it works in practice. According to James Lindsay, the author of several books on radical leftism, the administration of the CEI ranking functions more "like an extortion racket, like the Mafia." The group, as Lindsay describes it, "sends representatives to corporations every year telling them what kind of stuff they have to make visible at the company. They give them a list of demands and if they don't follow through, there's a threat that you won't keep your CEI score."[25]

When you look at what companies have to do in order to keep their scores at or near 100 percent, it becomes much clearer why we've seen so much woke nonsense over the past few years. According to the HRC, companies are graded on "marketing or advertising to LGBTQ consumers." The company also loses points on its score if it dares to give money to "organizations whose primary mission includes advocacy against LGBTQ equality," a description that could certainly, according to a recent report in the *New York Post*, include any Christian charity.[26]

I'm sure that if Chick-fil-A, for instance, were a publicly traded company—which, because of the company's commitment to Christian values and its admirable unwillingness to buy into the latest woke fads, it is not—it would have one of the lowest CEI scores in the country. And, sadly, even Chick-fil-A has given into the relentless pressure and named its own "diversity, equity, and inclusion" officer.[27]

In recent years, sucking up to groups like the HRC has become one of the top priorities for major American corporations. In some cases, this concern has overridden all others, often to the detriment of consumers and the American people.

"All the Right Shibboleths"

This is certainly what happened in the case of FTX, the supposedly groundbreaking cryptocurrency exchange run by Sam Bankman-Fried. Personally, I'm a big believer in Bitcoin and crypto more generally—I personally invest in Bitcoin and am working hard to make Texas an oasis for Bitcoin mining—but FTX turned out to be more of a Bernie Madoff–style Ponzi scheme than a sound financial institution.

For years, the head of this company was hailed in Washington and the financial world as the next Steve Jobs or Elon Musk—an eccentric genius in cargo shorts with messy hair who was worth close to $20 billion. If you believed the hype surrounding Sam Bankman-Fried, you would have thought that he had cracked the code to capitalism itself, figuring out a way to make billions of dollars every year by creating and trading a new form of money that very few people fully understood. For this reason, almost no one asked questions about what the hell was going on at FTX.

The best part?

Sam Bankman-Fried was the poster boy for ESG and the liberal social values it seeks to enforce on American companies—a high-profile, multi-million-dollar donor to Democrats and an evangelist for "funding research and policy initiatives that will have an outsized impact on the climate crisis" and "other climate related special projects." In July of 2021, his company launched the "FTX Climate Program" and announced that it would "become carbon neutral" that year.[28] And Bankman-Fried was richly rewarded for his embrace of ESG. As the *Wall Street Journal* would report, "ESG ratings company Truvalue Labs even gave FTX a higher score on 'leadership and governance' than Exxon/Mobil though the crypto exchange had only three directors on its board. The directors were Mr. Bankman-Fried, another FTX executive and an outside attorney."[29]

FTX executives donated more than $44 million to left-leaning PACs and similar organizations in the 2022 election cycle.[30] Sam Bankman-Fried personally donated $5.2 million to support the campaign of Joe Biden alone.[31]

Then, less than three years after the presidential election, FTX appears to have been nothing more than an elaborate system of smoke and mirrors—and, if the initial reports are to be believed, not a terribly well-constructed one. By the time FTX customers noticed that they were missing a collective $8 billion, it was too late; the company had no choice but to declare bankruptcy.

Sitting in the home of his parents in the aftermath of all this financial carnage, Bankman-Fried began a remarkably candid text exchange with a journalist from Vox who asked Bankman-Fried if the "ethics stuff" had "mostly been a front" to cover for the fact that he didn't really know what he was doing when it came to the business side of things.

His response was, "Yeah, I mean that's not *all* of it, but it's a lot."

Later in the same interview, when he was asked about some of the more technical details about *how* his company had managed to lose more than $8 billion—an absurd amount of money, even for someone who runs a large financial institution—Bankman-Fried seemed not to care very much. When the reporter pointed out that the scheme was "sketchy even if you get away with it," he seemed flippant.

"It was never the intention," he said. "Sometimes life creeps up on you."[32]

There are understatements, massive understatements, and then... whatever the hell *that* was.

FTX got a pass for years because it said all the right things, donated to the right causes, and gave money to the right left-wing politicians. If you asked the experts from the various foundations around the world who are currently in charge of deciding which companies are considered "good" according to the Great Reset crowd and which ones are not, they would have told you that FTX was an exemplary company, and that ordinary companies like Exxon should strive to be more like it. As we have seen, that global energy corporation was punished with a lower "governance" score than the crypto-bros at FTX—right up until the moment the whole thing came crashing down.[33]

Undoubtedly, more than a few company executives have been using ESG as a front to earn favor with the Left and (as with FTX) to distract outside observers from paying attention to business or ethical problems with the company. When Vox reporter Kelsey Piper asked Bankman-Fried about that, his response in the text exchange was stunningly honest:

> **Piper:** you were really good at talking about ethics, for someone who kind of saw it as a game with winners and losers
> **SBF:** ya
> hehe
> I had to be
> it's what reputations are made of, to some extent
> I feel bad for those who get f***ed by it
> by this dumb game we woke westerners play where **we say all the right shiboleths [*sic*] and so everyone likes us** [Emphasis added.][34]

In other cases, woke priorities may fatally divert a company's employees from the core purpose of the institution they are working for. Perhaps that's also what happened at the recently collapsed Silicon Valley Bank, which was more focused on ESG and "diversity, equity, and inclusion" than virtually any other bank in America. The executives of the bank were *so* concerned with these things, in fact, that they seem to have forgotten to check up on the actual…you know, *banking* part of their business—ultimately leading to the second largest bank failure in U.S. history.

For a full eight months, for instance, Silicon Valley Bank did not have a chief risk officer.[35] This is the person who is supposed to look at the bank's balance sheet, run the numbers, and assess whether the investments that the bank has made might lead to losses that the bank would be unable to cover. The chief risk officer is supposed to make sure that even in the event of a disaster (say, the Fed raising interest rates significantly) the bank will still be able to survive. If the chief risk officer finds that this is *not* the case—which is exactly what anyone who took that job would have found in the period from 2019 until about 2022—they're supposed to act quickly to remedy the situation.

But that didn't happen. Instead, executives focused on making sure that the bank's ESG score was in top shape, and that they came up with plenty of DEI initiatives. For a while, the top financial risk manager at Silicon Valley Bank UK was focused on instituting "safe spaces" for "coming-out stories" and planning "the company's first month-long Pride campaign," according to the *New York Post*.[36]

Then, the bank met the fate that eventually befalls many financial institutions that put wokeness over profit and good business: it failed in spectacular fashion, taking billions of dollars and many careers down with it. The Biden administration, which consistently protects its ideological allies, swiftly stepped in and saved the depositors at SVB, to the tune of $15.8 billion[37]—demonstrating that having friends in the Biden White House matters more than practicing sound financial risk management. Does anyone believe the Fed would have stepped in to bail out a bunch of oil and gas producers who had invested in a bank in Texas that went under?

This pattern goes on and on. If the last few years have taught us anything, it's that threats of government action and social ostracization are not enough to stop major corporations from obeying the pressure from investment funds, activist groups, and the various other far-left figures who control the flow of American capital. These companies have believed that, although a few customers may grumble and put up the occasional social media post when they push woke policies that most people don't agree with, the majority of customers will still buy the company's products, use its services, and allow the status quo to continue.

But there have been a few recent signs of hope.

Anyone who doubts this would do well to crack open a nice can of Coors Light and read about what happened to the beverage company Anheuser-Busch in April of 2023.

How to Fight Back

For as long as I can remember, Budweiser has been a brand that embraced everything that was good about America—simplicity, self-sufficiency, and, for some reason, a giant horse running wild over deserts and paved roads toward nothing. Most of the ads for Budweiser that I saw growing up were narrated by gravelly-voiced men who sounded like they might have just come in from a long afternoon of hunting and roping cattle. Bud was a beer for people who worked hard and wanted to enjoy a refreshing beverage at the end of the day.

Then the company got the message that they needed to start placating the left-wing activist groups and big investment funds of the world. Get woke quickly, or the company's CEI score might begin to fall, sending all the left-wing ESG money away toward other, more liberal beer brands.

That may help explain why Anheuser-Busch hired Alissa Heinerscheid, a relatively young liberal graduate of Harvard College and the University of Pennsylvania's Wharton School of Business, who became Bud Light's dedicated vice president of marketing in 2021.

It wasn't long before Heinerscheid betrayed her disgust with the brand she had taken over. Speaking on a podcast about women in leadership just a few months after taking the role, she said that she had a "clear mandate" when it came to the brand.

"It's like, we need to evolve and elevate this incredibly iconic brand," she said. "What I brought to that was a belief in, okay, what does evolve and elevate mean? It means inclusivity. It means shifting tone. It means having a campaign that's truly inclusive and feels lighter and brighter and different and appeals to women and to men."[38]

Now, it's been quite a while since I've been to the kind of parties where light beer is consumed in abundance. But in recent years I have taken quite a few long bus tours of the country—as part of my presidential campaign in 2016, in my Senate reelection in Texas in 2018, and most recently as part of my effort to get Republicans elected nationally in tough states during the 2022 midterms. When I stopped in bars and restaurants or gave speeches at large events along those bus tours, there were often bright blue cans of Bud Light as far as the eye could see. The same is true of most sporting events and concerts that I've been to recently. It seems that, out in the real world, where people didn't think much about ESG or how many transgender Wiccans were on a given company's board, the Bud Light "brand" was doing just fine.

Of course, as they probably would have told you themselves, Heinerscheid and her colleagues didn't have a problem with the *quantity* of people who were buying and drinking Bud Light. Their problem, it seemed, was with the perceived *quality* of those people.

"We had this hangover," Heinerscheid said later in the same interview. "I mean, Bud Light had been kind of a brand of fratty, kind of out-of-touch humor, and it was *really important that we had another approach* [emphasis added]."[39]

It's important to remember at this point that the need for a "new approach" was not simply the result of some young woman who'd been indoctrinated in business school coming in and pushing her personal whims on everyone else at a company.

This was coming right from the top—and, most important, from outside.

As we have seen, according to one of the most important criteria for CEI scores, companies needed to make specific efforts to reach out to customers that might be LGBTQ. If not, they could lose points and lose the approval of their biggest shareholders, which included BlackRock, among other ESG-focused funds.[40]

So they went looking for a brand ambassador who could appeal to LGBTQ folks. It wasn't long before they found him…or her, or them, or whatever Dylan Mulvaney has decided to be called this week.

For the previous few years, Dylan Mulvaney had been an effeminate man who sought attention wherever he could find it. In 2015, he began a career in musical theater singing in the deliberately offensive musical *The Book of Mormon*, which takes direct aim at religious Americans and includes numerous crude songs and jokes. From there he launched a career on social media, using his new platform to get on game shows.

But when the transgender craze began sweeping the United States, Dylan saw his moment. In front of his millions of followers, he began wearing makeup and small dresses and speaking about the joys of "transitioning" to a female. Dylan often made several videos a day, speaking frequently about how hard it was for him to let go of "boy Dylan" and become "girl Dylan."[41] He also launched a campaign to "normalize the bulge," meaning the sight of his intact male genitals, which were still visible under the tiny women's clothing he wore.[42]

Dylan put great effort into targeting young children, in particular, with his message. Using primarily TikTok and Instagram, Dylan put out a video lip-syncing "I am Eloise, I am six," while dressed as a small child; this video garnered 7.1 million views. Dylan put out multiple videos during his "Days of Girlhood" series, some of which were viewed over 11 million times.[43] Yet another video showed Dylan in Target shopping for Barbie dolls—according to market analysis, "the Barbie Toy market primarily target[s] young children aged 3–9 years"[44]—and that video gathered 8.3 million views.[45]

I'm not sure how the meeting went when partnering with Dylan was proposed to Bud Light leadership—what the exact pitch was that what Bud Light really needed was more transgender outreach to young children below the legal drinking age—but in any event the outcome was an enthusiastic green light. In mid-March, the marketing team at Bud Light sent Dylan Mulvaney a large can with his image on it, asking him to become one of the brand's new official "ambassadors."[46]

With that, a person who aggressively targets children nationally by pushing the ideology of transgenderism on TikTok, Instagram, and other social media platforms became the face of an iconic brand many Americans had been consuming their whole adult lives. I'm sure that company executives assumed, like always, that they would get praise for hiring Dylan Mulvaney from the institutions that grade companies on their adherence to ESG and other woke principles, while the company's main customer base—those "fratty" people who had been loyally consuming the brand for years—either wouldn't notice or wouldn't be able to do anything about it.

They were wrong.

A few days after the announcement, the singer Kid Rock filmed himself blasting to hell a stack of Bud Light cases with a rifle. His sentiments were concise: "F*** Bud Light." Other social media users vented their disappointment with the brand as well, albeit less colorfully.[47] More important, people who did not agree with the left-wing values that Bud Light was now shoving down the throats of the American people simply stopped buying the beer, successfully deploying the very kind of boycott that the Left had been using for many years.[48] Now that the shoe was on the other foot, of course, the Left didn't like it very much.

In the middle of April, it was announced that Bud Light's parent company had lost more than $6 billion in value over the course of just a few days. By June 1, that number had grown to *$27 billion.* In less than two months, the total market cap of Anheuser-Busch had plummeted from $135 billion to $108 billion.[49]

The company denied firing them, but Alissa Heinerscheid and Daniel Blake, who were in charge of marketing for the mainstream brands at Anheuser-Busch, both took a leave of absence,[50] and (I assume) the company took a long, hard look at whether it would be worth it in the future to completely change its iconic brand to try to make it more appealing to various left-wing activist groups like HRC and others.

As cases of Bud Light sat unpurchased by the thousands on store shelves—with retailers literally trying to give them away *for free*[51]—by June, Mexican beer company Modelo had surpassed Bud Light to become the top-selling beer in America.[52] Amazingly, it was so bad that Bud Light fell from the number-one-selling beer in America to, by July 2023, *no longer even in the top ten.*[53]

And then Target decided it wanted to follow Bud Light down the path of self-destruction.

Target is based in Minneapolis, Minnesota, and it has always been a left-leaning company. But in the spring of 2023, the company took it to another level. In celebration of "Gay Pride Month," Target hired a self-described Satan worshiper—yes, you read that right—to design a massive display for the front of its stores. The display deliberately targeted children, as young as infants. Among the first things you would see, as you walked in the store, were onesies for babies declaring their "gay pride." And there were children's T-shirts emblazoned with the slogan "TRANS PEOPLE WILL ALWAYS EXIST."[54]

Target's chosen designer also created clothing—with rams' horns and other occult symbols—proclaiming "Satan Respects Pronouns."[55]

At the time of this writing, it's not clear what imbecile at Target thought, *You know what our customers want? Devil worship! Transgender children!*

It turns out, moms weren't happy. Target's key demographic is the suburban mom, and suburban moms were outraged. They began posting viral videos online, showing the world the bizarre display.[56]

Target realized it had a problem. In the days that followed, Target held "emergency" strategy calls; one company insider told the *New York Post*, "I think given the current situation with Bud Light, the company is terrified of a Bud Light situation." Target leadership decided to move the displays to the back of the stores, but only in "Southern" locations.[57] (Apparently Target believed that people in the Midwest, New England, and the rest of America were fine with marketing transgenderism to young children.)

They tried to mitigate the damage. But the result was swift: from mid-May to June 9, Target's shares dropped 20 percent, eliminating *$15 billion* in market cap.[58]

And now, as a result, the next CEOs contemplating giving into the woke mob will have something serious to think about. They'll say, "I don't wanna be Bud Light. I don't wanna be Target." And maybe, just maybe, they'll decide to stay out of politics and focus on selling cheap beer or affordable clothing.

The reason that so many big companies give into this nonsense is that—at least until recently—incentives compelled doing so. If you were an apolitical CEO, a businessperson who just wanted to make money and run a successful business, the cost-benefit analysis strongly favored going woke. Why? Because historically conservatives have been terrible at boycotts, and the harm from giving in was minimal. (See, for example, the conservative boycott of MLB for boycotting Georgia.)[59] On the other hand, appeasing the angry twenty-somethings in your company, the Twitter scolds, the activist shareholders—all of that was tangible. And so the rational CEO surrendered to the woke mob.

Bud Light and Target may have helped change that calculus.

But we can do more. We can significantly increase the *cost* of going woke. We can change the cost-benefit analysis. How? Go after the money.

I almost always stay out of fights in the Texas legislature. I have enough fights in Washington, D.C., without getting into yet more fights in Austin. But Texas Senate Bill 13—to prohibit state pension funds or endowments from investing with firms that boycott oil and gas—was one of the very few exceptions to that rule. The reasoning behind the bill was simple: if you boycott oil and gas (which generates millions of jobs in Texas), then Texas is going to boycott you.

I picked up the phone and called the state House and Senate authors of the bill (both good friends of mine) and offered my help. I wrote an op-ed publicly urging the state legislature to pass SB 13.[60] And I sent that op-ed to every single state senator and representative.

SB 13 passed overwhelmingly. And, along with it, another bill that prohibited state funds from investing in firms that undermine the Second Amendment. Together, these two bills have already had a huge impact. Between university endowments and state employee pensions, the five Texas funds that were required to divest from energy boycotters control over $355 billion.[61] And that capital is now being withdrawn from banks and companies that go woke.

And other red states, collectively, control trillions of dollars. If we want to stop American corporations from embracing Cultural Marxism and using their economic might to try to force the rest of us to do so, then every one of those red states should use its economic muscle to change the cost-benefit analysis for corporate decision-makers. If the big banks and the big corporations stand to lose billions of dollars for going woke—if together we make the hashtag #GoWokeGoBroke a brutal reality—then we'll change the decision matrix for the next CEO. If the costs are high enough, he or she just might say, "Why don't we just stay out of politics?"

And these efforts are already working. In January, CEO Larry Fink said that BlackRock had *lost about $4 billion* in managed assets as a result of the public backlash against ESG.[62] Moreover, "in a conversation at the Aspen Ideas Festival [in June], Fink acknowledged that Florida Gov. Ron DeSantis's decision to pull $2 billion in assets hurt his firm in 2022."[63]

Fink elaborated, "I don't use the word ESG any more, because it's been entirely weaponized...by the far left and weaponized by the far right."[64] Instead, he said, he's using the term "conscientious capitalism"[65]—whatever the hell that means. And his backtracking continued. "When I write these [investment] letters, it was never meant to be a political statement....They were written to identify long-term issues to our long-term investors."[66]

Fink went on, "We had...one of the best years ever, but *I'm ashamed of being part of this conversation*."[67]

That's progress.

Looking back, some people may be tempted to minimize the impact of the Bud Light controversy and the Target debacle. But this was not just about Bud Light or Target. It wasn't even about the impact of the Left's current obsession with pushing an extreme transgender agenda.

Rather, the biggest impact, I believe, will be on the thousands of other woke young wannabe executives who are, at this very moment, graduating from the top business schools in our nation and getting jobs at our nation's top Fortune 500 companies. Some of them are going straight to the big investment funds where ESG and other woke values are being pushed, to great effect. During their time in business school, these students have learned that the principles of diversity, equity, inclusion, sustainability, kindness, unlimited access to abortion, and other radical left-wing values are far more important than making money or running a good business. If they don't get the message—loud and clear—that ordinary Americans are not going to stand for having far-left politics rammed down their throats by Big Business, there will be nothing to stop them from taking things one step further every fiscal quarter.

Imagine, for instance, what might have come next in the Dylan Mulvaney–Bud Light saga if so many Americans hadn't spoken up and stopped the whole campaign in its tracks. I'm sure that if the Dylan Mulvaney sponsorship had gone over quietly—allowing Bud Light executives to gain a few points on their CEI score and keep profits relatively healthy in the process—they might have reached out to other trans influencers, perhaps even giving several of them visible jobs at the company.

Had that been the case, the number of confused teenagers who would have fallen under the misapprehension that they are really transgender would have grown as these teens saw more and more confused adults rewarded for championing this extreme agenda. The number of "transgender youth" who choose life-altering hormone therapy and surgery might have increased dramatically.

One can imagine the inevitable final step in the process. Bud Light, having paid no price for its embrace of a radical ideology that most people in this country don't support, might have begun acting as an aggressive enforcer for laws that Democrats could not pass. The company could have identified states where "trans youth" were "under threat" (meaning states that have rightfully made it illegal to mutilate the genitals of children) and begun pulling their business from those states, just like MLB did from Georgia. I'm sure that in some of those states, the legislatures would have caved, not wanting to bring the ire of Big Business down on their constituents, and those bills to protect children would have stopped passing.

This is how the Left wins. It's the reason the long march through the institutions—which began in our universities and spread to business schools, high schools, and journalistic institutions—has been so successful. We have reached a point, in fact, where most people probably don't even notice the extent to which woke, neo-Marxist values have infiltrated our institutions. The fact that they have somehow been able to work their way into Fortune 500 companies and major investment funds, which were previously concerned with profit and selling goods and services to customers, is a testament to just how much power the radical Left wields.

Looking back through history, you'll find that Marxism often operates in this way. The long march, in other words, never goes to the next place you expect it to go. Even in the earliest days of the Marxist movement, for instance, no one believed that Russia would be the first country to have a Marxist revolution. Marx and his followers didn't believe that the country had developed enough industrially to be ripe for a communist revolution. But that's exactly what happened in 1917.

Similarly, most of the Marxists believed that capitalism was supposed to crumble quite early in the revolution; that was, in fact, the whole point of *having* a revolution in the first place. But as the virus of neo-Marxism moved slowly through every institution in the United States, it mutated along the way, adapting in such a way that its principles could now be applied *to* capitalism itself, giving the Marxists the kind of cover they needed to slip in all their worst ideas.

Of course, there are some instances when Cultural Marxism shows up *exactly* where you think it will—in the places where strange ideas and stranger people have been commonplace for decades. I am speaking, of course, about the entertainment industry, which has become by far the most effective method for spreading Cultural Marxism in modern history.

Anyone who doubts that should turn the page.

CHAPTER SEVEN

Entertainment

If you follow me on Twitter, you probably know that I'm no stranger to controversy. For years, I've found that social media is a great way to jump into conversations and engage in healthy debates with people who disagree with me (or, with some regularity, people who hate my guts).

I'm sure that the itch to get on Twitter and piss people off must come from the same part of my brain that made me want to join my high school debate team. I've always liked using words to solve disagreements and to fight in the battlefield of ideas. Some of my fondest memories were created in the heat of disagreement with good friends over a beer or two in my college dorm room.

But social media, as it turns out, is a much different place from a dorm room. When you send a message, you have no idea who's going to see it—and just how angry some of those people may get when they do.

As a result, I've found over the years that it's rarely the things you *think* are going to cause controversy that bring the mob to your door. I've sent tweets about hot-button cultural issues, for instance, that get nothing more than a few hundred retweets and messages of support from my followers. And, on the other hand, I've sent out what I thought were innocent holiday messages that ended up bringing me a torrent of online hate like nothing I'd ever seen.

But in all my time in public life, I have rarely managed to make the woke mob quite as angry as I have on the rare occasions when I have dared to talk about my favorite films, musical artists, and television shows.

Late in 2022, for instance, I recorded an episode of my podcast *Verdict with Ted Cruz* in which my co-host and I got to talking about some of the stranger claims that the environmentalist Left had been making in recent years. We spoke about how, in the eyes of your average climate change activist, human beings are a disease that has been inflicted upon the planet. They believe that the fewer human beings we make in the future, the better things will be for Mother Earth.

In this way, I said, they resembled Thanos, the CGI-created ultra-villain who wiped out half of humanity with a snap of his fingers in *Avengers: Infinity War.*

"Have you noticed," I asked, "in how many movies how often rabid environmentalists are the bad guys? Whether it's Thanos or go to *Watchmen*...the view of the Left is people are a disease. They buy into the Malthusian line that there are too many people in the world, that people are bad, and everything would be better if we had fewer people. I mean, Thanos wanted to eliminate 50 percent of the lifeforms of the universe with one finger snapping."

The outcry from the Left—and not just the rabid comic book fans who typically comment on this sort of thing—was immense. During my career, I've introduced many pieces of legislation that didn't get half the attention that my throwaway comments about *The Avengers* and *Watchmen* did.

Looking back, I think I know why. It's not simply because the Left hates conservatives and doesn't like the fact that I'm a hard-core movie buff who grew up watching movies with my parents and who loves to watch good (or even lousy) movies. It's not even that they really believed my interpretation of these films was wrong.

Rather, they got angry because my comments made them realize that their beloved stories *could*, in fact, be viewed seriously as critiques of the environmental Left. It made them consider the possibility that perhaps films—and all art, for that matter—are open to interpretation, and that my interpretation might be just as valid as their own. Maybe a few of them even considered the possibility that I was right, and that the creators of these films had made points that they hadn't intended to make when they created their art.

This, apparently, drove them insane.

To the woke, the notion that they might not have total control of the messages they stuff into their art, or how those messages will be interpreted, is incredibly dangerous. Wokeness, like the many forms of Cultural Marxism that came before it, relies on complete control. Artists who want the approval of the woke mob must ensure that their art contains exactly the right political messages, and that it does not contain anything that might be misconstrued by the public to say anything *other* than those messages.

As a result, there is something in the mind of dedicated leftists that makes them believe—and not, I should add, without reason—that all entertainment, whatever the quality of that entertainment or the politics of its creator may be, belongs to them, and *only* to them.

In the minds of the woke Left, all entertainment should be created to reinforce their political opinions. Any piece of entertainment that deviates even slightly from those politics is deemed unworthy of anyone's time. This means that when you go to the movies or watch television these days, you're likely to see all the tenets of neo-Marxism staring right back at you.

It's not quite clear when this tendency became so pronounced. Hollywood, after all, has always been known as a bastion of wacky left-wing ideas. According to Andrew Klavan, the political commentator and novelist who spent many years in Hollywood writing screenplays for hit films, the change really kicked into high gear sometime in the early 2000s.

In a wonderful foreword to the book *Virtue Bombs: How Hollywood Got Woke and Lost Its Soul*, written by the film critic Christian Toto, Klavan describes a meeting that he had some time in 2004 to pitch a horror film. He had written several at the time, which had all been big hits. This next one, he was sure, was the greatest idea he'd ever had.

But after Klavan gave what he calls "the best pitch [he] ever did," the producer he'd been pitching to looked at him blankly and asked a simple question.

"Do you think we could make the villains the American military?"

Because he was a person with integrity, and because he was especially mindful that thousands of soldiers were about to go overseas to fight a war on terror, Klavan left the room after giving a noncommittal response on whether he would be willing to change his film—a ghost story—into an anti-American screed to please the left-wing overlords who were then in the process of taking over Hollywood.

Shortly thereafter, he writes, his phone stopped ringing and "the jobs dried up." What had once been a promising career in screenwriting was now effectively over, all because Klavan was not willing to write the kinds of proto-woke scripts that were suddenly required of all people working in Hollywood. In a town that had been rocked to its core in the 1950s when many screenwriters who were suspected of being communists were placed on Senator Joe McCarthy's "blacklist," a new kind of blacklist had taken shape. Only this time, the list contained the names of screenwriters, actors, and producers who refused to churn out anti-American nonsense for big film studios simply because it was fashionable.

This left a vacuum. For every person who got his or her name put on a blacklist for having the wrong politics, there were ten more willing to step up and do the woke dirty work that studios were now demanding. Today, as Klavan puts it, "the blacklisters, encouraged, have come to run the town."

"In Hollywood right now," he writes, "it's not enough to disrespect your mother country onscreen. You have to despise it. You have to depict it as a cesspit of racism and cruelty. Your hero has to be a victim. Your victim has to be a minority. Preferably female. Preferably with a penis."[1]

Turn on a television and fire up almost any streaming show that has gotten acclaim over the past few years, and you'll find that Andrew Klavan (who now hosts a successful podcast with The Daily Wire and still writes excellent thriller novels) was exactly right. The top shows in the country all seem to have been created in the same sick, woke laboratory. The characters speak endlessly about oppression, microaggressions, and the racism that all "people of color" in the United States must live with. The plots of these films and shows depict life in the United States as an eternal struggle of good versus evil, in which minorities of all kinds are always fighting against the oppressive structures of the places they live.

And anyone who dares to point out that this does not quite reflect reality is immediately shamed.

Consider the case of Rainn Wilson, who played the offbeat character Dwight Schrute on NBC's *The Office* for nearly a decade. Not a right-wing guy by any means, Wilson took to Twitter to speak about a recent episode of the HBO series *The Last of Us*, based on a video game of the same name. The message was simple, and relatively surprising coming from someone who had spent so long in Hollywood—and who, by all outward appearances, was a dyed-in-the-wool leftie.

"I do think there is an anti-Christian bias in Hollywood," Wilson wrote. "As soon as the David character in 'The Last of Us' started reading from the Bible I knew that he was going to be a horrific villain. Could there be a Bible-reading preacher on a show who is actually loving and kind?"[2]

To me, this is the kind of message that Twitter was made for. It's a poignant piece of cultural criticism in miniature; on its face, it shouldn't offend anyone. It even includes a question, rhetorical or not, that seems intended to start a polite conversation.

For a while, that's what happened. Even left-wing accounts in the replies discussed the issue politely and insightfully, offering examples of films and shows in which Christian characters have been portrayed in a positive light.

Then, just a few hours later, Wilson issued a follow-up tweet lamenting the fact that Fox News had used his first message on the front page of its website. He noted that he did not agree with the positions of Evangelical Christians, who were, in his opinion, "Banning books – banning freedoms – denying inconvenient science, taking a grotesque anti-LGBTQ+ platform."[3]

Clearly, Rainn Wilson had stepped out of line. After vicious replies from left-wing accounts—and their quote tweets—to his original observation of Hollywood bias against Christians,[4] he had obviously felt the need to stand up and immediately signal once again that he was on the right team.

Scrolling through Twitter one day, I happened to see an article about this small controversy. This, as I recall, is when I first learned that the show *The Last of Us* existed. Given that the show seemed to be getting quite a bit of praise in the mainstream press, I wasn't surprised to find out that it featured a strong anti-Christian bias. Then, almost by accident, I scrolled down in the story and saw the series had been created and written by Craig Mazin, my old college roommate.

Now, I thought, it all made sense. Given his inveterate leftism, his prurient and juvenile sense of humor, and his dripping contempt for most Americans who didn't share his radical views, it came as no surprise that Craig was more than happy to write screenplays depicting Christians as arch-villains to be feared.

Over the past two decades, something happened. As Hollywood continued to blacklist principled writers who were unwilling to write woke nonsense—the trend Andrew Klavan outlined in his foreword to *Virtue Bombs*—the producers began looking for anyone who *would* write that kind of nonsense for a paycheck. Suddenly angry leftists are everywhere in Hollywood, slipping woke messages into their scripts and sending them out into the world, where they're praised by the critics and awards voters who also believe in those woke messages.

To visualize the scope of the problem, think back on your own life. Picture the whiniest, most entitled liberal brat you've ever come across. Maybe that person was your college roommate, your lab partner in high school, or someone who sat next to you on the school bus blasting Rage Against the Machine from his headphones.

There is a good chance that today that person (or somebody just like him) is a screenwriter working for a major Hollywood studio, churning out absolute crap to keep the powers that be happy (when he's not busy striking for higher wages, of course).

For a while now, the people who make the decisions in the American entertainment industry have been leftists. A lot of them are people who were educated at our top universities, taught to believe that this country is an evil place. I can only speculate about their motives; if the rest of them are anything like my old roommate, I know I will never truly understand how they think, or why they see the world the way they do. But from outside it sure looks like they believe that the purpose of art—even blockbuster films—is to let everyone know just how evil America is. They seem to believe, in typical Cultural Marxist style, that films and television are some of the best vehicles for radical ideas—possibly because the people who consume the films and television shows will not know that they are being slowly indoctrinated.

This idea isn't new. In China under Chairman Mao Zedong, one of the primary ways that the government got its message out was by making smarmy, propagandistic films about the glories of communism. The same thing happened in the Soviet Union, where citizens were subjected to films in which communist heroes fought valiantly against the capitalists for control of the world. In these films, Americans were usually depicted as stupid, fat, and rich, while the Soviet Marxists were cunning and noble. The idea was to inundate people with Marxist messaging in ways that were not immediately obvious. Eventually they would be exported to other countries to further the revolution.

Now it's Hollywood regularly churning out films that push the tenets of Marxism, albeit the strange American variant that is obsessed with race and gender rather than class. Recently, it was announced that in order to be eligible for the Academy Awards, a film must meet certain rigid "diversity" standards imposed from above.

According to these new standards, films must pass muster in several categories before they can be considered for an Oscar. "The categories," according to the *New York Post*, "would require new diversity measures to be met through 'On-screen Representation,' 'Creative Leadership and Project Team,' 'Industry Access and Opportunities,' and 'Audience Advancement.' 'On-screen Representation' is classified as at least one lead character from an underrepresented racial or ethnic group, having at least 30 percent of secondary roles be from two underrepresented groups or the main storyline has to focus on an underrepresented group."[5]

If you've ever spoken to anyone who works in Hollywood, you know just how important the Oscars can be. Studios and producers will do just about *anything* to increase their chances of winning one. Now, it is no longer just implicit that these studios must consider "audience advancement"—read: reeducation—when writing the scripts of their films. They must consider it from the very beginning, measuring how well a given film aligns with the predetermined opinions of those on the Left.

In May of 2023, the actor Richard Dreyfuss—famous for his fabulous portrayal of the shark expert Matt Hooper in *Jaws* and of the devoted music teacher in *Mr. Holland's Opus*—said that, as an artist, he found the new guidelines made him want to "vomit."

Asked why, he said, "Because this is an art form, it's also a form of commerce, and it makes money, but it's an art. And no one should be telling me, as an artist, that I have to give in to the latest most current idea of what morality is. And what are we risking? Are we really risking hurting people's feelings? You can't legislate that."[6]

As expected, Richard Dreyfuss—an outspoken liberal—has been widely condemned for sharing his opinion on this highly sensitive matter.[7]

But he's exactly right. Once art and politics begin to mix, we are left not with art, but with propaganda. As the Left imposes more rules on the people who make art, the art will get worse, and the people who watch it will become more indoctrinated than ever.

However bad things are now, they stand to get much worse in the years to come.

And things, in case you haven't noticed, are *very* bad now.

Stepping Out of the Shadows

For a long time, the woke messaging in film, television, sports, popular literature, and music was subtle. The woke, even before they were called that, knew that if they wanted to keep people buying movie tickets and watching television, they couldn't insult the intelligence or the values of their audience in ways that were too obvious.

Then, around the same time that the rest of society began to grow more radical, an even greater shift happened in Hollywood. This has proven to be especially true in the era of so-called "prestige television," when screenwriters and showrunners have been given more power than ever before. Now, it's difficult to find anything to watch on a major network that does not include at least some left-wing, neo-Marxist talking points as part of the plot or dialogue.

Take *Watchmen,* for example, a show whose writer-producer attacked me on Twitter.[8] In the original 1986 comic, as well as the fantastic 2009 film that was made from that comic, one of the central plotlines concerns a villain named Ozymandias who believes the world can avert nuclear war if he simply kills half of the people in Manhattan (an idea that AOC and the Democrats might bring to a vote in Congress soon, if we're not careful). It was for this reason that I analogized him to Thanos in *Avengers,* as yet another radical environmentalist whose solution is eliminating people.

When HBO decided to reboot the series during the Trump years, however, the plotline was completely rewritten, so that the show contained very little of the original source material. Instead of a crazed anti-nuke activist who wanted to eliminate half of New York's population for leftist utopian reasons, the new plot revolved around police violence and White supremacy—secret Klansmen hidden in plain sight in Oklahoma.[9] Apparently these are the greatest dangers we face as a nation.

This sort of thing has become incredibly common in recent years. Take something everyone loves, stuff it full of woke neo-Marxist ideas, and then put it on the air. If people point out that the ideas (and the show) are bad, you can always claim that they're racists, fascists, or both. By now, it has happened too many times to count.

Disney's reboot of the beloved *Little Mermaid* was a case in point. Fans complained that the 2023 live-action film starring Halle Bailey was a poorer version of the original animated tale of the mermaid Ariel and her handsome human prince—even NPR called this "latest of Disney's poor unfortunate remakes" a "cynical exercise," complained about its "dull, forgettable" new music, and judged it "creatively uninspired."[10] But instead of admitting that Disney had managed to ruin a classic, defenders of the subpar remake—including its star—accused the public of racism. When the trailer to the film was universally panned, CNN published an "Analysis" purporting to offer a "Definitive Rebuttal to Every Racist 'Little Mermaid' Argument."[11] And after the film itself met with scathing criticism, Halle Bailey "opened up" in an *Entertainment Weekly* interview "about all the racists who are butt hurt about her casting as Ariel in Disney's Live action/CG-animated *The Little Mermaid*": "As a Black person, you just expect it and it's not really a shock anymore."[12]

Meanwhile, what parents have come to "just expect" from Disney is relentless propagandizing for the woke agenda. Pixar's 2022 *Lightyear* hijacked the beloved "Buzz Lightyear" franchise to acclimate small children to the sight of lesbians kissing. That same year, Disney also released the aptly named *Strange World*: "a focal point" of that film is "a scene in which 16-year-old Ethan tells his grandfather, Jaeger, about his crush on another boy."[13] (It's all part of the "not-at-all-secret gay agenda" that one Disney employee—who bragged about "adding queerness" to programs for children—was seen boasting about on video leaked to Christopher Rufo.)[14]

When it comes to children's television, the messages are, if possible, even less subtle. Maybe this is because the producers and screenwriters responsible don't think that parents spend much time watching television over their children's shoulders. Maybe they believe that even if the parents *do* notice all the woke nonsense being force-fed to their kids, they won't do anything about it.

That would certainly explain how strange and outwardly woke most programming for children has become. Consider, for instance, the scene in *Muppet Babies*, a popular television show for children, in which one of the (supposedly male) characters announces that he wants to wear dresses and become a pretty princess. Rather than treating this as some kind of silly joke—which is certainly what would have happened in any of the cartoons we watched when we were kids—the other characters in the show deliver long impassioned speeches about how people who believe they're the opposite gender should be fully supported.

"Oh, Gonzo," says Miss Piggy, apologizing for questioning the Muppet baby Gonzo for wanting to change genders and go to the ball as "Gonzo-rella." "We're sorry. It wasn't very nice of us to tell you what to wear to our ball."

The message of this show, and too many others like it, is clear. Dressing up in clothing meant for the opposite gender is no longer a silly game for children. It is a profound proclamation of transgender identity, which must be treated with profound respect.

The same stilted, deadly serious dialogue is often deployed on children's TV shows with regard to race—a topic that has become inescapable even on the silliest of children's cartoons.

Consider the recent reboot of Disney's cartoon series *The Proud Family*, which ran quite successfully in the early 2000s as the story of an African-American family living in California. The original version was an ordinary children's cartoon that featured jokes, gags, and occasional lessons about the values that mattered to all human beings. It taught children about things like sharing, bullying, and looking out for one another.

The new version, however, is a far cry from the nice, easy children's programming that defined the original series. This time around, it is left-wing politics, not story, that takes the lead. Rather than emphasizing our common humanity by telling stories that might appeal to all children, the writers of *The Proud Family: Louder and Prouder* seem to have opened a textbook on Critical Race Theory, copied down the most ludicrous phrases and assertions, and then written some light scene direction to turn the textbook into a television show.

Below is an excerpt of the dialogue, with absolutely no edits or additions.

This country was built on slavery, which means SLAVES built this country. Tilled this land from sea to sea to sea. First there was rice, tobacco, sugar cane....Built this country! The descendants of slaves continued to build it. Slaves built this country! And we, the descendants of slaves in America, have earned reparations for their suffering, and continue to earn reparations every moment we spend submerged in systemic prejudice, racism and white supremacy! That America was founded with and still has not atoned for. Slaves built this country! Not only field hands but carpenters, masons, blacksmiths, musicians, inventors built cities from Jamestown to New Orleans to Banneker's Washington. Forty acres and a mule? We'll take the forty acres! Keep the mule! We made your families rich! From the southern plantation heirs to the northern bankers to the New England ship owners. The founding fathers. Current senators. The Illuminati, the New World Order. Slaves built this country! We had Tubman,

Turner, Frederick D. Then they say Lincoln freed the slaves! But slaves were men. And women. And only we can free ourselves. Emancipation is not freedom!

Amazingly, it goes on from there.

Images of chains, whips, and a crumbling Mount Rushmore flash on the screen as the characters perform their monologue in a kind of strange, semi-religious chant, apparently written to stir the kids watching from home into revolutionary anger.

This, in the neo-Marxist Left's ideal world, is what our children would watch all day. This is the nonsense that would air in the time slots once occupied by *Bugs Bunny* and *Tom and Jerry*. Rather than raising a generation of kids who have fun, play outside, and care about one another, they hope to raise a revolutionary class of young Marxists eager to tear down the United States and everything it stands for.

I can't imagine the damage that has already been done to children who sit down in front of radical, revisionist entertainment like this, filled as it is with such hate and division. When I was young, parents worried that allowing their kids to watch Tom whack Jerry with a hammer might lead to too much violence on the playground. Later, parents worried that too many episodes of *Rugrats* might make their children use coarse language such as "Shut up" too early in life.

Now the parents of young children need to worry that their kids are going to run up to people of other races and scream, "*Slaves* built this country!"

Even parents who would like to shield their children from this nonsense by showing them old films and cartoons aren't safe. Given that the entire library of Disney, to take just one example, now lives on streaming services accessed through smart televisions, the company can now alter these films in any way that it sees fit. A few years ago, Disney began adding "trigger warnings" and "racial sensitivity notes" to some of its most beloved cartoons, implying that there was something somehow wrong and offensive with classic films such as *The Aristocats* and *Peter Pan*, which, Disney now tells children, "portray Native people in a stereotypical manner that reflects neither the diversity of Native peoples nor their authentic cultural traditions." And that's not all. "Peter and the Lost Boys engage in dancing, wearing headdresses and other exaggerated tropes. . . ."[15] The horror! According to Disney this "appropriation of Native peoples' culture and imagery" is "a form of mockery."[16] Silly me. I always thought kids like to wear those head-dresses because they think Native Americans are *cool.*

Apparently, in the view of the folks at Disney, the headdress scene in *Peter Pan* is far more harmful than the insane ranting in *The Proud Family*, which teaches children to be obsessed with racial division and class conflict rather than showing them how we can all get along. And more worrisome than the "not-at-all-secret gay agenda" that Disney is busy inserting into its new programming for children. Latoya Raveneau, the director of *The Proud Family* reboot and a self-identified "biromantic asexual," is the Disney official who was caught on tape bragging about that.[17]

Given how extreme and political children's television has become, you might wonder what the Left expects our children to watch as grown-ups. How, after all, can you go up from a show that includes lines directly lifted from some of the most unhinged left-wing literature on the planet?

Apparently, you simply take the most insane left-wing literature and film it, which is exactly what Hulu did when it turned the 1619 Project into a documentary series. For the Left, it's not enough simply to allow this project to exist in its initial magazine format, or as a book; it's not even enough to turn it into lessons for schoolchildren to learn at their desks, as we covered in Chapter Two of this book. In their eyes, the messaging must come from everywhere, even the smart televisions that are now in almost every living room in the country.

Although I have not seen the entirety of Hulu's *The 1619 Project*, I have seen enough to know that it goes even further—and contains more outright falsehoods—than the original magazine story, which was debunked by numerous major historians at the time of its release.[18] In the show, which offers the same dim view of the history of the United States as its source material, Nikole Hannah-Jones (who narrates most of the series) doubles down on her demonstrably false assertion that "one of the primary reasons the colonists decided to declare their independence from Britain was because they wanted to protect the institution of slavery."[19]

This time, however, there are even stranger claims. Near the end of the series, for instance, Hannah-Jones speaks over video clips showing workers in a modern-day Amazon factory about how the institution of slavery, in which every living American is complicit, never really ended.[20] The implication is that the people who work in Amazon factories today—who, in fact, make decent wages and live in nice apartments in major cities such as New York City and Seattle—are somehow comparable to the slaves who were denied all human rights and were forced to work the fields of this country and suffer horrific abuse in the eighteenth and nineteenth centuries. The comparison is absurd. And it is also unadulterated Marxism.

The "project" of this show is clear. It is meant to rewrite not only American history, but the American present as well. It is meant to demoralize and confuse young people into believing that their country is racist, uncaring, and cruel. It does this, amazingly, by attempting to convince viewers that working for wages is somehow analogous to slavery, and that there is no way out other than a complete embrace of left-wing revolutionary ideas—reparations, for one.

Other shows have made similar points. For instance, a couple years ago Netflix released a television show hosted by Colin Kaepernick, the former quarterback of the San Francisco 49ers who found himself unable to get rehired as a free agent after staging several racial justice protests from the side of the football field. In that show, titled *Colin in Black & White*, Kaepernick speaks about the horrible racism he faced while playing in the NFL.

During one memorable episode, he narrates a scene in which NFL players are shown being weighed and evaluated before being recruited by teams—which, as I understand it, is common practice in all sports leagues—and intersperses that footage with animations of slaves being measured before being sold to their White slave masters.[21] The implication, I suppose, is that making millions of dollars to play football is the modern-day version of slavery. (Only today's oppressed slaves drive Lamborghinis.)

This kind of playacting is necessary to sustain the myth that the United States is a White supremacist country. If this is the worst example of the terrible racism that Colin Kaepernick has suffered in his life, it would appear that he hasn't experienced much *real* mistreatment or prejudice on account of his race. In order to maintain the fiction that "people of color" are victimized even when they are paid millions of dollars and widely adored by every media institution in the United States, the woke must overanalyze every aspect of their lives looking for racism.

This, as it happens, is something that Colin Kaepernick is quite good at. He's certainly better at it than he ever was at playing football. Early in 2023, just as his children's book about racism was going to print, Kaepernick spoke about all the ways that his White parents—two people who'd adopted him and shown him nothing but love—were secretly racist against him when he was a child.

"I know my parents loved me," he said, "But there were still very problematic things that I went through. I think it was important to show that, no, this can happen in your home, and how you move forward collectively while addressing the racism that's being perpetuated."

The "racism that was being perpetuated," according to Kaepernick, was his mother's aversion to cornrows, which she said made her son look like "a little thug."[22] To most sane people, this sounds like a mother trying to ensure that her son looks good when he goes out into the world. As a matter of fact, according to Kaepernick's story, his mother told him cornrows weren't "professional."[23] That's not much different from memories a lot of us have of our own parents telling us not to wear a wrinkled shirt, shave our heads, get a mohawk, or acquire a tattoo in a place where potential employers might be able to see it. In my case, I remember leaving the house more than once in high school demonstrating truly horrific teenage fashion sense—dressed in parachute pants and billowy shirts reminiscent of Michael Jackson's *Thriller*—and my father asking me, "Why do you want to look like a bum?"

To Kaepernick, however, his mother's question was evidence of latent racism—which, when your career depends on finding racism wherever you go, everything is.

The damage that Colin Kaepernick and others like him have done to our culture is immense. They stoke the fires of racial hatred, knowing that as long as people are looking for reasons to hate one another, they will keep selling books and finding audiences for their terrible streaming shows.

Consider the trail of destruction that Kaepernick has left behind him in the world of professional sports.

Music and Sports

As the woke neo-Marxists have infiltrated the institutions of the United States, it's become increasingly difficult to find apolitical pastimes. In recent years, it seems that everything people used to do to unwind, whether it be going to the movies on a Friday night, watching a television show on the couch, or even cracking open a Bud Light at the end of a hard day, has become a political statement.

This is by design.

In the neo-Marxists' worldview, everything is political. They believe that we are so close to fascism in the United States (by which they mean that a Republican might be elected) that all art, commerce, and personal interactions must be used to further antifascist and anti-racist goals. Anyone who doesn't go along with this is contributing to the problem.

As they often put it, "Silence is violence."

Still, not long ago there used to be some places where you could reliably waste a few hours without having to hear a political speech. One of them was a concert. Growing up, I went to lots of concerts, from The Police, to Genesis, to Billy Idol to Pink Floyd. I saw a bunch of fans getting stoned, but I don't recall any of the musicians giving long political speeches.

Now I'm not saying I was under the impression that many (or even any) of these artists shared my political views. I'm well aware of the tendency of musical artists to lean left. Nobody expects Willie Nelson to be a conservative.

But slowly, as the pressure campaigns grew during the Trump years, it seemed that there were no musical artists left who did *not* regularly weigh in on political issues. When President Trump was inaugurated in 2017, news organizations took delight in publishing articles about how he could not get A-list musical artists to perform at the ceremony.[24]

In the aftermath of the "summer of love," things got even more serious. Citing a "racial reckoning," many groups issued statements filled with the nonsensical language of neo-Marxism. The Dixie Chicks, who had once taken heat for criticizing President George W. Bush over the Iraq War, now found themselves under fire because their name vaguely referenced the Confederacy. On June 25, 2020, they announced that their band name would be changed to "The Chicks."[25] (I'm shocked that they're still willing to acknowledge that they're female.)

Of all the areas that have fallen to Cultural Marxism in recent years, however, the most surprising may be sports. Since I was a little kid, I've loved going to basketball and football and baseball games. I was there when the Rockets won game 7 of the NBA Finals in 1994 to win Houston's first championship in any sport. I was at the Rose Bowl in 2006 when the University of Texas beat USC for the national championship. I was at Kyle Field when Texas A&M beat #1 ranked Alabama in 2021. And I was at Minute Maid Park just last year (with my twelve-year-old daughter, Catherine) when the Astros won the World Series (for the second time in six years).

For as long as I can remember, football games, especially, have been largely patriotic events. Anyone who has stood in the stands at a stadium while the national anthem is sung or witnessed the touching displays to our military that often occur at these games will likely agree. I'm sure that if you went back about twenty years in a time machine and told anyone standing in an NFL stadium that these games would soon become bastions of anti-American nonsense, they'd have been quite surprised.

But that's exactly what happened.

By most accounts, the woke movement in sports began with the aforementioned Colin Kaepernick, who decided (like many mediocre celebrities before him) that the best way to distract from his faltering career[26] was to appeal to left-wing politics. In the beginning, this was all small gestures. Kaepernick began kneeling during the performances of the national anthem that always open football games. When journalists asked him why, he made vague references to the supposed epidemic of police violence against African-Americans in the United States[27] and claimed the American flag "oppresses Black people."[28]

Eventually he would sue the NFL and suggest that the only reason he hadn't been recruited since the 2016 season was that the owners and coaches of various NFL teams who *could* have recruited him were secretly racist.[29]

In response, some critics claimed he was ignorant.[30] I'm not sure that was necessarily true. I think there's a high probability that Kaepernick knew exactly what he was doing, even if what he was doing was morally reprehensible. I'm guessing that sometime around the year 2016, when the nation was becoming more divided than ever and Cultural Marxism was well on its way to becoming ascendant in all of this nation's major institutions, Colin Kaepernick must have realized that there was more currency in being a victim of oppression than there was in being a professional athlete. Since then, a number of other celebrities—Meghan Markle and Jussie Smollett, to name just two examples—seem to have come to the same realization.

But Kaepernick was early to this game of victimhood, and he played it better than most. And the heightened rhetoric and baseless accusations of racism worked for him. Even when his career in the NFL had ended, he was rewarded with book deals, television shows, and other opportunities to appear in the media and spread his message. The fact that this happened so quickly illustrates how streamlined and monolithic our cultural institutions have become.

Watching from the sidelines, I was annoyed at Kaepernick and the other athletes who followed him. I was disgusted by the tendency of other players and coaches to bow to his beliefs and the beliefs of those who agreed with him. I was dismayed to see that professional sports—one area of American culture that truly remained a meritocracy—had been consumed with this new woke ideology.

In 2019, I saw that Colin Kaepernick had posted a few lines on Twitter from a speech of great historical import. He was using it to further his usual thesis that the United States of America and everyone in it are hopelessly racist and irredeemable.

The speech he quoted was "What to the Slave Is the Fourth of July?" by the legendary abolitionist Frederick Douglass. As a piece of rhetoric alone, this speech is almost unmatched. And it was written by a man who loved his country. Douglass says as much in the speech itself. But Kaepernick didn't quote that part. Instead, he tweeted:

> "What have I, or those I represent, to do with your national independence? This Fourth of July is yours, not mine.... There is not a nation on the earth guilty of practices more shocking and bloody than are the people of these United States at this very hour."[31]

Taken alone, this excerpt gives the impression that Douglass hated the country he lived in—that he shared the leftists' view that America is irredeemable. Many of Kaepernick's followers may have gotten the impression that the only acceptable position for someone looking to honor Douglass's legacy was the rabid anti-Americanism that many modern leftists openly embrace.

I thought I would add some context.

In response to Kaepernick's tweet, I shared a thread that went viral over the next few days. Taken together, the tweets said this:

> You quote a mighty and historic speech by the great abolitionist Frederick Douglass, but, without context, many modern readers will misunderstand.
>
> Two critical points:
>
> This speech was given in 1852, *before* the Civil War, when the abomination of slavery still existed. Thanks to Douglass and so many other heroes, we ended that grotesque

evil and have made enormous strides to protecting the civil rights of everybody.

Douglass was not anti-American; he was, rightly and passionately, anti-slavery. Indeed, he concluded the speech as follows:

"Allow me to say, in conclusion, notwithstanding the dark picture I have this day presented, of the state of the nation, I do not despair of this country. There are forces in operation, which must inevitably, work the downfall of slavery. 'The arm of the Lord is not shortened,' and the doom of slavery is certain.

"I, therefore, leave off where I began, with hope. While drawing encouragement from 'the Declaration of Independence,' the great principles it contains, and the genius of American Institutions, my spirit is also cheered by the obvious tendencies of the age."[32]

I then sent another tweet with a link to the full speech[33]—encouraging everyone to read it in its entirety—believing that if people could read and decide for themselves what Douglass meant, they would get much closer to the truth of the matter.

Although my answer was broken up into 140-character tweets, it seemed to resonate with people. Multiple news outlets wrote or ran stories on it, and it was shared widely in political circles. There were, of course, leftists who seemed annoyed that I had shared a link to the entire speech—as if they were afraid that people might find out that the great Frederick Douglass did not share their reductive neo-Marxist view of the world. I replied to as many as I could.

This, I believe, is a critical weapon that we have against the woke. Whenever they say something wrong or easily disprovable—especially if it's on social media—we can say so. Most of the time, the source material they're using is easy to find. So are good, science-based studies that contradict whatever ridiculous claims they're making. This may seem like a small thing, but you'd be amazed how far a simple correction can go. At the very least, it lets the woke know that they cannot simply spread lies to a credulous public with impunity.

Another similar exchange happened with Alexandria Ocasio-Cortez, or AOC, who like Kaepernick routinely trumpets neo-Marxist dogma. It started with the NAACP issuing an absurd "travel advisory" in May of 2023 advising African-Americans not to travel to Florida because Governor Ron DeSantis's policies constitute "an all-out attack on Black Americans."[34] I thought that was ridiculous, and said so:

> This is bizarre. And utterly dishonest.
> In the 1950s & 1960s, the NAACP did extraordinary good helping lead the civil rights movement.
> Today, Dr. King would be ashamed of how profoundly they've lost their way.

At this point, Norm Ornstein, a left-wing "scholar" at AEI who has become more and more partisan in his old age, jumped in, tweeting:

> Guess who would've been first in line to filibuster against the voting rights act, and the civil rights act. Yes, Ted Cruz!

To which I responded:

> Nonsense. That shameful filibuster was led by Democrats—your party. My party—the Republicans—proudly voted for the Civil Rights Act in much higher percentages than the racist Dems.

At which point AOC chimed in, tweeting:

Why don't you go ahead and tell people what happened to the parties after that, Ted.

I was more than happy to oblige. Here's the tweet thread I put out:

Sure.
- First, the Dem party founded the KKK.
- Then the Dem party wrote Jim Crow laws.
- Then the Dem party filibustered the Civil Rights Act.
- Today, the Dem part[y] filibusters school choice—trapping millions of Black kids in failing schools.
- Today, the Dem party pushes abolishing the police, which results in many more Black lives murdered.
- Today, every Dem senator voted against my bill to stop DC from throwing 40% of Black kids out of schools bc of vax mandate.
- The Republican Party was founded to oppose slavery.
- Our first Republican President was Abraham Lincoln, who won the Civil War and ended slavery.
- It was Republicans who voted for the civil Rights Act in a much higher percentage than racist Dems.
- Today, we produced the lowest African-American unemployment EVER, under the Trump economic boom.
- Today, we produced the lowest African-American poverty levels EVER, under the Trump economic boom.
- Today, (in 2017) I passed the largest expansion of federal school choice EVER (making 529 plans cover K-12), over the objection of every single Senate Dem.

- Also, just two years ago, the Dem governor of Virginia had put the photo of A MAN DRESSED AS A KKK KLANSMAN on his personal yearbook page.

- And today, the sitting Dem President—Joe Biden—gave in 2011 a flowery eulogy for an "Exalted Cyclops" of the KKK.

- And to add to all that, the Dem party aggressively supports open borders—which has led to the deaths and brutal assaults of thousands of Hispanics, and @aoc somehow can't seem to find her White pantsuit to cry over their suffering.[35]

AOC…never responded.

Why push back so vigorously? Well, her initial post had 19.3 million views.[36] The only way to counter the propaganda of the neo-Marxists is to respond forcefully on the merits. They are wrong. But they hope that the people hearing their dishonest messages never hear the truth.

Moreover, engaging immediately, with facts and substance, is a small way of changing the calculus for institutions that are faced with the constant threat of boycotts and cancellations from the Left. Right now, these institutions believe that caving to the mob is the safest, most efficient way to keep the money rolling in. Sadly, they are not always wrong.

Some of them have even begun preempting the mob.

In August of 2022, an anchor on ESPN suggested that the term "Mount Rushmore," often used to list the four greatest athletes in a given category, be retired because it is offensive.[37] A few months later, the National Hockey League held a draft in Middleton, Wisconsin, meant only for trans players. When fans of the league reacted with bafflement, the league tweeted, "Trans women are women. Trans men are men. Nonbinary identity is real."[38] Over the same period, the

National Basketball Association—recently voted #1 on the "Worst of the Woke" list compiled by the New Tolerance Campaign[39]—has made countless statements about what a horrible place the United States is to live in for people who are members of "marginalized" groups.[40]

In 2020, for instance, countless players in the NBA replaced the names on the backs of their jerseys with slogans coined by the radical Left. Suddenly, "Anti-Racist" was passing the ball to "Justice," then jumping over "Black Lives Matter" to score.[41] (Notably, the NBA refused to allow "Free Hong Kong" because woke virtue cannot get in the way of the almighty dollar—and China drives much of this nonsense.[42] More about that in Chapter Nine.)

That same year "Black Lives Matter," which also happens to be the name of an explicitly Marxist organization, was emblazoned on the hardwood of NBA basketball courts.[43] Players fell to their knees to protest systemic oppression as fans watched from home, confused and annoyed at the sudden infiltration of politics into one of the few areas of life that were supposed to stay apolitical.

During that season, according to Sports Media Watch, NBA viewership fell to 1.36 million, compared to 2.51 million just ten years earlier.[44] Today, those numbers have rebounded, but only slightly, to around 1.59 million.[45] As long as players keep shoving left-wing politics down the throats of their fans, many fans won't return.

When players and coaches are asked about the new tendency to take left-wing political stands on television, they often talk about the right of all people to criticize their government. This is understandable. Given that nearly all of these people have lived in the United States for most of their lives, it's only natural that they would hold the ability to speak out against the government in high esteem. But, alas, very few of them dare speak out against the Cultural Marxism that allows one and only one message to be conveyed in sports.

How to Fight Back

Entertainment will be the hardest commanding height to retake. But it is, in my judgment, the most important. It is the most ubiquitous, the most subtle, and the most effective. And its takeover by the Cultural Marxists has been thoroughly complete.

The only answer is either to create new avenues of entertainment or to retake the old ones. Both routes need to be pursued. When it comes to new avenues, The Daily Wire is investing heavily in creating a new movie studio. I recently returned from filming a cameo in its upcoming comedy about a group of guys who decide to dominate women's sports by claiming to be transgender. (Spoiler alert: I do *not* wear a skirt in the scene.) The script is hysterical—think an anti-woke *Dodgeball*—and it will certainly offend all the right people. At the filming, I saw one of the cast members of the Babylon Bee's side-splittingly funny series *Californians Move to Texas* (in which I also got to make a cameo).

The week before, I met with Jim Caviezel and Eduardo Verástegui about their new movie *The Sound of Freedom*, a true story about the heroic work of DHS officer Tim Ballard, who risked his life rescuing children from child-trafficking networks in Latin America. A few weeks earlier, I joined my friend Steve Deace for the premier of his new movie *Nefarious*, a horror film exploring demonic possession from a Christian perspective.

All of these efforts are good. We need more. Much more.

And the demand is there. Think back to 2004. When Mel Gibson wanted to produce *The Passion of the Christ*, no major studio was interested. Hollywood doesn't do Christian films that are biblically faithful. So Gibson made the courageous decision to produce the film himself. He cast Jim Caviezel in the title role, he bore the financial risk...and the film ended up *grossing over $612 million worldwide*.[46] Much of the country longs for positive films, for comedy that's actually funny, for art that doesn't attack their faith and their values and their very existence with contempt. Parents want shows that kids can watch...without being indoctrinated by woke ideology.

Late-night TV is virtually unwatchable. I love comedy, but watching angry leftists scream about how much they hate Donald Trump isn't remotely funny. It's pitiful.

The talent is there. I remember, back in 2013, I was invited to speak to the Friends of Abe, a right-of-center group in Hollywood that met surreptitiously. To my astonishment, I arrived to find over four hundred people (the largest group they'd ever had) gathered to hear me speak. There were a few big-name stars there. Jon Voight. Gary Sinise. Bruce Jenner. (And yes, he was Bruce then; it was long before Caitlyn.) But the bulk of the room was filled up with relatively unknown actors, writers, cinematographers, and others who worked in movies. Friends of Abe had a strict policy: ZERO pictures. This is markedly different from most other political events, where just about everybody wants a selfie. Here, virtually everyone was terrified for there to be any evidence that they were even in the room. If you're already a star, maybe—maybe—you might survive, but if you're a little guy, one whiff that you're conservative and your career in Hollywood is over. I still remember the palpable fear in the room; I don't think it would have been worse if we were at a midnight meeting murdering puppies under a full moon (indeed, in Hollywood, that might even be a plus!).

Friends of Abe no longer exists. But the talent is still there. It's just underground. For example, actress Gina Carano was fired from the hit Disney show *The Mandalorian* after she posted on Instagram: "Jews were beaten in the streets, not by Nazi soldiers but by their neighbors...even by children. Because history is edited, most people today don't realize that to get to the point where Nazi soldiers could easily round up thousands of Jews, the government first made their own neighbors hate them simply for being Jews. How is that any different from hating someone for their political views?"[47]

This was not her first "offense." Prior to that, she had been on social media criticizing mandatory masking (the horror!) and making fun of "preferred pronouns." Here's what happened on the pronouns:

> Lucasfilm's choice to remove Carano from *The Mandalorian* likely came as a relief to *Star Wars* fans who have been calling for her firing since September, when she put the words "boop/bob/beep" in her Twitter bio, in lieu of pronouns. Many saw this as Carano openly mocking trans people. After being accused of this, Carano removed the words from her bio, but fired back at fans, writing that "Beep/bop/boop has zero to do with mocking trans people" and everything "to do with exposing the bullying mentality of the mob that has taken over the voices of many genuine causes." But she said *she finally removed the words because her co-star on The Mandalorian, Pedro Pascal, helped her understand why* people specify their pronouns in their social media bios. [Emphasis added.][48]

So Lucasfilm fired her. Her talent agency, UTA, fired her as well.

Because deviating from the neo-Marxists in Hollywood is a firing offense.

Fortunately, Gina got hired by The Daily Wire to star in its films.

But there are hundreds of other Gina Caranos out there. Actors, writers, directors. Some are not even conservative. Take, for example, Richard Gere. Yes, seriously. Gere, of course, was an A-list actor. He starred repeatedly in major films, including *Looking for Mr. Goodbar*, *American Gigolo*, *An Officer and a Gentleman*, *Pretty Woman*, and *Chicago*. He's also a liberal Democrat who donated to Hillary Clinton.

But Gere committed a cardinal offense: He criticized China. Gere is a vocal advocate for human rights in Tibet and regularly visits

Dharamshala, the headquarters of the Tibetan government-in-exile. In 1993, he was *banned from being an Academy Awards presenter* after he denounced China's occupation of Tibet and China's "horrendous, horrendous human rights situation."⁴⁹

As a result, Gere has been blacklisted. I met him when he came to the Senate to advocate for Tibet, and he told me he hadn't done a major studio movie in two decades. Here's how one Hollywood paper explains it:

> But now that Hollywood is cozying up ever closer to the authoritarian superpower, and studios are careful not to offend the government that oversees what has become the world's second-biggest box-office market, the star also is paying a price. "There are definitely movies that I can't be in because the Chinese will say, 'Not with him,'" he acknowledges matter-of-factly. "I recently had an episode where someone said they could not finance a film with me because it would upset the Chinese."⁵⁰

If we're tired of the arrogant censorship and abuse of power of the neo-Marxists, our alternatives are simple: build "counterinstitutions"—ironically, as suggested by Marcuse so many decades ago—or buy back the existing institutions. Ideally, we would pursue both. So, for any conservatives with resources: BUY a damn movie studio. BUY a network. BUY CNN or Paramount Pictures or Universal or Warner Bros. or MGM or somebody. BUY a country music label. BUY a streaming service. Put together the financing, raise the equity, secure the debt, and invest in saving America. Or invest real capital in one of the multiple endeavors right now to create counterinstitutions.

There is no better investment. It is not about maximizing returns. Sure, make a profit, but the stakes are much, much higher than that.

Ronald Reagan put it perfectly in 1964 in his speech "A Time for Choosing": "You and I have a rendezvous with destiny. We will preserve for our children this, the last best hope of man on earth, or we will sentence them to take the first step into a thousand years of darkness. If we fail, at least let our children and our children's children say of us we justified our brief moment here. We did all that could be done."[51]

If we can create "safe spaces" for free speech, sanctuaries for those who dare criticize China, havens for those who think freely and refuse to succumb to the neo-Marxists...many more will come. America will reemerge. As they said in *Field of Dreams*, "If you build it...they will come."

CHAPTER EIGHT

"The Science"

I believe The Science.

If you've spoken to a woke leftist in the past few years, you've probably heard some variation of this phrase. In their minds, it's the ultimate way to win an argument, especially when the facts don't seem to be on their side.

In the spring of 2020, for instance, when people on the left were confronted with the suggestion that maybe, just *maybe*, they didn't need to wear masks while taking long walks alone on the beach, they fought back viciously, insisting that they only did so because they "believed The Science." More recently, we've heard the same refrain from leftists who are told that they cannot change their genders at will using only their thoughts.

"The Science," they insist, says that they can.

Now, if this were a bunch of lunatics pretending that science gave them permission to do and say crazy things, that would be one thing.

But it's not. In recent years, we have seen a sharp increase in actual scientists—that is, people with degrees in the hard sciences from major universities who regularly receive money to conduct actual scientific research—using their credentials to parrot the talking points of the woke neo-Marxist Left.

Many people started to notice this phenomenon in the early months of the Covid-19 pandemic, when a group of over 1,200 scientists from labs and universities all over the country—the very same people who had been insisting that the country needed to lock down immediately in order to stop the spread of Covid—signed a letter declaring that while a pandemic was indeed bad, the scourge of "systemic racism" was far worse. "White supremacy," they wrote,

> is a lethal public health issue that predates and contributes to COVID-19. Black people are twice as likely to be killed by police compared to [W]hite people, but the effects of racism are far more pervasive. Black people suffer from dramatic health disparities in life expectancy, maternal and infant mortality, chronic medical conditions, and outcomes from acute illnesses like myocardial infarction and sepsis. Biological determinants are insufficient to explain these disparities. They result from long-standing systems of oppression and bias which have subjected people of color to discrimination in the healthcare setting, decreased access to medical care and healthy food, unsafe working conditions, mass incarceration, exposure to pollution and noise, and the toxic effects of stress.
>
> Black people are also more likely to develop COVID-19. Black people with COVID-19 are diagnosed later in the disease course and have a higher rate of hospitalization, mechanical ventilation, and death. COVID-19 among Black

patients is yet another lethal manifestation of white supremacy. In addressing demonstrations against white supremacy, our first statement must be one of unwavering support for those who would dismantle, uproot, or reform racist institutions.[1]

This, you may notice, is hardly the language of science. The claims are not backed up by any significant data or by double-blind studies. Instead, they are supported with the same thing that leftists use to support all their most radical claims: *their feelings.*

It may not be true, for instance, that "racism" explains the death rates from police shootings and Covid among the Black population—multiple studies have established other causes.[2] But it *feels* true to leftists. You'll notice that the authors of this letter did not cite any data to support their claim that the disparities in health outcomes or fatal police shootings between Black and White people are the result of "long-standing systems of oppression." But in the summer of 2020, that *felt* true to them too. More important, it was functionally impossible to say anything else and hope to keep your job.

Consider what happened that spring to the physicist Stephen Hsu, who was forced to resign from his position as senior vice president for research at Michigan State University because he had supported research that did not explicitly align with the new tenets of woke science. His crimes, according to the *Wall Street Journal,* "included doing research on computational genomics to study how human genetics might be related to cognitive ability—something that to the protestors smacked of eugenics," and "supporting psychology research…on the statistics of police shootings that didn't clearly support claims of racial bias."[3]

It's important to note that Stephen Hsu was not forced to resign because he was a bad scientist, or because he had fostered and promoted bad science. Even his harshest critics—many of whom were themselves qualified scientists—couldn't find any flaws in the data or problems with the methods of the research he had supported. He was forced to resign, rather, because that research did not *feel* good to the woke activists who were now calling the shots.

Amazingly, even getting the man fired was not enough for the mob. Like all good Marxists, these woke ideologues also had to smear the man's name in public, attack the research that was done under his supervision, and make sure that his story served as a warning to anyone else considering committing acts of scientific wrongthink. Shortly after Hsu resigned, the co-authors of the psychology paper about police shootings retracted it, claiming that they were afraid the research they had done might be "misused" by journalists and other scholars for undesirable ends.[4]

There was a time when scientists simply conducted research to find out what the truth was. In the early 1600s, for instance, the Italian astronomer Galileo did thousands of experiments and calculated equations to arrive at the conclusion that the heliocentric model of the universe, first proposed in 1543 by Nicolaus Copernicus, was correct. He did this research despite knowing that it was illegal to endorse, teach, or write about this theory, according to the established leaders of the Church. But he persisted because he believed he knew what the truth was, and he was unwilling to allow dogma to get in the way of his data. The feelings of the clergy or the masses did not matter to him as much as the truth.

For centuries, Galileo has been a hero to scientists everywhere, admired not only for his unwillingness to back down in the face of tyranny but also for the way he relied on facts and the scientific method to reach his conclusions. In the early twentieth century, Albert Einstein cited *Two Modern Sciences*, the book Galileo wrote while under house arrest mandated by the Church, as one of the biggest inspirations of his own career, calling him "the father of modern science."

Over the past few decades, however, as the long march through our institutions has ramped up in pace and severity, the model established by Galileo and other legendary scientists is crumbling. Today, woke doctors and science researchers reach their conclusions first, then make sure that their experiments are conducted in a way that ensures those conclusions. If, heaven forbid, the results reveal something that doesn't align with the principles of equity, antiracism, or wokeness, they simply retract them and try again.

In laboratories and universities all over the country, the scientific method is running in reverse.

In July of 2020, as the protests backed by "The Science" were raging in the streets, physicist Lawrence Krauss wrote an excellent op-ed in the *Wall Street Journal* bemoaning the new tendency of scientists to put equity and antiracism before the scientific method and objective facts. In that op-ed Professor Krauss recalled how in the late 1980s, when he was a professor of physics and astronomy at Yale University, he and his colleagues would "scoff at the lack of objective intellectual standards in the humanities, epitomized by a movement that argued against the existence of objective truth itself, arguing that all such claims to knowledge were tainted by ideological biases due to race, sex, or economic dominance."

They didn't believe the same thing could happen in the hard sciences, where objective facts were paramount, and feelings were not supposed to matter.[5]

But it did happen.

In July of 2020 at Princeton University, an institution that I loved when I attended and that I am saddened by more and more each day, Krauss reports that more than one hundred faculty members

> including more than 40 in the sciences and engineering, wrote an open letter to the president [of Princeton] with

proposals to "disrupt the institutional hierarchies perpetu-
ating inequity and harm." This included the creation of a
policing committee that would "oversee the investigation
and discipline of racist behaviors, incidents, research, and
publication on the part of faculty," with "racism" to be
defined by another faculty committee, and requiring every
department, including math, physics, astronomy and other
sciences, to establish a senior thesis prize for research that
somehow "is actively anti-racist or expands our sense of how
race is constructed in our society."[6]

    This letter, much like the one signed by more than 1,200 public
health officials endorsing race riots, was not written in the language of
science. Instead, both letters were written in the language of dogma.
Princeton University then established a committee to "oversee the investigation and discipline of racist…research," which represents an explicit
threat to free inquiry and the pursuit of truth. This especially true in light
of the fact that the definition of "racism," at least according to Princeton's
various statements on the matter, will now be determined by a committee
of university professors, many of whose members will likely have made
careers out of finding racism in places where it doesn't really exist.[7]

    In the early 1600s, when Galileo first published and defended his
research on the heliocentric model of the universe, censorship and tyranny
came from religious leaders who believed that they alone could interpret
God's will and decide what was true. And they had the power to enforce
their decrees. Anyone who dared go against the established dogma, as
Galileo soon found out, could be accused of heresy and punished severely,
and could face imprisonment, torture, or death.

    In Germany during the 1940s, censorship came from the regime
of Adolf Hitler, who mounted campaigns to rid universities of
"non-Aryan" scientists who might object to the barbaric "experiments"

that the Nazis later carried out. Similarly, in Soviet Russia, Josef Stalin ordered a campaign against the science of genetics, in which, according to Professor Krauss, "literally thousands of mainstream geneticists were dismissed in the effort to suppress any opposition to the prevailing political view of the state."[8]

Today, that same censorship comes from the woke neo-Marxist Left, whose long march through the institutions has given them near-total control of our universities, professional organizations, and other institutions where knowledge is made. Like the religious hierarchy of the 1600s, these people believe that they are on a divine mission, and that anyone who stands against them must be a heretic. Rather than books of the Bible, they have the impenetrable writings of Marxist scholars, plus big stacks of bestselling books on antiracism by Ibram X. Kendi, Robin DiAngelo, and Ta-Nehisi Coates, among other race-baiting charlatans.

And since these people don't have the power to lock people up for their beliefs—at least not *yet*—they punish heretics by pulling their funding, signing petitions to get them fired, and ruining their reputations on social media.

By now, the insight that wokeness has become a new religion—in some sense, a replacement for the Judeo-Christian religion that Marxists have been trying to tear down for over a century—is hardly novel.

Over the past few years, something similar has happened with science, which has been taken over by those who believe in the new religion of antiracism. Today, many on the woke Left speak about "The Science" as if they're talking about their religion, reciting the slogans of their faith and shaming anyone who expresses even mild skepticism or disagreement—two things that were once hallmarks of the scientific method—in the same way that clerics used to shame and punish heretics.

Look around you, and you'll find people repeating slogans as if they're sitting in church. Democratic candidates for political office will claim that they "trust The Science," or "believe in The Science" in the way that politicians used to say they had faith in God. Often, it seems, science merits a definite article and full capitalization. And The Science™ conveniently aligns perfectly with whatever left-wing orthodoxy is currently being enforced by the mob.

Public official Dr. Anthony Fauci, one of the woke Left's most venerated saints, self-righteously declared, "Attacks on me, quite frankly, are attacks on science."[9]

Fauci's smug certainty evokes King Louis XIV, "the Sun King," who infamously declared, "*L'État, c'est moi*, I am the State." For King Fauci, *I am The Science* is his *cri de coeur*.

In the same spirit, whenever someone presents argument or data or evidence that goes against the leftist dogma of impending climate catastrophe, the bellowing response is inevitably, "The Science is settled!"

Galileo would be horrified.

As most people know, science can be good, and religion can be good too. But when you start treating science *like* a religion—as a set of eternal truths handed down from on high that cannot change (until it does) and must be "believed in" without question—things can go south very quickly.

As anyone who has taken an introductory course in biology or chemistry knows, science is not a set of unfixed beliefs. Rather, it is a method by which we can find out what is true about the world and what isn't. The body of knowledge we call "science" changes every day. As scientists conduct new experiments and gather new data, the conclusions that seemed irrefutably true yesterday might come to seem ridiculous today.

Consider that up until the late 1800s "The Science" told us that the best way to treat hundreds of diseases (including acne, cancer, diabetes, and leprosy) was to bleed the patient with leeches. Then, with little fanfare, "The Science" changed its mind (thankfully!). To give another example, as recently as the early 1900s doctors were telling us that cocaine and heroin could cure all sorts of medical ailments:

In 1884, an Austrian ophthalmologist, Carl Koller, discovered that a few drops of cocaine solution put on a patient's cornea acted as a topical anesthetic. It made the eye immobile and de-sensitized to pain, and caused less bleeding at the site of incision—making eye surgery much less risky. News of this discovery spread, and soon cocaine was being used in both eye and sinus surgeries. *Marketed as a treatment for toothaches, depression, sinusitis, lethargy, alcoholism, and impotence, cocaine was soon being sold as a tonic, lozenge, powder and even used in cigarettes.* It even appeared in Sears Roebuck catalogues. Popular home remedies, such as Allen's Cocaine Tablets, could be purchased for just 50 cents a box and offered relief for everything from hay fever, catarrh, throat troubles, nervousness, headaches, and sleeplessness. In reality, the side effects of cocaine actually caused many of the ailments it claimed to cure—causing lack of sleep, eating problems, depression, and even hallucinations.

You didn't need a doctor's prescription to purchase it. Some states sold cocaine at bars, and it was, famously, one of the key ingredients in the soon-to-be ubiquitous Coca-Cola soft drink. By 1902, there were estimated an 200,000 cocaine addicts in the U.S. alone. In 1914, the Harrison Narcotic Act outlawed the production, importation, and distribution of cocaine. [Emphasis added.][10]

Regarding heroin:

In the late 1880s...heroin was introduced as a safe and non-addictive substitute for morphine. Known as diamorphine, it was created by an English chemical researcher named C. R. Alder Wright in the 1870s, but it wasn't until a chemist working for Bayer pharmaceuticals discovered Wright's paper in 1895 that the drug came to market.

Finding it to be five times more effective—and supposedly less addictive—than morphine, *Bayer began advertising a heroin-laced aspirin in 1898, which they marketed towards children suffering from sore throats, coughs, and cold.* Some bottles depicted children eagerly reaching for the medicine, with moms giving their sick kids heroin on a spoon. Doctors started to have an inkling that heroin may not be as non-addictive as it seemed when patients began coming back for bottle after bottle. Despite the pushback from physicians and negative stories about heroin's side effects piling up, Bayer continued to market and produce their product until 1913. Eleven years later, the FDA banned heroin altogether. [Emphasis added.][11]

Everyone knew that scientists could be wrong, and that the essence of science is to challenge prior assumptions, until along came the Covid-19 pandemic, which elevated scientists—at least the ones who spouted the regime's preapproved talking points—to positions of near sainthood on the Left. No matter what these people said, even if it was totally wrong from the moment it left their mouths, everyone was mandated to follow it, or face immediate cancellation. In the time since Covid has disappeared from our daily lives, we've learned just how much these supposedly infallible scientists got wrong during the heat of the pandemic.

In the beginning, they claimed that masks were not effective. For example, when Sylvia Burwell (Obama's health and human services secretary) asked Dr. Fauci whether she should wear a mask while traveling, he replied via email on February 5, 2020:

Masks are really for infected people to prevent them from spreading infection to people who are not infected rather than protecting uninfected people from acquiring infection.

The typical mask you buy in the drug store is not really effective in keeping out virus, which is small enough to pass through material. It might, however, provide some slight benefit in keep[ing] out gross droplets if someone coughs or sneezes on you.

I do not recommend that you wear a mask, particularly since you are going to a very low risk location. [Emphasis added.][12]

And on February 29, 2020, Surgeon General Jerome Adams tweeted, "Seriously people- STOP BUYING MASKS! They are NOT effective in preventing general public from catching #Coronavirus, but if healthcare providers can't get them to care for sick patients, it puts them and our communities at risk!"[13]

Next, on March 8, Fauci said on *60 Minutes*, "There's no reason to be walking around with a mask," in part because "it could lead to a shortage of masks for the people who really need it."[14]

But by April, "The Science" had changed, and Fauci was recommending that *everyone* wear masks. When asked in June of 2020 why his recommendation had changed, why people "weren't...told to wear masks in the beginning," he replied:

"Well, the reason for that is that *we were concerned the public health community*, and many people were saying this, were concerned that it was at a time when personal protective equipment, including the N95 masks and the surgical masks, *were in very short supply*. And *we wanted to make sure that the people namely, the health care workers*, who were brave enough to put themselves in a harm way [*sic*], to take care of people who you know were infected with the coronavirus and the danger of them getting infected" [emphasis added].[15]

There are three and only three possible explanations for this wildly contradictory "scientific" advice. *First,* the scientific understanding of the efficacy of masks genuinely changed in the course of a couple months. But there is no empirical basis for concluding that actually happened.

Second, it could be that masks were always beneficial to prevent the spread of Covid, but *Fauci deliberately lied to the public for several months* because he didn't want a shortage of masks for health workers.

Or *third,* perhaps cloth masks were never beneficial in stopping the spread of Covid (as Fauci told Burwell in February 2020), but "The Politics" changed by April and Fauci decided to claim "The Science" supported mandating masks.

We may never know, but, whether the answer is #2 or #3, the inevitable conclusion is that Dr. Fauci was deliberately dishonest with the American people and was more than willing to subjugate science to his own political objectives.

If members of any other profession had made such egregious public errors, or engaged in such naked deceptions, there might have been a reckoning. People certainly would have been allowed to ask questions—in particular, who was making millions of dollars off of the erroneous diktats.

But in this case, anyone who raised doubts was silenced by the regime. They had to toe the line, or they were kicked off social media.[16] As we've seen repeatedly throughout history, this is what happens under Marxist governments. The state controls what information gets out to the people, and anyone who resists must be punished. Anyone who even *supports* anyone who resists must be punished as well.

If Covid taught us anything, it was that the top government scientists are far too often working to preserve government control—even during a Republican administration; that's why they call it "the Deep State." This is what happens to bureaucrats who remain in their posts for too long.

What has been less remarked upon, though, is how far the woke ideology has spread—not just throughout the National Institutes of Health and other government agencies, but to medical schools, doctors' offices, and hospitals all over the country.

Bad Medicine

In August of 2021, a group of about 140 first-year medical students at Columbia University gathered in the university's auditorium for the school's annual white coat ceremony. This ceremony, which is held at medical schools all over the country, typically proceeds in routine fashion: students stand up, recite the Hippocratic Oath, and receive the white coats they will wear during their time in training.

For a little over 250 years, the words of the Hippocratic Oath that the students were made to recite remained mostly the same. Students promised to "do no harm," and recited the rest from there, just as doctors had been doing for decades (although in recent decades, the prohibition on providing an abortion was conveniently omitted).[17]

This year, however, the students—who had come to medical school from universities all over the country, where they had majored almost exclusively in hard sciences, not humanities—wrote their own version of the oath, which they later recited in unison.

A video of this oath, which made the rounds on Twitter shortly after the ceremony took place, ranks among the creepiest things you're likely to find on the internet. Even the most recent season of *Stranger Things* doesn't quite provide the same level of unsettling terror.

"We enter the profession of medicine with the appreciation for the opportunity to build on the scientific and humanistic achievements of the past," said the new recruits, sounding more like the Children of the Corn than future doctors. They continued:

> We also recognize the acts and systems of oppression effected in the name of medicine. We take this oath of service to begin building a future grounded in truth, restoration and equity, to fulfill medicine's capacity to liberate.
>
> I acknowledge the past and present failures of medicine to abide by its obligation to do no harm and affirm the need to address the systemic issues in the institutions I uphold.
>
> I promise to critically examine the systems and experiences that impact every person's health and ability to receive care. I vow to use this knowledge to uplift my patients and disrupt the injustices that harm them as I forge the future of medicine.
>
> I promise to self-reflect diligently, to confront unconscious prejudices, and develop the skills, knowledge and character necessary to engender an inclusive equitable field of medicine. Let us bow our heads in recognition of the gravity of this oath, we swear to faithfully engage with these ideals and obligations for the ongoing betterment of medicine and humanity.

When the future medical students finished reciting these words, the audience applauded. Then, over the next couple years, these young doctors went through their medical school classes, learning about drugs, anatomy, and how to treat patients. By the time this book is released, they will be nearing graduation, and then soon practicing "medicine" in a place near you.[18]

Increasingly, the medical profession is staffed by people who believe in the strange neo-Marxist views expressed by these students at Columbia medical school. These doctors and nurses believe that the mission of medicine is not simply to heal the patient that is in front of them on any given day—which, in any normal world, would be their only concern—but, as one training document from the Association of American Medical Colleges (AAMC) put it, to do "health equity work," to disrupt "dominant narratives...grounded in white supremacy."[19]

In the same document, the AAMC, which controls what new doctors are taught in medical schools all over the country, says, "narratives that uncritically center meritocracy and individualism render invisible the genuine constraints generated and reinforced by poverty, discrimination, and ultimately exclusion."[20] Read that again. "The Science" is now telling us that "meritocracy" and "individualism" are simply tools of oppression.

Amazingly, medical students are now being taught to treat patients differently based on their race. As a matter of principle, this is utterly wrong. It has no place in medicine. It will inevitably distract doctors from the work of healing their patients. Rather than simply treating patients, a job that takes a serious amount of focus and brain space, doctors must now be focused on the race, gender, and social class of whatever patient they're presented with.

The medical schools themselves must, in the words of a statement published by the American Medical Association, "prioritize and integrate the voices and ideas of people and communities experiencing great injustice and historically excluded, exploited, and deprived of needed resources such as people of color, women, people with disabilities, LGBTQ+, and those in rural and urban communities alike."[21]

In order to meet this goal, as the writer Heather Mac Donald has pointed out, it has become necessary for medical schools to drastically reduce the standards for admission and advancement. In 2021, for instance, a student at Yale Medical School complained that the Step One test—which is administered to second-year medical students and tests their knowledge of "the body's anatomical parts...biochemistry, physiology, cell biology, pharmacology, and the cardiovascular system"—was taking time away from his antiracism work. Shortly thereafter, the school announced that it would now grade the exam on a pass-fail basis.

It is also a fact, as Mac Donald points out, that "virtually all medical schools admit black and Hispanic applicants with scores on the Medical College Admission Test that would be all but disqualifying if presented by white and Asian applicants, and some schools waive the MCATs entirely for select minority students. Courses on racial justice and advocacy are flooding into medical school curricula; students are learning more about white privilege and less about cell pathology."[22]

Woke neo-Marxism has reached medicine, capturing yet another of the many institutions that we once believed would be immune to it.

If the doctors of tomorrow do not leave these institutions completely brainwashed by woke ideology, they will, at the very least, leave them with an inferior understanding of medicine and the human body—if only because of how much time they wasted on things *other* than how to stop people from suffering and to save lives.

Not for the first time, the tenets of Marxism are *literally* going to kill people.

Of course, there are doctors who will somehow manage to get a good education and serve their patients well, despite their insane experiences at medical school. They'll learn all the right things and do all the right things when it counts. But as soon as they step out of line, they'll put themselves in grave danger of being kicked out of their chosen profession.

Consider what happened to Jordan Peterson, the brilliant Canadian psychologist. In December of 2022 he received a letter in the mail from the College of Psychologists of Ontario, a professional medical organization to which he belonged, telling him that he needed to undergo what they called, rather ominously, a "coaching" program. According to this letter, he "may have lacked professionalism" *in his social media posts*, and the issue needed to be addressed.

If not, he would lose his license to practice psychology.[23]

By the time the letter arrived, Jordan Peterson had been attacking the ideology of woke neo-Marxism with passion and precision for years. Jordan is a friend of mine, and he came to the attention of millions in 2016 when he campaigned against Bill C-16 in his home country of Canada, which would have made it illegal not to refer to a person who claimed to be transgender by their preferred pronouns. Since then, he had posted almost daily on Twitter about the threats posed to society by the twin ideologies of transgenderism and neo-Marxism.

By all accounts, Dr. Peterson is an excellent psychologist. He has taught at the University of Toronto and Harvard, among other places, and his classes were always extremely well attended. At the time he received the letter from the College of Psychologists of Ontario, he had just completed a tour with thousands of people packing multiple arenas to listen to him speak night after night.

To no one's surprise, some of Peterson's supposed offenses touched on the trans community—whom the woke Left have recently decided are the new oppressed minority who must be fought for and represented for the sake of "equity." As reported by The Daily Wire,

> Some of Peterson's offenses, according to the regulator, include retweeting Conservative Party leader Pierre Poilievre's criticism of Trudeau, criticizing a former senior Trudeau aide, and expressing opposition to the idea of the Ottawa police taking custody of the children of Trucker Convoy protesters.
>
> Other supposed offenses do not involve direct criticism of the Canadian government, such as Peterson saying on Joe

Rogan's podcast that accepting radical gender theory is a sign of "civilizations collapsing," calling climate change models unreliable, and criticizing Sports Illustrated for putting a plus-sized swimsuit model on the cover.

Peterson also previously criticized a Canadian law that criminalized using the incorrect pronouns for trans-identifying people.[24]

At the time of this writing, it is not clear how the Ontario College of Psychologists will resolve the proceeding. Their stated position is that the "remedial training" they are trying to mandate is not punitive; it's simply the case that "members are required to uphold the standards and ethics of the profession and they remain subject to the regulation of their professional body for as long as they remain members."[25]

Of course, I might not be able to observe Peterson's situation with perfect objectivity. On May 18, 2022, the leftist "65 Project" asked that the Texas Bar Association revoke my law license. Their reason was that in January of 2021 I had agreed to represent Texas before the Supreme Court. In particular, President Trump had called and asked if I would be willing to argue the state of Texas's election challenge before the Court; I told him that it was highly unlikely that the Court would take the case, but if four justices decided they wanted to set oral argument, then Texas deserved effective representation, and so I would be happy to represent my state.

The complainants before the Texas Bar recounted my willingness to represent Texas as if they had uncovered some kind of giant secret—as if I had not myself told the story dozens of times in public, in the press, on television, and in an entire chapter in the pages of my last book, *Justice Corrupted*.

Thankfully, the Texas Bar is not entirely captured by the woke Left, and it doesn't disbar lawyers for agreeing to represent clients. And so the complaint did not succeed. Rather, it was summarily dismissed.

But the incident reminded me, once again, of how much power the woke Left—whose members, hilariously, still believe they are "oppressed" by society—can exert on professional organizations, even the ones that govern supposedly neutral, apolitical professions such as medicine and the law.

The complaint against me failed. But if current trends continue, attempts to revoke the professional licenses of anyone who opposes the woke Left will be increasingly common—and increasingly successful.

Licensing boards have already disciplined doctors for going against the official narrative on Covid vaccines and treatments—some even had their licenses yanked. Because far be it from medical professionals to apply their own training, expertise, and judgment to the treatment of their patients in defiance of the (ever-changing) government recommendations.

In September of 2021, an NPR headline complained: "This Doctor Spread False Information about COVID. She Still Kept Her Medical License." Dr. Simone Gold had told her patients to avoid the new and experimental vaccines, and she had prescribed drugs that weren't recommended by the government (at least not at that time) for treating the coronavirus. As NPR reported, "The Federation of State Medical Boards issued a statement in late July warning that 'Physicians who generate and spread COVID-19 vaccine misinformation or disinformation are risking disciplinary action by state medical boards, including the suspension or revocation of their medical license.'"[26]

And in February of 2022, Politico reported on the cases of eight other doctors sanctioned by their state licensing boards for spreading Covid "misinformation"—in other words, for treating their patients according to their best medical judgment when their own expertise didn't jibe with the official narrative and Dr. Fauci's ever-changing Covid recommendations:

> Medical boards have sanctioned eight physicians since January 2021 for spreading coronavirus-related misinformation, according to the Federation of State Medical Boards, which has recommended that health officials consider action against medical professionals who dispense false medical claims in public forums. The eight penalized doctors, who've been hit with discipline from suspension to revocation of licenses, represent a surprising figure, considering the time it takes for state boards to mete out punishment. The targets of investigations have cited their own scientific expertise in recommending alternative courses of treatment.[27]

How dare they?

And I'm sure that soon this trend will spread beyond Covid "misinformation"—and beyond the practice of medicine. Already, agreeing to represent Donald Trump or to pursue legal remedies with regard to the 2020 election seems like a surefire way for a lawyer to put his or her legal license in jeopardy.[28] And scientists who go against the dictates of the woke Left will increasingly find themselves blacklisted, unable to get research grants or university appointments if they don't go along with the current dogma about the Left's pet issues. Look at what already happened to Stephen Hsu when he supported research that was inconvenient to the reigning myth about racism. And ask yourself how long your career as a scientist would last if you questioned the strangest, most cultish belief of them all: that we're all about to die from "climate change."

The New Malthusians

By the time I became a United States senator, the notion that the world would soon end in a climate disaster—and by "soon," I mean within my own lifetime—had already been around for decades.

Every few months, it seemed, we had a new expert come testify before Congress about how *this* time it was very serious. The witness would say that if we didn't act within the next ten years, or ten months, or even ten days, we would do irreparable damage to the planet—damage that would end, they assured us, with major cities being swallowed up by the ocean and the rest of us dying a fiery death on land as we scrambled and killed one another for resources.

Needless to say, this hasn't happened yet. But the predictions haven't stopped coming. In 2019, during an interview to promote her Green New Deal, Representative Alexandria Ocasio-Cortez claimed that the world was going to end "in twelve years" if we don't do something about climate change. I'm not being unfair to AOC here, nor am I misquoting her. Representative Ocasio-Cortez *actually* said the world was twelve years away from ending.[29]

Her source for this outrageous claim, it turns out, was a special report published one year earlier by the Intergovernmental Panel on Climate Change, a group of nearly two hundred scientists around the globe overseen by the United Nations. Immediately after this report was released, almost every major newspaper in the United States reported its findings with total credulity.[30]

In 2019, shortly before AOC sat down with a reporter to tell us all that we had just over a decade to live, the *New York Times* warned in a "news" story that "floods, drought, storms and other types of extreme weather threaten to disrupt, and over time shrink, the global food supply," which a NASA scientist who was quoted in the story called a "multi-breadbasket failure."[31] In other words, human beings had now screwed up the world so bad—by building too many cities, having too many children, and staying alive for too long—that we were all inevitably going to starve and die horrible deaths, courtesy of Mother Nature.

In fact, there is some debate about that, even among scientists.

In the days following AOC's assertion that we were all just twelve years from starvation or drowning in surging water from melting polar ice caps, the news outlet Axios published a piece that included quotes from scientists who disagreed with her claim. The responses, which the independent journalist Michael Shellenberger (who would later gain notoriety for heroically and exhaustively digging into the Twitter Files) collected in his excellent book *Apocalypse Never*, are amusing, if slightly troubling.

One of the scientists, who studies climate change at NASA, said that "time-limited frames" like the ones that AOC and other Democrats constantly throw around were "bullshit." He explained, "Nothing special happens when the 'carbon budget' runs out or we pass whatever temperature targets you care about, instead the costs of emissions steadily rise."[32]

Shellenberger also includes a quote from Andrea Dutton, a paleo-climate researcher, who said that "for some reason the media latched onto the twelve years (2030), presumably because they thought that it helped to get across the message of how quickly we are approaching this and hence how urgently we need action. Unfortunately, this has led to a complete mischaracterization of what the report said."

What the report that AOC was quoting *actually* said, as Shellenberger pointed out, was that "in order to have a good chance of limiting warming to 1.5 degrees Celsius from preindustrial times, carbon emissions needed to decline 45 percent by 2030. The IPCC did not say the world would end, nor that civilization would collapse, if temperatures rose above 1.5 degrees Celsius."

So a bunch of scientists from various countries got together and released scientific research about the climate—which did *not*, as Michael Shelleberger notes, say that the world was going to end anytime soon. Then a larger group of Democratic politicians and media figures spun the report to fit their predetermined political agenda—namely, that we need to tear down society and rebuild it so that it becomes more environmentally friendly—and began screaming their heads off about how the apocalypse would soon arrive.

In other words, a bunch of political activists had taken a study that had at least the patina of science, twisted it around, and used it to further their political ends. You'll recall that when the woke mob came at Stephen Hsu of Michigan State University, they bullied the authors of the study on police shootings into retracting their results—however accurate they were—because they might be "misused."

Shouldn't the mob be just as concerned about the alarmists who take dry, relatively boring research about our climate and use it to make grand and false pronouncements about the apocalypse? It certainly seems like the kind of thing that anyone interested in stopping bad science and misinformation should be on the lookout for.

After all, the consequences of such misinformation will be devastating. In many cases, they already have been. Consider what it might be like, for instance, to walk into school as a nine-year-old kid and hear that by the time you go off to college, it'll already be too late to stop yourself, your parents, and all your friends from being burned up by the sun. Even if that *were* going to happen—which it's not—we wouldn't want to run around alarming children needlessly about something they can't control.

But that's exactly what we've done, and countless children have suffered for it. According to a recent story in the *Washington Post*, more children than ever have reported suffering from "eco-anxiety" over the past few years. The story cites a Washington Post–Kaiser Family

Foundation report, which revealed that 57 percent of young people said that "climate change made them feel scared and 52 percent said it made them feel angry." The same poll revealed that because of climate change only 29 percent of teenagers said they were "optimistic" about the future.[33]

As the father of two teenage girls, I can tell you that young people have more than enough to feel stressed out about. I'm sure that anyone whose children are nearing adolescence would say the same. During their teenage years, kids should be worried about passing their exams, keeping their friends, and getting tickets to Taylor Swift's *Eras* tour. They should *not* be worried that they and everyone they love will soon be engulfed in balls of flame because of human-caused climate change.

Of course, no one on the political left has said a word about pulling climate change research because it might lead to exaggeration or inaccurate reporting. They haven't said a word about this because when it comes to climate change, the exaggerations and distortions of "The Science" uniformly go in the direction they like—that is, toward the proposition that we're all going to die unless we give unlimited power to the Democrats and the United Nations so they can "fix" the climate for us.

You'll notice that whenever Democrats talk about "The Science," the next thing out of their mouths is usually a request for more power or more money. Usually, it's both.

I'm sure that if you confronted one of the many people who have exaggerated research about climate change over the past few years—meaning just about every left-wing activist and elected Democrat in the country—they'd claim that the exaggerations aren't so bad. If you forced them to confront their errors, they might argue that although their numbers were off (often by factors of a few thousand), they were nonetheless doing the right thing to wake people up and alarm them about the very real threat of climate change. They might suggest that even if the world isn't going to end sometime in the next decade, it is going to end *very soon* unless we do something about it.

They are, in other words, lying to us for our own good. This is exactly what they did, if you'll remember, when they claimed masks were not effective against the spread of Covid, then flip-flopped on that position as soon as they were sure that there were enough masks for frontline workers.[34] It's what they did when they claimed, with absolute certainty and moral authority, that the Covid-19 vaccines would stop people from getting and then spreading Covid-19—something that later turned out to be false.[35]

Whenever leftists are called out on these lies, they equivocate, claiming that their hearts are in the right place and that they couldn't have known better at the time. Then, usually in the span of the same paragraph, they'll give us the next piece of draconian regulation—supposedly required by "The Science"—that we must shackle our economy with, or else risk imminent death.

They've been doing this for decades—at least as long as I've been alive.

Most people of a certain age will remember, for instance, that some of the first predictions that the world would soon run out of food or become barren due to climate change were made not by Al Gore or some member of the Green Party but by university professors in the early 1970s. Some of these professors, as author Alex Epstein has pointed out, became quite famous for their predictions of our doom.

If you were a regular viewer of *The Tonight Show* with Johnny Carson in the mid-1970s, for instance, you might have seen a professor from Stanford University named Paul Ehrlich. Ehrlich had become famous for his book *The Population Bomb*, which argued that the world's population would soon spiral out of control, resulting in famines and disaster for everyone. In 1971, as Epstein points out in his book *The Moral Case for Fossil Fuels*, Ehrlich claimed, "By the year 2000 the United Kingdom will be a small group of impoverished islands, inhabited by some 70 million hungry people." Needless to say, 2000 came and went, and Ehrlich's prediction proved laughably false.

Over the course of the next few decades, Paul Ehrlich and his protégés made dozens more ridiculous predictions of this sort. In 1989, for instance, a scientist named Bill McKibben predicted that failing to act on climate change by banning the use of all fossil fuels would "lead us, if not straight to hell, then straight to a place with a similar temperature.... A few more decades of ungoverned fossil fuel use and we will burn up, to put it bluntly." Three decades later, we're still here.

Another Ehrlich protégé named John Holdren predicted that, by the year 2020, "carbon-dioxide climate-induced famines could kill as many as a billion people."[36] The year 2020 came and went, and yet another prediction proved to be nonsense.[37]

It should surprise no one, of course, that Bill McKibben and John Holdren have not perished from climate-induced famines. No one has. In fact, the use of fossil fuels has *saved* millions more lives from weather-related disasters in recent times than have been saved at any other point in human history.[38]

But these false prophets have nevertheless been elevated by the Left, despite being factually wrong on almost every claim they've ever made. During the Obama administration, John Holdren became a special advisor to the president on science; Bill McKibben regularly writes for mainstream publications and gives speeches to packed crowds all over the country.

Have you ever noticed how many people who claim the earth is about to perish from rising seas nonetheless own oceanfront property? Barack and Michelle Obama, for example, spent $11.75 million to buy a massive estate in Martha's Vineyard in 2019.[39] If they actually believed their apocalyptic rhetoric, you might think mountain property would be more appealing.

Unsurprisingly, scientists like Holdren and McKibben still regularly assure crowds that the Earth is only a few years away from overheating, claiming that if we don't accept whatever radical policies the Democrats happen to be pushing that year, soon we'll all die.

Amazingly, their mentor Paul Ehrlich, who just turned ninety-one years old, is still widely celebrated for his contributions to science. He recently published an autobiography titled *Life: A Journey through Science and Politics*. To this day, despite having seen his predictions about population, climate, and food scarcity proven flat-out wrong time and time again, Ehrlich continues to insist that the best way to go about "saving" our planet is to curb the growth of the human population.

Paul Ehrlich and his disciples have pushed this idea in various writings over the past half century, claiming that the fewer people we have on Earth the better. As Alex Trembath and Vijaya Ramachandran recently pointed out in *The Atlantic*, Ehrlich explains in his autobiography that he was inspired to begin speaking out against the rapid growth of the human population after reading the work of William Vogt, an early-twentieth-century writer who proposed that governments offer "sterilization bonuses" to the poor in order to avoid having to support the "hordes of offspring that, by both genetic and social inheritance, would tend to perpetuate the fecklessness [of their parents]."[40]

Trembath and Ramachandran point out, "In the beginning of the previous century, there was simply no contradiction in being a 'liberal conservationist' and being a eugenicist. Vogt was the national director for the Planned Parenthood Federation of America, which has recently reckoned with the eugenicist commitments of its founder, Margaret Sanger."[41]

Actually it's not so clear when exactly Planned Parenthood stopped endorsing the hateful, anti-human views of its founder Margaret Sanger, who explicitly supported the racist view that fewer babies, especially poor, Black babies, would be a good thing for the world.[42] Indeed, the entire project of Planned Parenthood—and the Left in general—seems predicated on the notion that human beings are somehow a disease on this planet and that the fewer of them we have, the better.

Humans, according to the woke, neo-Marxist Left, contribute to the destruction of the planet. They cause pollution. They are racist, they are cruel, and they take up too much space. It should surprise no one that a left-wing historian and climate researcher from Harvard University recently published an op-ed in *Scientific American* titled "Eight Billion People in the World Is a Crisis, Not an Achievement."[43]

The Left has bought into the view of Thomas Malthus, the eighteenth-century economist who believed that the food supply on planet Earth would not be able to keep up with the world's growing population. Malthus became famous for his belief that human beings needed to stop having children immediately if they wanted to have any hope of eating in the near future.

In the years after Thomas Malthus died, of course, the human race did what it always does. It adapted. We found new ways of growing food and spreading it around so that people everywhere could have enough to eat. The same thing, unsurprisingly, happened again in the late twentieth century, when the top scientists in the world realized that we could still grow enough food to support our even larger and still growing population. Advances were made, mostly in the United States, with the use of fossil fuels, which are employed in much greater amounts today than they were in the 1970s, when neo-Marxist scholars were warning us every day that the world's supply of oil and gas was about to dry up at any moment.

How to Fight Back

Fighting back on science is necessarily intertwined with the fight to undo the woke takeover of universities, discussed in Chapter One; the two are intertwined. All the strategies for winning back the universities will help in the battle to restore science as well. Critically important is that we follow the money—and condition the government money on scientists' and universities' staying out of politics. Much like my successful legislation to cut off Department of Defense language school funding for universities that allowed Chinese-controlled Confucius Institutes (discussed at length in Chapter Nine), we need to cut off funding for politicized faux science. That is true whether at universities or within government.

Covid presents a real opportunity to save science. The pandemic made it so obvious to so many people—even those who hadn't been paying attention—that "The Science" had become politics. So that we now have a real chance to press back. But we need to seize the moment—to counter every politicized "scientific" claim with facts, data, evidence...you know, actual science.

And everywhere possible we need to expose "The Science" for the political agenda it really is. For example, in 2015, Sierra Club president Aaron Mair testified before the Senate Judiciary Subcommittee on Oversight, Agency Action, Federal Rights and Federal Courts, of which I was the chairman. He was repeating the standard leftist talking points, devoid of actual facts and evidence. And so I exposed him:

> **Cruz:** How do you address the fact that in the last 18 years the satellite data show no demonstrable warming whatsoever?
> **Mair:** Sir, I would rely upon the Union of Concerned Scientists, and I would rely upon the evidence, again, of our own NOAA officials, the data are there.
> **Cruz:** Is it correct that the satellite data over the last 18 years demonstrate no significant warming?
> **Mair:** No.

Cruz: How is it incorrect?

[At this point, Mair leaned back to listen to a Sierra Club staffer whisper in his ear. After *eight seconds of silence*, Mair replied.]

Mair: Based upon our experts, it's been refuted long ago, and there is no longer, **it's not up for scientific debate.**

Cruz: I do find it highly interesting that the President of the Sierra Club when asked what the satellite data demonstrate about warming, apparently is relying on staff. The nice thing about the satellite data is these are objective numbers. Are you familiar with the phrase, "the Pause"?

[Mair again leaned back again for help, and the same staffer whispered in his ear. After *14 seconds of silence*, Mair replied.]

Mair: The answer is yes and, uh, essentially, uh, we rest on our position.

Cruz: You said you are familiar with the Pause, so to what does the phrase "the Pause" refer?

[Mair again leaned back to listen to the staffer. After *another 14 seconds of silence*, I asked him again:]

Cruz: I'm sorry, you said you were familiar with that term. So I asked to what does it refer?

Mair: Essentially it is a slow in global warming during the '40s, sir.

Cruz: During the '40s? Is it not the term that global warming alarmists have used to explain the 'inconvenient truth,' to use a phrase popularized by former Vice President Al Gore, that the satellite data over the last 18 years demonstrate no significant warming whatsoever? Global warming alarmists call that "the Pause" because the computer models say there should be dramatic warming, and yet the actual

satellites taking the measurement don't show any significant warming.

Mair: But Senator, 97 percent of the scientists concur and
agree that there is global warming, and anthropogenic
impact with regards to global warming.

Cruz: The problem with that statistic that gets cited a lot is that
it's based on one bogus study. And indeed your response...I
would point out your response is quite striking. I asked about
the science and the evidence, the actual data. We have satellites, they're measuring temperature. That should be relevant.
And your answer was, "Pay no attention to your lying eyes,
and the numbers, that the satellites show. Instead, listen to
the scientists who are receiving massive grants, who tell us,
'do not debate the science.'" [Emphasis added.][44]

To fight back effectively, we have to know the evidence. Few do it
better than *The Moral Case for Fossil Fuels* author Alex Epstein,
whose website Energy Talking Points provides essential data for anyone confronting climate alarmists. We need to rely on *facts*, to counter
their hyperbole. Alex recently tweeted out answers to "loaded questions" for presidential candidates, which I in turn urged every candidate and officeholder to understand and use. Here are key excerpts:

[Q:] Do you believe in "climate change"?
[A:] If by "climate change," you mean some human impact
on climate, yes. But I don't believe in "climate crisis." As the
world has warmed ~1°C in the last century, *climate disaster
deaths have fallen 98% thanks in large part to fossil fuels.*
    Fossil fuels' CO_2 emissions have contributed to the
warming of the last 100 years, but that warming has been
mild and manageable—~1°C, mostly in the colder parts of

the world. And *life on Earth thrived (and was far greener) when CO2 levels were at least 5 times higher than today's.*

Fossil fuels have actually made us far safer from climate by providing low-cost energy for the amazing machines that protect us against storms, protect us against extreme temperatures, and alleviate drought....

The intent of the vagueness of "Do you believe in climate change?" is to get you to say "yes" because you (correctly) believe in some human impact on climate, then take that "yes" to mean that you (falsely) concede a catastrophic human impact on climate—a "climate crisis."

[Q:] What about the 97% of climate scientists who agree that we must rapidly eliminate fossil fuels?

[A:] The "97%" studies reflect widespread agreement that humans have some climate impact, *not catastrophic impact.* They don't justify the disastrous policy of rapidly eliminating fossil fuels. [Emphasis added.][45]

Critically, America's rise to the position of number-one producer of oil and gas in the world directly coincided with a sharp *decline* in air pollution. Indeed, in the twenty-first century the United States has been *leading the world in total carbon reductions.*[46]

The largest polluter in the world is...China, which Democrats and the international planners routinely try to exempt from the massively costly regulatory burdens supposed to solve "climate change." Indeed, right now China is in the process of building more new coal capacity than *every single U.S. coal plant combined.* (U.S. current total coal capacity is 198 GW; China is currently planning or building 365 GW of new coal capacity.)[47]

Another important expert on the climate issue is Bjorn Lomborg, the Danish president of the Copenhagen Consensus Center think tank.

His book *The Skeptical Environmentalist* injected much-needed reason into the climate debate, focusing on ways that are far more cost-effective than phasing out fossil fuels to (1) reduce pollution, (2) promote economic prosperity, and (3) save lives. As he wrote recently,

> [Eight years ago] the United Nations and world leaders came up with a hodge-podge, absurdly long list of 169 targets for the world to achieve from 2015–2030: the Sustainable Development Goals.
>
> The SDGs do promise to do incredibly important things, like eradicating poverty and hunger, getting rid of disease, ending war and global warming. They also set targets for more peripheral issues like providing green spaces. . . .
>
> This year, we are at halftime of the SDGs. . . . So how do we fix things from here?
>
> First, we need to prioritize which targets matter most. For most people, less hunger and better education matters more than well-meaning pledges of increased recycling and global awareness of lifestyles in harmony with nature (two of the 169 targets).
>
> Second, we need to acknowledge that some challenges can be fixed with cheap and simple policies and some cannot. Promising peace and an end to all violence, crime, and corruption is laudable, but it is likely impossibly difficult to achieve, and there is little knowledge of how to get there.
>
> In contrast, we know how to fix many pervasive problems effectively at low cost. Tuberculosis is entirely treatable and has been so for more than half a century, yet it still quietly kills more than 1.5 million people annually. While nine out of ten rich country 10-year-olds can read and write, only one-in-ten can do so in the world's poorest countries. And each year,

more than two million children and 300,000 women die around childbirth. All these problems have cheap, effective solutions. They should get our full attention, but don't.[48]

Of course, pointing out such possibilities of real progress and sensible priorities is forbidden on the Left. That would get in the way of their plan to tear down the private sector, shut down fossil-fuel companies, take total control of the world economy, and rebuild everything from the ground up according to woke principles. Shortly after Alex Epstein announced that he was publishing yet another book on the topic of fossil fuels, for instance, which brilliantly refuted some of the woke Left's most important claims, he received a call from a reporter at the *Washington Post*, letting him know that they'd be running a hit piece on him. Luckily, thanks to his experience in media, Epstein was able to refute many of the major claims, including several accusations that he was—what else?—a racist.[49]

The details of the piece that was ultimately published[50] are too stupid to mention here, but it is worth noting that those who dare disagree with the Left's views on climate usually find themselves in the same place: backed up against a wall, fighting accusations from the mob that they are racist, sexist, and somehow responsible for the deaths of millions of people.

It has been happening to me for years—so long, in fact, that the ridiculous accusations no longer really stick. By now, I've endured just about every epithet that the Left can come up with (including a few that probably aren't even in wide circulation yet), and I've come out the other side just fine. By now, I've developed an immunity to accusations from the Left in much the same way that Westley, the hero of *The Princess Bride*—which is still my favorite film, even after hundreds of viewings—developed his immunity to iocane powder. Anyone who sticks around long enough and keeps saying things that are true will find himself in the same position: able to speak those unpopular truths without being afraid of getting cancelled.

This is what allowed me to point out in September of 2022—when we supposedly had only nine years to live, according to the Left—that going on the most recent data from NASA there had been no warming in the past eight years, despite tons more carbon dioxide being released into the atmosphere.[51] The replies to the tweet in which I pointed this out were vicious, of course, but nothing that was going to succeed in getting me cancelled. The same can't be said for other people who deviate from "The Science"—and report the actual science—in a way that the Left finds offensive.

My resistance to insults and attacks from the Left is what has allowed me to question scientists, most notably Dr. Fauci and numerous left-wing environmentalists, with such rigor in the Senate. I believe that this is one of the most important parts of my job. While other people may have doubts about the validity of what these people are saying, too many of them are afraid to speak out.

CHAPTER NINE

China

During my time in the Senate, I've met with hundreds of foreign leaders. I've sat across from dozens of heads of state and hundreds of ambassadors, dignitaries, and emissaries from other countries. Some of these countries have terrible human rights records, or their leaders have said openly hostile things about the United States, the American people, or even me personally. Communicating with your adversaries is important, even if it is not always pleasant.

But one particular meeting, which took place in June of 2022, still haunts me to this day. Even now, writing these words, I can picture the blank, malevolent look on the face of the man I met with that afternoon.

That memory still sends a shiver down my spine.

The man was Qin Gang, who at the time was the Chinese ambassador to the United States. Today, he's the Chinese foreign minister. He had requested this meeting, I believe, because of some...let's just say *"unkind"* comments that I had been making about the Chinese Communist Party, the organization he is tasked with representing to foreign leaders all over the world.

Although I'm not sure exactly what the offending phrases were, I believe they included some candid descriptions of the "murder," "torture," "lies," and "genocide" routinely carried out by the Chinese Communist Party. The phrase "communist bastards" may have also been invoked.

All true, of course.

But that didn't mean that the ambassador would be any less offended. He certainly wasn't going to greet me with a fruit basket at the door when he arrived. (Nor would I eat the fruit if he did.) This meeting was going to be tense; it might very well entail raised voices from both ends of the table.

For a few days, I wrestled with whether to take the meeting at all. To begin with, I didn't think there was much to gain from it on my end. As I had been dealing with the Chinese Communist Party, I had learned a few things, chief among them that its representatives cannot be trusted. They are representatives of the largest openly Marxist nation on earth, and they have been indoctrinated in ways that most of us in the West can only imagine.

But there was at least one good reason to take the meeting. At that point the Chinese government had been holding a man from Texas named Mark Swidan in custody for nearly ten years. In many ways, his story represents nearly everything that is corrupt and evil about the Chinese Communist Party. In 2012, Mark Swidan had been traveling around China on business when he was abducted by members of China's Public Security Bureau. They accused him of engaging in a criminal conspiracy, along with eleven other people, to manufacture and traffic drugs.

Swidan denied the charges. But the Chinese authorities attempted to elicit a false confession from him anyway. Repeatedly, he refused. When his case finally went to trial almost exactly one year later, in November of 2013, he pleaded not guilty. The prosecution did not produce any forensic evidence to back up their allegations. No drugs had been found on Mark Swidan or in his hotel room. Records, as well as Mark's passport, showed that he *wasn't even in China* at the time the alleged offenses occurred. None of the eleven men with whom Mark was supposedly engaged in a criminal conspiracy could even identify him.

Nevertheless, a Chinese court sentenced Mark to death in 2019. By the time the Chinese ambassador sent in his request to meet with me, Mark had been languishing in a Chinese prison for nearly a decade. By all accounts, he had endured deplorable conditions. The location of his cell meant that he was often exposed to extreme heat and extreme cold. The guards who kept him there regularly deprived him of sleep and withheld food. As a result, he had lost more than a hundred pounds, and his health situation was dire.[1]

As is often the case in diplomacy, the situation was delicate. As much as I would have liked to see President Biden send in the Navy SEALs to break Mark Swidan out of prison, starting a shooting war with China was not something anyone wanted to do. During several conversations with Mark's mother—a wonderful, sweet woman from Luling, Texas, who has never stopped praying for and fighting for her son—we had developed a strategy to apply escalating pressure through diplomatic channels to try to secure his immediate release. A face-to-face meeting with the ambassador hadn't been part of that plan at first, but I was glad to get the opportunity.

So I said that I would take the meeting, if only to convey the message about Mark Swidan directly.

In the weeks leading up to Qin's arrival, I tasked my staff with finding a good place for us to meet. It could not, under any circumstances, be held in my own office—given the penchant that CCP officials seem to have for planting listening devices wherever they go in the

United States. I also didn't want to go too far from my office, considering how much other business I had to conduct that day. In the end, we settled on a small, secure conference room on a different hallway in the Russell Senate Office Building.

Now, I'm sure that there are some public officials who would have prepared for this meeting by crafting a diplomatic, prewritten apology to the Chinese ambassador for giving offense to his government. I imagine others would have figured out ways to appeal to the vanity of the Chinese ambassador or maybe thought of a way to strike some kind of a deal. Given the tense situation between our two countries at the time, perhaps that would have been the smart thing to do.

But that's not what I did.

Short of looking up different ways to say "Piss off!" in Chinese, I didn't see how doing any research in advance could prepare me for the meeting ahead.

I arrived at the meeting room not quite knowing what to expect. My national security advisor, Omri Ceren, a brilliant, incisive foreign policy thinker, sat alongside me. The plan was to hear whatever Ambassador Qin had to say, make my direct appeal on behalf of Mark Swidan, and see if any other business came up along the way, though I doubted it would.

From the moment Qin entered the conference room, there was a sense of foreboding. I'm not the kind of person who typically uses the word "evil" in casual conversation, but there was no mistaking it in the room that day.

Qin, who had arrived from China not long before, carried himself with the air of a man with immense authority. I got the impression that he was accustomed to taking people who had made comments like mine—about the murderous, dictatorial regime he represented—and having them thrown in a small cell to rot forever. Or worse.

At the time Qin and I began speaking, more than 1.3 million people were sitting in "reeducation camps" in the Xinjiang Province of China.

The vast majority of these people were Uighur Muslims who'd been sent there because of their religion. In these camps—which were, for all intents and purposes, prisons—the rape of female (and some male) inmates is extremely common. So too is physical abuse, torture, and murder. Men and women alike are forced to do hard labor, producing many of the goods that Chinese companies (which are effectively run by the state) sell to the rest of the world.

Some of my loudest and most strident attacks on the Chinese Communist Party were attacks on this horrific concentration camp system, which I view as an abomination that should be addressed immediately.

After a few formalities, Qin got down to business. His first priority, it seemed, was to read off a few of the most offensive comments I'd made about his government and various of its leaders back home. They included quotations from speeches I had given, things I'd said in interviews, and even off-the-cuff comments from my podcast and other media appearances.

After reading the last one, he asked if I would please stop saying these things about his government.

I paused. Then I declined.

"No," I said. "In fact, in the future, I will make sure to keep saying those things, more loudly and to as many people as possible." I continued calmly, "When your government stops committing horrific atrocities, when you stop lying, stealing, torturing, and murdering, then I will stop calling you lying, stealing, torturing, murdering bastards."

Qin seemed taken aback, though he maintained a tight, controlled smile as I spoke.

"Your government has over one million Uighurs imprisoned in concentration camps. It's the largest concentration of human slavery on the face of the planet," I observed.

Qin leaned back, closed his eyes, and smiled.

"Oh, Senator," he said. "You misunderstand. Those are not *concentration camps*."

I asked what they were.

"You see, in China, we unfortunately have a great many people who suffer from mental illness. They criticize the government, and they refuse to go along with our agenda, which proves they are mentally ill. And so these are centers to help *reeducate* these people. To help them. To *cure* them of their illness."

There was a calmness in his voice that made me think of the poignant phrase employed by the great Hannah Arendt: "the banality of evil." Qin described the concentration camps in exactly the same tone one would use to describe a local clinic helping people with cuts and bruises and other minor medical needs.

I smelled sulfur in the air.

Nevertheless, I pressed forward with the purpose of the meeting. I demanded that China release Mark Swidan. I told Qin that Swidan was wrongfully imprisoned, that he was a Texan, and he needed to come home.

Qin said that Swidan had been convicted in a Chinese court. I told him the conviction was bullshit.

"China aspires to be a great nation," I told him. "Great nations don't hold political prisoners."

Qin gave a noncommittal answer, saying only that he would bring the issue back to his superiors. I told him bluntly that, if Mark Swidan was not released, I would continue raising the issue on the global stage, calling out the horrific injustice. At the date of this writing, Swidan still has not been released, and I have continued ratcheting up the pressure. In the Senate, I authored and passed—*unanimously*—a resolution condemning China's unjust imprisonment of Swidan. I worked with colleagues in the House, and the House, too, unanimously passed the very same resolution. I've repeatedly gone to the Senate floor, and on national TV, denouncing China's keeping Swidan as a hostage. And I've pressed Secretary of State Blinken to make releasing Swidan a top priority in his negotiations with now–Foreign Minister Qin.

Walking back to my office that June afternoon, still shaking off my unease at how calmly Qin had described mass imprisonment, torture, and murder, I considered what it must be like to live in a country where men like President Xi Jinping make the rules. It's something that most Americans who've never experienced communism—who don't even know someone who's experienced it—can never quite understand. As the great writer Ayn Rand once said during a moving speech in front of Congress, "It is almost impossible to convey to a free people what it is like to live in a totalitarian dictatorship."[2]

In China and other communist nations, the threat of being sent to "reeducation camp" by the government isn't hyperbolic. It is something that has happened to millions of people in China who fail to live up to the arbitrary standards of the Chinese Communist Party. Every day, citizens live with the same fear that has consumed millions of people throughout history who've lived under communism. They fear that today is the day the security forces will knock on the door and carry them away to a jail cell for something they didn't even know was a crime. They fear that if they say the wrong thing, they'll be sent to a reeducation program, where the regime will stuff all the right propaganda into their heads.

This is the world my family fled when they came to the United States in the 1950s and '60s. It's the world many of my relatives lived and died in during the Castro years. As of this writing, millions of people—in China, Cuba, North Korea, and other nations—continue to live with this same constant, brooding fear.

This is why I have been so strident in my condemnation of the radical Left and its neo-Marxist project of remaking this nation. It's why I spoke out about the case of Jack Phillips, to take just one example, who was forced by the state of Colorado into what was for all intents and purposes a "reeducation program," in Justice Neil Gorsuch's powerful words, after he refused on religious grounds to bake a cake for a gay wedding.[3] No matter what you think of this man's religious beliefs or his personal opinions, it was beyond the purview of the state to force him to do something that went against his faith. I was extremely pleased to see that when the case finally went to the Supreme Court, the Court upheld his religious liberty.

So too with Jordan Peterson, and the "social-media communications retraining" that the Ontario College of Psychologists mandated he undertake because he had dared say out loud, among other things, that he believed that the radical gender theory behind the trans movement is a sign of civilizational collapse.[4]

I've repeatedly pointed out that this kind of "retraining"—especially when it's mandated by the government—is as clear an example of Marxism as we're likely to see in the United States or Canada. Of course, it seems perfectly normal in a country where Cultural Marxists have successfully infiltrated and captured our major institutions, insisting that people like Jordan Peterson or Jack Phillips be forced to learn woke beliefs as mandatory dogma from which no dissent is possible.

What many people don't realize, however, is just how many of our institutions and key figures in the United States have become inextricably tied to China—a country that is run by *actual* Marxists who openly cheer for the demise of the United States and the global order we've upheld for decades.

Today, with the cover they're given by Cultural Marxists in the media, they no longer make any real attempts to hide it.

The Soft Spot

Before the Covid-19 virus reached our shores, I suspect most Americans didn't think very much about China. When they did, I'm sure it was because they'd noticed that many of the things we wear and use every day are made there; perhaps they had heard predictions that the Chinese economy would soon overtake ours, and wondered how that could be possible.

But all that faded quickly into the background when we learned that the novel coronavirus that began spreading early in 2020 had come from Wuhan, China—a place most people in the world had never heard of until it began appearing in cable news chyrons and newspaper headlines. Suddenly, the eyes of the world were on China, and they were looking at some pretty horrific things.

During the early stages of the pandemic, when it may have still been possible to prevent the virus from becoming a global pandemic, some of the top scientists in China warned their government of the danger posed by this new disease. In response, the government made these whistleblowers retract their statements and locked them up. Some of them were "disappeared" by the government. One of them, a scientist named Li Wenliang, eventually died from the disease he had been attempting to warn the world about.[5]

Once the virus was unleashed, the Chinese government did everything in its power to deflect blame for as long as possible. We now know that while the world was scrambling during those key first months, China was actively destroying samples from its novel coronavirus lab in Wuhan, which had been working on mutating viruses that bore a striking resemblance to the one that eventually escaped and killed millions of people.[6]

Even in 2020, I was making the case everywhere I could that the Covid-19 virus had almost certainly leaked from a Chinese laboratory. In March and April of 2020, I devoted four separate podcast episodes on *Verdict with Ted Cruz* to laying out the evidence that the Covid virus had escaped from a Chinese government lab.[7] Four facts, known very early, were compelling:

First, the Chinese government ran the Wuhan Institute for Virology (WIV) where they studied…coronaviruses.

And not just coronaviruses, but coronaviruses…from bats.

Those bats did not occur naturally anywhere near Wuhan; the closest they could be found in China was in caves…nine hundred miles away.

Second, the first outbreak of Covid-19 occurred in the wet market in downtown Wuhan, which is…9 miles away from the Wuhan Institute of Virology. To put that into context, there are a total of 51 biosafety-level-4 labs on the planet, spread across 27 countries. The WIV is the *only* biosafety-level-4 lab in China. There are roughly 57,269,000 square miles of land on the planet. The odds against the outbreak of a serious contagious virus occurring naturally within 10 square miles of one of those 51 labs are—doing some quick back-of-the-envelope math—roughly 11,229 to 1. In other words, extremely unlikely.

Third, in 2018—before the pandemic—the State Department sent two official wires raising serious concerns about the risk of a coronavirus pandemic breaking out from the Wuhan Institute of Virology, due to their very poor security protocols. The wires warned that "during interactions with scientists at the WIV laboratory, [the U.S. scientists] noted the new lab has a serious shortage of appropriately trained technicians and investigators needed to safely operate this high-containment laboratory."

And *fourth*, in the wake of the pandemic, the Chinese government ordered the scientists at the Wuhan Institute for Virology to destroy the original samples of their research on coronaviruses. As the government-controlled *South China Morning Post* admitted on May 15, 2020, "China…confirmed it had ordered unauthorised laboratories to *destroy samples of the new coronavirus in the early stage of the outbreak*, but said it was done for biosafety reasons" [emphasis added].[8]

In a court of law, if somebody destroys evidence, a judge in civil trial can instruct the jury that it can draw a negative inference from that destruction of evidence, namely that the evidence destroyed would have been unfavorable to the party responsible for its spoliation.

Despite this overwhelming evidence, in 2020 the corporate media were united in trying to shut down any discussion of the origins of Covid-19 likely coming from a Chinese government lab. They insisted it was "racist" to say so, and a "conspiracy theory" to boot. Bizarrely, the media insisted it wasn't racist to assert that the virus must have come from backwards Chinese peasants eating raw or undercooked bats from the Wuhan "wet market," but it was definitely racist to put one iota of blame on the Chinese Communist Party.

To give just one example of this nonsense, the *Washington Post* ran a story in 2020 entitled "Tom Cotton Keeps Repeating a Coronavirus *Conspiracy Theory That Was Already Debunked*" [emphasis added]. The "conspiracy theory" Cotton kept repeating was that Covid had come from a Chinese lab. In June 2021—conveniently, *after* the 2020 election—the *Post* was forced to formally correct that story with the following explanation: "Earlier versions of this story and its headline inaccurately characterized comments by Sen. Tom Cotton (R-Ark.) regarding the origins of the coronavirus. *The term 'debunked' and The Post's use of 'conspiracy theory' have been removed* because, then as now, there was no determination about the origins of the virus."[9]

Similarly, the *Baltimore Sun* in 2021 denounced former CDC director Robert Redfield as "toss[ing] viral kindling on anti-Asian fires" because he had said the virus "most likely" originated in a Chinese lab. The *Sun*'s editorial board sneered that "it's probably untrue" (on the grounds that the heavily Chinese-influenced World Health Organization disagreed) and said it was "feeding the mob" and contributing to "an epidemic of hate crimes directed at Asians."[10]

And it was not just the media. The Deep State—Dr. Fauci in particular—was deeply vested in silencing any discussion about Covid-19 coming from a Chinese government lab. So much so that Dr. Fauci worked hand in hand with Big Tech to help silence any inquiry into the topic. Specifically, on March 15, 2020, Facebook CEO Mark Zuckerberg made Dr. Fauci the following offer, in an email exchange that, as we discussed in Chapter Four, was made public in June of 2021:

> Tony:
>
> I wanted to send a note of thanks for your leadership and everything you're doing....I also wanted to share a few **ideas of ways we could help you get your message out**. . . .
>
> This isn't public yet, but **we're building a Coronavirus Information Hub** that we're going to put at the top of Facebook for everyone (200+ million Americans, 2.5 billion people worldwide) with two goals: (1) make sure people can get authoritative information from reliable sources and (2) encourage people to practice social distance. . . .
>
> As a central part of the hub, I think it would be useful to include a video from you. . . .
>
> I'm also doing a series of livestreamed Q&As with health experts to try to use my large following on the platform (100 million followers) to get authoritative information out as well. . . .
>
> **Finally, [REDACTED]** [Emphasis added.][11]

The REDACTED portion of the final paragraph is widely assumed to be an explicit offer to censor so-called Covid "misinformation." And that inference is reinforced by the fact that Facebook made the following public announcement ten days later, on March 25. Nick Clegg, Facebook's VP of global affairs, explained:

We do not allow misinformation to circulate on Facebook which can lead to real-world harm. So if people say drinking bleach is going to help you vaccinate yourself against coronavirus—that is dangerous. We will not allow that to happen. We won't even allow folk to say social distancing makes no difference in dealing with this pandemic. . . .

What politicians say on the campaign trail about each other is not what a medic or an epidemiologist says about a pandemic. They're completely different forms of information. One is underpinned by science and established expertise, which no one questions. [It's easier for the company to act under the] strict expertise and guidance [from institutions like WHO and CDC]. [Emphasis added.][12]

No doubt part of the reason that Big Tech, the Deep State, and the corporate media all aligned to silence discussion of the compelling evidence of a Chinese lab leak is that, in 2020, President Trump was calling Covid the "Chinese virus" and making the point (as only he could) that it was from "CHI-nah," and all three of those powerful forces were aligned in wanting Trump to lose the 2020 election to Biden. Now, ironically, two different agencies of the Biden administration have publicly confirmed that the lab-leak theory is likely correct. Specifically, in 2023, the Biden FBI publicly concluded that Covid-19 "most likely" originated from a lab incident in Wuhan. As FBI director Chris Wray explained, "The FBI has for quite some time now assessed that the origins of the pandemic are *most likely a potential lab incident* in Wuhan. The Chinese government, seems to me, has been doing its best to try and thwart and obfuscate the work here, the work that we're doing, and that's unfortunate for everybody" [emphasis added].[13]

Likewise, also in 2023, the Biden Department of Energy has publicly concluded that Covid-19 "most likely" came from a lab leak, although it stated that its judgment was with "low confidence." The FBI's conclusion was given with "moderate confidence."[14]

Not only is there strong evidence that Covid-19 escaped from a Chinese government lab, there is considerable (albeit disputed) evidence that it was *created* in that lab, using "gain of function" research to make existing coronaviruses more lethal and more transmissible to humans. As former CDC director Robert Redfield testified before the House on March 8, 2023, in his scientific judgment Covid-19 was "more likely…the result of an accidental lab leak than the result of a natural spillover event. This conclusion is based primarily on the biology of the virus itself, including its rapid high infectivity for human to human transmission which would then predict rapid evolution of new variants.…In my opinion, the Covid-19 pandemic presents a case study on the potential dangers of [gain-of-function] research."[15]

But leftists don't want to hear any of this. Despite their serious dedication to analyzing and tearing down everything that they believe is wrong with the United States—a country that ended slavery, led the world to victory in two world wars, won the Cold War without firing a shot, and developed a vaccine for Covid-19 in record time, to name just a few accomplishments—they seem pathologically unable to say anything in public that might make China look bad.

On first impression, that would seem to have a certain logic to it. China is a country filled with "people of color." So in the strange mindset of the woke neo-Marxists, saying anything bad about their country—or the totalitarian government that runs it—would be racist.

It doesn't seem to bother the radical Left that the Chinese government, unlike the government of the United States, is *itself* systemically racist. Today in China it is impossible for anyone who is not Han (the dominant ethnic group) to rise to a leadership position in the government, or even to advance in society.

According to James Fallows, who covered the issue in *The Atlantic*, "what we would consider racism in the West is simply a deeply ingrained cultural characteristic of mainland Chinese people. White skin (the Chinese like to consider themselves white) and or being a Han (the dominant ethnic group) means a person is good. Dark skin or not being Han means a person is inferior (and more likely to be a bad guy/a thief/ incompetent etc)."[16]

But the radical Left's unwillingness to criticize China comes from more than just a misguided commitment to "antiracism." Many media figures, business leaders, star athletes, and Democratic politicians have a vested financial interest in the success of China. Despite the crimes that this openly communist government has committed on the world stage—the Covid-19 pandemic being just one example—these Americans have come to believe that the rise of China is inevitable, and that they had better profit from that rise while they can.

Some of these figures have famous names. I'm sure there are very few people left in the United States, for instance, who don't know that Joe Biden's son Hunter has made millions of dollars in China over the years, often by using his father's name for clout. In 2013, while his father was still vice president, Hunter flew on Air Force Two on an official trip to China with his father. At the time, Hunter was in the process of forming a Chinese private equity fund to collect massive amounts of cash from all around the world. The venture also involved Devon Archer, who had been a close adviser to John Kerry.

During that trip, Hunter Biden arranged for a photo-op in the lobby of a hotel with his father and several of the Chinese officials he wanted to work with. Shortly thereafter, Hunter's new fund cut a deal with a subsidiary of the Chinese Communist Party that would eventually come to be worth about $1.5 billion."[17]

It would appear that there was virtually nothing that Hunter Biden and his associates—including Joe Biden's brother Jim—did that did not involve the former vice president. Thanks to files that came off the Hunter Biden laptop—and to the *New York Post*, which, as we saw in Chapter Four, was censored by social media for reporting the contents of that laptop when other media outlets chose not to cover the story and hurt Joe Biden's chances in the 2020 election—we know quite a few disturbing details of those business deals, including one, involving a joint venture with a Chinese energy conglomerate, in which the partners put aside "10 percent for the Big Guy," meaning Joe Biden himself. According to a *New York Post* reporter, when an employee of that Chinese company was arrested at JFK airport in 2018 on a bribery charge, his first phone call was to Jim Biden "to try to track down Hunter, who he had paid a whopping $1 million legal retainer." Despite the former vice president's repeated denials that he knew anything about Hunter's business deals with the Chinese, shortly after the arrest was reported in the *New York Times*, Joe Biden left Hunter a voice mail saying, "I think you're clear."[18]

An IRS whistleblower revealed to the public in June of 2023 that Hunter Biden, on July 30, 2017, sent the following WhatsApp encrypted text to Chinese businessman Raymond Zhao:

> **I am sitting here with my father** and we would like to understand why the commitment made has not been fulfilled. Tell the director that I would like to resolve this now before it gets out of hand, and now means tonight. And, Z, if I get a call or text from anyone involved in this other than you, Zhang, or the chairman, **I will make certain that between the man sitting next to me and every person he knows** and my ability to forever hold a grudge that you will regret not following

my direction. I am sitting here waiting for the call **with my father.** [Emphasis added.][19]

Anyone interested in a detailed analysis of the Biden family's deep, strange ties to China would do well to read Peter Schweizer's excellent book *Red-Handed: How American Elites Get Rich Helping China Win.* This book also explores the sordid connections that other Democratic politicians and public figures have to the Chinese Communist Party.

Senator Dianne Feinstein, for instance, has benefited massively from several deals that her husband has made with Chinese companies. Not coincidentally, she often speaks about China in glowing terms. As Schweizer points out, she even said once that that "China is perhaps more Democratic than the United States."[20] That's a ludicrous statement, even for someone who is far past her prime as a legislator.

The list of Democratic representatives with big ties to the Chinese Communist Party—who also happen to be extremely soft on the country in their public statements—is long. We have Nancy Pelosi, whose son is involved in several major funds with ties to China.[21]

Famously, the Chinese government attempted to recruit Representative Eric Swalwell using a Chinese spy, and it appears that he fell easily for the honey pot trap. It is almost incredible that Nancy Pelosi allowed Swalwell to remain on the House Intelligence Committee—with full access to classified information—even *after* his alleged intimate relationship with Chinese spy Fang Fang was revealed; thankfully, in 2023, Republican leadership corrected that misjudgment.[22]

It's not just Democratic politicians who are in bed with China—sometimes literally—it is also nearly all of the Democrats' major stakeholders. From Big Business to Big Tech to Big Universities to Big Hollywood...all earn billions from their ongoing business interests in China. As a result, the modern Democratic Party is functionally pro-China, because their most important supporters depend on China for a massive percentage of their profits.

The heads of many major American investment funds and Fortune 500 companies—who, as we saw in Chapter Six, have no problem pointing out flaws in their own country—have become very hesitant to talk about the flaws of China. Consider Ray Dalio, for instance, bestselling author and head of Bridgewater Associates, the largest hedge fund in the United States.

For the past few decades, Ray Dalio has been attempting to drum up interest in various Chinese investments within the United States. He views China, as he's said often, as "the future." The country's rise is inevitable, in Dalio's opinion.[23]

Unsurprisingly, Larry Fink, who was the leading champion for ESG investing until widespread negative attention to the concept made him "ashamed" of the term—though not of the underlying idea[24]—says largely the same thing. Despite lecturing American investors about the need to consider values like global warming and feminism when making their investment decisions, Fink makes no such proclamations about the Chinese companies that BlackRock invests in. Instead, he offers praise for the Chinese government and tells his Chinese counterparts that "BlackRock should be a Chinese company in China."[25]

The woke CEOs pushing ESG on corporate America—and the congressional Democrats pressing the Green New Deal agenda[26]—are in reality working to undermine U.S. security and make America profoundly dependent on China. Consider the following.

Today the United States is the world's leader in oil and natural gas production; we produce roughly 20 percent of all the oil and gas produced worldwide.[27] As a result of the shale revolution, America now produces more energy than we consume.[28] But, what do Democrats and the ESG proponents demand? That we shift our energy consumption from fossil fuels—which generate more than 75 percent of the energy we consume,[29] and which we produce in massive quantities, considerably more cleanly than most of the rest of the world[30]—to wind and solar. And who controls wind and solar? China.

China controls refining capacity for 73 percent of the world's cobalt, 40 percent of the copper, 59 percent of the lithium, 68 percent of the nickel, and 83 percent of rare earth metals. Every one of those is necessary for wind and solar power.[31]

And when it comes to the finished products that Democrats want to produce all our domestic energy, China is responsible for 80 percent of global solar panels manufacturing,[32] 70 percent of global wind turbine manufacturing,[33] and 77 percent of global lithium-ion battery manufacturing.[34]

So, understand, every time you hear a Democrat saying, *We must immediately have an energy transition from oil and gas to wind and solar,* what they are really saying is that *We should trade American energy independence for complete and total dependence on China for our energy.* That would render the American economy completely defenseless to China's cutting off our energy, and would enable the Chinese communist government to almost totally cut off energy from the American military, making us utterly powerless to stand up to Chinese aggression.[35]

Why would anyone who loves America want that outcome?

And it's not just Democrats and Big Business. The executives who run Hollywood likewise appear to be thoroughly in bed with the Chinese government. In an era when nearly every big-budget Hollywood film is marketed to global audiences—including the billions of people in China—studios have shown that they are more than willing to edit, censor, and otherwise alter the final cuts of films to please the Chinese Communist Party. For years, studios have removed scenes from films and adjusted dialogue to avoid offending the sensibilities of the Chinese government.

One studio did a re-cut of the film *Bohemian Rhapsody* to remove any hint that Freddie Mercury was a homosexual—truly astonishing given the virtue signaling Hollywood typically does on LGBT issues, not to mention the impossibility of telling Mercury's story without acknowledging his sexuality. Another studio cut several scenes from *Pirates of the Caribbean: Dead Man's Chest* to avoid any mention of "ghosts" or "cannibalism"—only to find that the Chinese censors rejected the film anyway. During the production of *Iron Man 3*, according to *The Atlantic*, Chinese regulators even visited the set of the film to ensure compliance with their standards.[36]

When a trailer for the film *Top Gun: Maverick* was released, people noticed that two patches Tom Cruise's character had worn in the original *Top Gun* movie back in the 1980s—one from Japan, the other from Taiwan, both considered enemies of China—were mysteriously missing from his jacket. What's curious about this, of course, is that as far as we know, no one had asked the makers of the movie to remove the patches. Apparently, they had simply done it hoping that they would be able to stop Chinese censors from getting upset. I publicly blasted the studio for their cowardice, noting that "Maverick would not be afraid of the Chinese communists!" Ultimately, the studio did the right thing and replaced the patches...but only after the movie had already been banned in China.[37]

While the woke neo-Marxist revolution is teaching ordinary Americans to censor themselves before speaking because they don't want the woke mob to come for them, the old-fashioned Marxist Chinese Communist Party—the most prominent representative of the original old-fashioned brand of Marxism on the world stage—is successfully training our powerful institutions to censor themselves because they don't want to pass up on lucrative business opportunities.

China, one of the most repressive nations on earth, which should have seen its power *decline* as the world grew democratic, is more powerful than ever—and the woke Left in the United States is enabling it.

Bowing Down

Over the past few years, citizens of the United States have grown quite used to seeing people grovel in public. We've seen celebrities who've committed sins against the woke ideology issue apologies for their behavior, practically begging not to be cancelled. We've seen ordinary people who've done nothing wrong do the same thing.

In China, this isn't a new phenomenon. It has been going on for decades. During the 1966–76 Cultural Revolution, in the last ten years of the reign of Chairman Mao Zedong, it was common for mobs of revolutionaries to hold "struggle sessions" in the town square, where people who held views deemed offensive by the regime were publicly humiliated, beaten, and forced to recant their beliefs.

This era, which came to a close only with the death of Mao, ended horribly. Millions of Chinese citizens died as the result of execution or starvation (the two reliable outcomes of communism everywhere that the Marxists have succeeded in implementing it). Even as late as the early 1990s, the Chinese economy was still extremely poor. The primary method of transportation for the average Chinese citizen, even in major cities, was the bicycle.

Slowly, however, things began to change. In the 1990s, the United States led a worldwide effort to bring China into the global economy. The leaders of our country believed that if we allowed China to experience the benefits of capitalism, the Chinese Communist Party would grow less authoritarian and more democratic.[38] Some of the top political scientists in the world argued that this would lead to prosperity for everyone in the world.[39]

That didn't happen.

Today, the Chinese Communist Party is more brutal and authoritarian than ever. During the CCP's celebration in 2021 to mark one hundred years since its founding, President Xi Jinping warned that anyone who stood against the rise of China on the world stage would have "their heads bashed bloody against a Great Wall of steel."[40]

There was a time when China could only exert that kind of power within the borders of its own country. Chinese citizens who spoke out against the government were jailed, or even killed. Anyone who said things that the regime deemed offensive was forced to publicly recount his views and issue a prompt apology for having expressed them in the first place. This is what happened, as you'll recall, to the scientists and doctors who attempted to blow the whistle about Covid-19. They were forced to issue retractions, and they were jailed. At least one of them died.[41]

But lately, the power of the Chinese Communist Party has been extending outward. Today, largely because American corporations depend so heavily on Chinese consumers to make money, the CCP has the ability to force citizens of *other* countries to issue public apologies when they offend the sensibilities of the regime.

It happens all the time.

Consider what happened when John Cena, a popular WWF wrestler-turned-actor who was promoting a film, gave an interview in which he referred to Taiwan as a country.[42] I'm sure that Cena didn't think carefully about using the word "country" in reference to Taiwan. He had just been there during the promotional tour. But in China—and now, if the Chinese communists get their way, in the United States as well—using that word in reference to Taiwan is forbidden.

The controversy stems from the Chinese Civil War, which took place intermittently between 1927 and 1949. During this war, which was extremely bloody, two parties fought for control of China. The nationalists, led by the Western-supported leader Chiang Kai-shek, eventually lost to the communists, who were led by Mao Zedong. The "winning team," so to speak, took over the Chinese mainland including the capital city, while the nationalists fled to the tiny island of Taiwan, where they established a small democratic outpost in the largely authoritarian East that is still (barely) hanging on today. Taiwan is an economic powerhouse, one of the most prosperous nations in the world. But it faces enormous military peril.

The Chinese Communist Party, of course, sees this island as a rebel territory of communist China, not a country in its own right. President Xi Jinping and other members of his party believe that one day—possibly very soon—the Chinese people will reclaim Taiwan and bring the country together again. Anyone who goes against this notion—even if that person is not a Chinese citizen—risks giving offense to the Chinese government.

And these days, giving offense to the Chinese government means losing the opportunity to show films and hold sports events in the country, which in turn means the loss of a *lot* of money. Which, it seems, is what Western celebrities, even those who indulge in endless moral preening about the supposed sins of the United States and other Western powers, seem to care about most.

Within days, Hollywood tough guy John Cena had recorded a message to the people of China (remarkably, he was speaking in Mandarin Chinese) in which he personally apologized for giving offense to the Chinese people[43]—the ones under the regime of President Xi Jinping, that is, not the Chinese in the free country of Taiwan.

All this over the use of one word that the Chinese government didn't like.

Unfortunately, Cena is not alone in his willingness to be silenced, censored, and otherwise pushed around by the Chinese Communist Party. That totalitarian government has also exerted pressure on star athletes such as LeBron James, who in recent years has been much nicer to China than he's ever been to the government of the country he lives in.

Late in 2019, for instance, as thousands of young pro-democracy protestors were filling the streets of Hong Kong to speak out against the CCP's repressive policies, Daryl Morey, the general manager of the Houston Rockets (in my parochial opinion, America's finest basketball franchise), tweeted out a message of solidarity with the protestors.

"Fight for freedom," he wrote. "Stand with Hong Kong."

Again, this might seem innocuous at first glance, especially to American citizens who have long been used to being able to speak their minds without consequences. What Daryl Morey was supporting, oddly enough, was the notion that everyone in the world—not just Americans—should enjoy these same rights, or at least have the opportunity to fight for them.

LeBron James, who surely knows that NBA executives make millions of dollars every year through deals with the Chinese Communist Party (and who personally benefits from those millions), did not agree. Asked about Morey's comments in October of 2019, James said Morey "wasn't educated" about the subject he had tweeted about.

"So many people could have been harmed," James said, "not only financially, but physically, emotionally, spiritually, so, just be careful what we tweet, what we say, what we do. Even though yes, we do have freedom of speech, there can be a lot of negative that comes from that."[44]

Clearly, these are the words of someone who *has* freedom of speech—who has it because he lives in the United States of America, where that right is guaranteed even for people who say things that are vile, racist, and stupid in public.

When LeBron James goes on Twitter to suggest, for instance, that he lives in a systemically racist society where Black people are routinely murdered by police officers, as he did several times in 2020,[45] he is able to do so because he has freedom of speech. The same is true when he speaks about the United States' response to the Russian detainment of WNBA star Brittney Griner, wondering aloud on a television show whether Griner would "even want to go back" to such a horrible country.[46]

This, apparently, is the kind of "education" (or "reeducation," to use the term of LeBron's preferred government) that he wishes Daryl Morey had gone through before speaking about current events. In athletics today—and in entertainment—nothing but the most rabidly neo-Marxist, anti-American sentiments will do when it comes to politics.

This kind of anti-American propaganda never fails to make the woke here at home feel good. It reinforces their belief that the world they live in is cruel and repressive, and that they're noble for speaking out against it.

The Chinese Communist Party also loves it. In recent years, it has become extremely common for Chinese leaders and diplomats, on the increasingly infrequent occasions when they are presented with China's horrific history of human rights abuses, to rattle off the talking points of the woke, neo-Marxist American Left to defend themselves.

When confronted with their horrific human rights record, the Chinese communists predictably respond, *How can the Americans criticize anyone when they have a police force that routinely murders Black citizens with impunity?*[47]

This is, of course, a lie. Most normal people in America know it. But as long as the lie is out there, the Chinese Communist Party will be able to use it on the world stage as a weapon against the United States.

In March of 2021, for instance, the U.S. ambassador to the United Nations—an African-American woman named Linda Thomas-Greenfield—got up in front of the U.N. General Assembly and said that racism "continues to be a daily challenge" in the United States, and that "for millions, it's more than a challenge. It's deadly."

Later in the speech, Thomas-Greenfield made reference to the horrible human rights abuses committed by China and other nations.

When the Chinese representative to the United Nations rose shortly thereafter, she scolded the United States for daring to talk down to other nations, given its own "abuses." The woman denied that there was a "genocide" in Xinjiang province, sporting the same creepy, Orwellian affect that I'd heard from the Chinese ambassador in Washington years earlier.

"If the U.S. truly cared about human rights, they should address the deep-seated problems of racial discrimination, social injustice and police brutality, on their own soil."[48]

At some level, it shouldn't be surprising to hear the Chinese communists repeating the U.S. ambassador's words back at her. Before she was nominated, Thomas-Greenfield had been paid $1,500 to give a speech effusively praising China at Savannah State University's Confucius Institute, which is controlled and funded by the Chinese Communist Party.[49] I opposed her nomination on those grounds, but every single Democrat nevertheless voted to confirm her.[50]

Here, we can see how destructive anti-American sentiment can be—not only to students who are forced to learn it in their classrooms from the age of five, or to academics who have to waste their time studying it in American universities. This kind of talk, especially when it's based on complete lies, is destructive to all American citizens, who may soon see our nation weakened significantly on the world stage as those lies spread.

How We Fight Back

Since I arrived in the Senate over a decade ago, I have been warning about China—which I maintain poses the single greatest geopolitical threat facing the United States for the next century.[51] My first year as a senator, I gave a speech urging that we can't deal with China "by embracing arm-in-arm and singing kumbaya."[52] At the time, that was very much a minority view; all the Democrats and most of the Republicans disagreed. When they looked to China, they saw nothing but dollar signs.

The Covid pandemic opened millions of people's eyes to the evils of the Chinese government. As a result, mine is no longer a lonely voice in the wilderness; now, I've been joined by a growing number who realize just how malevolent the Chinese communists are.

For me, it's visceral: *I hate communists.*

And we very much need clear vision and a detailed, systemic strategy to defeat them. Our approach should be modeled after Reagan's strategy that won the Cold War and defeated the Soviet Union.

It should start by shining a light of truth on the communists. Reagan astonished the intellectual elites when he referred to the Soviet Union as an "evil empire." When he said Marxism-Leninism would end up "on the ash heap of history" and when he said his strategy in the Cold War was "very simple: we win, they lose," Democrats and the intelligentsia derided him as an ignorant philistine. But when he stood before the Brandenburg Gate and demanded, "Mr. Gorbachev, tear down this wall!" his words changed history.

We need to do the same with China. Speak with clarity. Call out their evil. Their murder, torture, thievery, concentration camps, oppression.

Like the Soviets, the Chinese are incredibly sensitive and vulnerable to the power of sunshine. For example, in 2016 I introduced legislation to rename the street in front of the Chinese embassy to be "Liu Xiaobo Plaza," after the 2010 Nobel Peace Prize laureate who was imprisoned multiple times for standing up to Chinese oppression.[53] Repeatedly, I went to the Senate floor to try to pass my bill. And repeatedly, Senator Dianne Feinstein, the Democrat from California, objected. She argued that my legislation would irritate the Chinese government. Yes, I replied, that was the point. To shame them.

In the face of Democrat obstruction, I placed a hold on every Obama State Department nominee. And the Obama White House freaked out, coming to me and asking what they could do to get me to lift my holds. "Pass my bill," I replied. So the White House leaned on Feinstein, and she lifted her objection. And my legislation passed the Senate *one hundred to zero*. Unfortunately, the Republican House refused to take up the legislation (as I said, being soft on China is a bipartisan problem), and so it did not get enacted into law.[54]

However, there's an epilogue to the story. In the spring of 2017, I was having breakfast with Trump's new secretary of state Rex Tillerson at his office in Foggy Bottom. We were discussing many aspects of foreign affairs, but China was front and center. Rex told me he had recently been visiting with his counterpart, the Chinese foreign minister, who had relayed China's "top three" foreign-policy priorities. Rex continued, "Ted, it's the darndest thing. One of their top three priorities is stopping your legislation renaming the street in front of their embassy."

At the time, Liu Xiaobo had just passed away. But his widow Liu Xia had been placed under house arrest and was not allowed to leave China.[55] Indeed, she still had not been able to collect the $1.5 million for her husband's Nobel Peace Prize.[56] I said to Rex, "Tell China, if they release Liu Xia I will stop pushing the bill. But, if they don't release her, tell them I will continue to push it, and I will pass it. And you can tell them I'm not bluffing. They've seen that we've already passed it through the Senate unanimously once, and next time I'll get it through the House as well, and President Trump will sign it."

The next year, after eight years under house arrest, China released Liu Xia.[57]

Why? Because communist regimes fears accountability. They fear being called out. Our strategy for Liu Xiaobo Plaza was inspired by

Reagan's strategy decades earlier, when he renamed the street in front of the Soviet embassy "Sakharov Plaza," after the famed Soviet dissident. A street renaming may seem unimportant, but it means everyone writing the embassy must write the name of the dissident. Everyone looking up directions on Google has to see the name of the dissident. And there is power in *saying his name.*

Just this year, I followed the very same strategy to call out Cuba, and unanimously passed legislation out of the Senate to rename the street in front of the Cuban embassy as "Oswaldo Payá Way," after the heroic democracy activist who was murdered by the communist regime.[58] When it passes the House (and I believe it will), every day the Cuban communists at the embassy—and everyone who comes to visit them—will be forced to look upon the name of the martyred hero.

China fears its dissidents. And it fears Taiwan. And Hong Kong. The reason is simple: both Taiwan and Hong Kong show that Chinese people can live in freedom—and the result is enormous prosperity. Xi is terrified that the 1.3 billion Chinese people suffering under communist oppression will look to Taiwan and Hong Kong and say, *We want what they have.*

For that reason, in 2019, I traveled to Pearl Harbor, and Japan, and India, and Taiwan, and Hong Kong, on a "friends and allies" tour surrounding China. The objective was to highlight the threat of China, and to rally support from our allies in the region. In Hong Kong, millions of democracy activists were in the streets. They were risking their lives, fighting against the brutal communist crackdown. Amazingly, they were waving American flags and holding signs with words from our nation's Founding Fathers. I met with democracy activists, including the great Jimmy Lai (who has since been wrongfully imprisoned). And I gave a satellite interview on *Face the Nation* from Hong Kong, dressed in all black to show solidarity with the democracy protestors. I called out the CCP's horrific human rights abuses. And called for us to stand with Hong Kong.[59]

Tragically, the Chinese government continued its vicious oppression, stripping the residents of Hong Kong of the civil liberties and economic freedom that they had enjoyed for a century under British rule and for two decades under the initial terms of China's takeover. In response, I passed legislation to make sure the United States recognized that reality (the idea being that it endangered the safety and security of Americans not to acknowledge that China was exploiting Hong Kong to undermine our national security). Specifically, I filed the Hong Kong Reevaluation Act, which mandated a determination by the president on whether Hong Kong was still independent—and, if not, imposed countermeasures ending Hong Kong's special status. My bill was incorporated into the Hong Kong Human Rights and Democracy Act of 2019, which President Trump signed into law. And, pursuant to the language of my bill, the Trump administration did indeed find that it could no longer determine Hong Kong was independent, and therefore implemented the countermeasures against China.[60]

We need to contest China, and not just overseas. We also need to fight against Chinese espionage and propaganda here at home. And we need to use every tool we have to fight back. In the Senate, I've introduced dozens of pieces of legislation fighting back against the misdeeds of the Chinese communists. In my first term in the Senate, one of the key pieces of legislation I authored and passed was to cut off Department of Defense language-program funding for any university that allowed a Chinese-controlled Confucius Institute. At the time, there were over one hundred Confucius Institutes at American universities across the country, all funded and controlled by the Chinese Communist Party. The centers engaged in both espionage and propaganda: directly monitoring what students and professors were saying and doing on campus (and what they were researching), and actively pushing the preferred narrative of the CCP (including suppressing discussion of human rights abuses and democratic uprisings such as Tiananmen Square). As a result of my legislation, passed in 2018, dozens of Confucius Institutes closed permanently.[61]

Nevertheless, China continues to flood money into our universities. To take just one notable example: the University of Pennsylvania, home of the "Biden Center," a think tank named after the president, has accepted *over $100 million from communist China*.[62] This was no doubt in significant part as a result of the active solicitation of then former vice president Biden; the desire of politicians to erect monuments to their own hubris is strong, and China is more than willing to exploit that vanity to try to purchase a major U.S. university.

Combatting Chinese propaganda also requires confronting the American media. When it comes to Chinese influence, the CCP seeks to control what Americans see, hear, and ultimately think about China. And Hollywood, as we have seen, has been more than happy to comply. In response, I filed the SCRIPT Act, which stands for Stopping Censorship, Restoring Integrity, Protecting Talkies (as silly as it sounds, sometimes creative acronyms help legislation get traction). The SCRIPT Act doesn't try to put a mandate on Hollywood; instead, it would prohibit the Defense Department from providing technical assistance or access to government assets for U.S. companies that censor their films for screening in China (where censoring meant altering "the content of the film in response to, or in anticipation of, a request by an official of the Government of the People's Republic of China or the Chinese Communist Party"). The federal government often allows movie producers to use government assets—think jets, ships, tanks, aircraft carriers, helicopters—to film action scenes in movies. The SCRIPT Act simply says, *If you're going to actively censor on behalf of the CCP, the U.S. government isn't going to help you out.*

When the SCRIPT Act was introduced, Big Hollywood freaked out. They launched a major lobbying campaign trying to stop it, including contacting all the other members of the Senate Foreign Relations

Committee (on which I serve) to try to kill the bill. They planned op-eds attacking the bill. And they worked with Democrats to try to gut the language. Nevertheless, last year we had a partial win: a version of SCRIPT was included in the FY23 National Defense Authorization Act and signed into law. It was, alas, watered down—subject to a waiver, and requiring "good faith" implementation. But it is in there: "None of the funds authorized to be appropriated by this Act may be used to knowingly provide active and direct support to any film, television, or other entertainment project if the Secretary of Defense has demonstrable evidence that the project has complied or is likely to comply with a demand from the Government of the People's Republic of China or the Chinese Communist Party, or an entity under the direction of the People's Republic of China or the Chinese Communist Party, to censor the content of the project in a material manner to advance the national interest of the People's Republic of China."[63] And, in June of 2023, the Department of Defense issued formal guidelines implementing the SCRIPT Act and barring DOD production assistance to any movie that is likely to be complicit in CCP censorship.[64] That's a step in the right direction—and a big one.

I also filed another bill called the BEAMS Act, which was designed to prevent the Federal Communications Commission (FCC) from granting a license to any America radio station controlled by China and broadcasting CCP propaganda. Specifically, the Chinese wanted to get an American license to broadcast Chinese-language radio out of Mexico and into the Southwest United States, in order to spread their propaganda directly to Americans. Here we scored another victory when, in significant part because of the legislation I had filed, the Trump FCC denied the license and stopped the Chinese effort.[65]

Finally, we need to act to reduce the American economy's dependency on the Chinese supply chain. The Chinese government has systematically targeted our critical infrastructure, from advanced semiconductors to pharmaceuticals to critical minerals. During Covid, one state-controlled Chinese newspaper demanded that China cut off America's supply of life-saving pharmaceuticals—literally putting the lives and health of millions of Americans at risk.[66] The upside of their making that threat? It made obvious to anyone with any sense that America must not remain dependent on China for our vital needs.

Over the past decade, I've introduced multiple bills to delink our economy from China, so that the Chinese government will no longer have the ability to hold the American people hostage. One of those was the ORE Act, the Onshoring Rare Earths Act of 2020. The objective of that bill was for the United States to take control of the top of the critical minerals supply chain, which is a billion-dollar industry of mining and recycling that could be kick-started domestically. The key to doing so is to address the problem of U.S. investment capital money staying on the sidelines of the industry because of uncertainty regarding downstream domestic capacity and demand. The bill would have allowed a new tax deduction for 200 percent of the cost of purchasing or acquiring such critical minerals and metals extracted from deposits in the United States. Unfortunately, at least so far, Democrats have blocked the bill.

However, section 5 of ORE extended an existing Buy American mandate on the Defense Department to the entire supply chain: previously, the DOD had only been mandated to source critical mineral components from the United States if they were at the end of the supply chain, that is, "melted or produced." My language expanded that mandate to the top of the whole supply chain, that is, "mined, refined, separated, melted, or produced." And that language became law via the 2021 National Defense Authorization Act. It will become effective January 1, 2026.[67]

Getting Democrats to stand up to China is a difficult task. That was never clearer than in 2021, when I forced a vote on the Senate floor to ban the importation of electric vehicles or EV parts manufactured *using slave labor in concentration camps in China*. With over one million Uighurs currently imprisoned in concentration camps in China, that should have been an easy vote. Indeed, when I tell Texans about the vote, they assume everyone agreed that America should not be actively supporting slave labor. Tragically, *every single Senate Democrat* except Joe Manchin voted no. When John Kerry was asked about the Biden administration buying millions of dollars of EVs and EV parts from Chinese concentration camps, he replied, "That's not my lane."[68]

My response, only slightly tongue in cheek, was to name John Kerry the concentration camp "Customer of the Year."[69]

I wish that were hyperbole, but it's not. The Democrats persistently enable the use of slave labor by the Chinese. And the corrupt corporate media, themselves fully in bed with China, say nary a word about it.

◆　◆　◆

The Marxists' long march through our institutions, commenced six decades ago, has succeeded in capturing the commanding heights of virtually every organ for the transmission of ideas. Education (K–12 and the universities), journalism, Big Tech, Big Business, science, and entertainment...all have been overtaken by the Cultural Marxists. And communist China is a central nexus intertwined with it all.

But, fortunately, Marxism survives only in darkness. The more of us who stand up, who shine the light, who speak the truth, the more readily we'll take our country back. The Berlin Wall fell, and so will the Woke Wall of Idiocy. America remains, I believe, a center-right country. Our people continue to have a deep reservoir of common sense. That's why the Cultural Marxists operate quietly, because they know their ideas are not widely shared. But every time another one of their abuses is exposed, more and more people wake up to the threat. More and more of us are fighting back. And, if that keeps happening—if we are smart, strategic, systemic, and relentless (just like the Marxists have been)—I fully believe we will take America back.

Acknowledgments

This is my fourth book, and I enjoyed writing it immensely. I'm grateful to my family—to my best friend Heidi and my precious girls Caroline and Catherine—who endured long nights and countless hours while I worked on the draft.

I want to thank the terrific team who helped me complete it. My agent Keith Urbahn did his always excellent job. Writers Sean McGowan and Dylan Colligan provided enormous assistance with research, brainstorming, and writing. Their talent and dedication is considerable.

The team at Regnery, led by Tom Spence and my editor Elizabeth Kantor, were diligent and effective partners in writing the book.

The following reviewed portions of the book and provided very helpful edits: Aaron Reitz, Steve Chartan, Nick Maddux, Ethan Zorfas, Sam Cooper, Jeff Roe, Jason Johnson, Omri Ceren, Victoria Coates, Duncan Rankin, Judd Stone, and Nick Gangei. I appreciate their help, friendship, and insight.

All errors are my own, but any material mistakes should be blamed on the communists.

Notes

Prologue

1. "The Vengeful Visionary," *Time*, January 26, 1959, https://time.com/3641153/the-vengeful-visionary/.

Introduction: The Long, Slow March through the Institutions

1. Paul Kengor, *The Devil and Karl Marx* (Gastonia, North Carolina: TAN Books, 2020), 124.
2. Walter E. Williams, "Did You Know That Karl Marx Was a Racist and an Anti-Semite?," *Panama City News-Herald*, August 16, 2020, https://www.newsherald.com/story/opinion/2020/08/16/many-marxists-dont-realize-their-hero-racist-and-anti-semite/3369024001/.
3. Walter Williams, "The Devil and Karl Marx," *Amarillo Globe-News*, September 15, 2020, https://www.amarillo.com/story/opinion/2020/09/15/williams-rsquothe-devil-and-karl-marxrsquo/114031312/.
4. Williams, "Did You Know That Karl Marx Was a Racist?"; Jonah Goldberg, "Karl Marx's Jew-Hating Conspiracy Theory," *Commentary*, April 2018, https://www.commentary.org/articles/jonah-goldberg/karl-marxs-jew-hating-conspiracy-theory/.
5. Nate Hochman, "The Long March Back," *National Review*, March 6, 2023, https://www.nationalreview.com/magazine/2023/03/06/the-long-march-back/.
6. Ibid.
7. Herbert Marcuse, *Counterrevolution and Revolt* (Boston: Beacon Press, 1972), 55.
8. Ibid., 56.
9. See, for example, Charles W. Mills, *From Class to Race: Essays in White Marxism and Black Radicalism* (Lanham, Maryland: Rowman & Littlefield Publishers, 2003); Keeanga-Yamahtta Taylor, "Race, Class and Marxism," *Socialist Worker*, January 4, 2011, https://socialistworker.org/2011/01/04/race-class-and-marxism.

10. Christopher F. Rufo, "The Long March through the Institutions: Ep. 2," YouTube, August 5, 2022, https://www.youtube.com/watch?v=NEt9XepeGt4.

11. Joshua Rhett Miller, "BLM Removes Page on 'Nuclear Family Structure' amid NFL Vet's Criticism," *New York Post*, September 24, 2020, https://nypost.com/2020/09/24/blm-removes-website-language-blasting-nuclear-family-structure/.

Chapter One: The Universities: The Wuhan Labs of the Woke Virus

1. Michael Mechanic, "Ted Cruz's College Roommate Can't Stop Talking Smack about Him," *Mother Jones*, February 2, 2016, https://www.motherjones.com/politics/2016/02/ted-cruz-princeton-roomate-won-iowa-caucuses-victory/.

2. "Official Protest to Remove Ted Cruz as the Commencement Speaker," Facebook, April 11, 2007, https://www.facebook.com/groups/2309564055.

3. Ibid.

4. Ibid.

5. Ibid.

6. Sheila Flynn, "Wyoming Senator Booed during Graduation Speech at Alma Mater after 'Two Sexes' Comment," *The Independent*, May 16, 2022, https://www.independent.co.uk/news/world/americas/cynthia-lummis-wyoming-commencement-lgbtq-b2080376.html.

7. "Halloween Costume Controversy," FIRE, https://www.thefire.org/research-learn/halloween-costume-controversy.

8. Felicity Barringer, "The Mainstreaming of Marxism in U.S. Colleges," *New York Times*, October 25, 1989, https://timesmachine.nytimes.com/timesmachine/1989/10/25/061089.html?pageNumber=39.

9. Russ Latino, "Free Speech? Fifth Circuit Judge Shouted Down by Stanford Law School Students and Faculty," *Clarksdale Press Register*, March 13, 2023, https://www.pressregister.com/index.php/most-recent/free-speech-fifth-circuit-judge-shouted-down-stanford-law-school-students-and-faculty-640f624caa182?e_term_id=14432&e_sort_order=week; "Transcript of Stanford Law Shutdown of Judge Kyle Duncan, March 9, 2023," FIRE, https://www.thefire.org/research-learn/transcript-stanford-law-shoutdown-judge-kyle-duncan-march-9-2023.

10. "Policy on Campus Disruptions," University Policies and Standards, Stanford Law School, https://law.stanford.edu/office-of-student-affairs/university-policies-and-standards/#slsnav-the-fundamental-standard.

11. National Review, "Stanford's Dean of DEI Embarrasses Herself," YouTube, March 13, 2023, https://www.youtube.com/shorts/G2gy4rS9rFQ.
12. "Transcript of Stanford Law Shoutdown."
13. Latino, "Free Speech? Fifth Circuit Judge Shouted Down."
14. Vimal Patel, "A Lecturer Showed a Painting of the Prophet Muhammad. She Lost Her Job.," *New York Times*, January 8, 2023, https://www.nytimes.com/2023/01/08/us/hamline-university-islam-prophet-muhammad.html.
15. Greta Reich, "President, Law School Dean Apologize to Judge Kyle Duncan for 'Disruption' to His Speech," *Stanford Daily*, March 12, 2023, https://stanforddaily.com/2023/03/12/president-law-school-dean-apologize-to-judge-kyle-duncan-for-disruption-to-his-speech/.
16. Aaron Sibarium, "Student Activists Target Stanford Law School Dean in Revolt over Her Apology," Washington Free Beacon, March 14, 2023, https://freebeacon.com/campus/student-activists-target-stanford-law-school-dean-in-revolt-over-her-apology/.
17. Aaron Sibarium, "'Dogs—t': Federal Judge Decries Disruption of His Remarks by Stanford Law Students and Calls for Termination of the Stanford Dean Who Joined the Mob," Washington Free Beacon, March 10, 2023, https://freebeacon.com/campus/dogshit-federal-judge-decries-disruption-of-his-remarks-by-stanford-law-students-and-calls-for-termination-of-the-stanford-dean-who-joined-the-protesters/.
18. "WFB Reporter Explains Why Woke Stanford Law Students Who Tried to Censor Him Are Hypocrites," Washington Free Beacon, March 19, 2023, https://freebeacon.com/media/aaron-sibarium-fox-and-friends-stanford/.
19. *Terminiello v. Chicago*, 337 U.S. 1 (1949); *Brown v. Louisiana* 383 U.S. 131 (1966).
20. Jeremiah Poff, "Stanford Law School DEI Dean Placed on Leave Following Outburst at Trump Judge," *Washington Examiner*, March 22, 2023, https://www.washingtonexaminer.com/restoring-america/faith-freedom-self-reliance/stanford-law-school-dei-dean-placed-on-leave.
21. Valerie Richardson, "Two Judges Extend Boycott on Yale Clerks to Stanford after Students Shout Down Conservative Jurist," *Washington Times*, April 3, 2023, https://www.washingtontimes.com/news/2023/apr/3/james-ho-elizabeth-branch-boycott-stanford-law-stu/; John F. Banzhaf, "14 Federal Judges Will Not Hire Yale Law Grads—Report," ValueWalk, March 31, 2023, https://www.valuewalk.com/14-federal-judges-will-not-hire-yale-law-grads-report/.

22. "Read: Judge James Ho's Remarks Announcing a Hiring Boycott from Stanford Law School," Washington Free Beacon, April 1, 2023, https://freebeacon.com/campus/read-judge-james-hos-remarks-announcing-a-hiring-boycott-from-stanford-law-school.

23. Madison Alder, "Stanford Law Added to Clerk Hire Boycott by US Judges Ho, Branch," Bloomberg Law, April 2, 2023, https://news.bloomberglaw.com/us-law-week/stanford-law-added-to-clerk-hire-boycott-by-us-judges-ho-branch.

24. Young America's Foundation, "Chipping Away at Democracy: Verdict with Ted Cruz Live at Yale University," Facebook, April 11, 2022, https://www.facebook.com/watch/live/?ref=watch_permalink&v=1020041045575029.

Chapter Two: "Malleable Clay": K–12 Education

1. Alberto Benegas Lynch Jr., "My Cousin, El Che," qtd. in Guillermina Sutter Schneider, "Are You Gay? Che Guevara Would Have Sent You to a Concentration Camp," HuffPost, October 9, 2017, https://www.huffpost.com/entry/are-you-gay-che-guevara-would-have-sent-you-to-a-concentration_b_59cc0d9ee4b0b99ee4a9ca1e.

2. Allison Aldrich, "Column: Che Guevara: Exposing Myths about a Murderer," *Collegiate Times*, March 11, 2008, http://www.collegiatetimes.com/opinion/article_7392ebfe-329b-5736-881e-d37e10ce733f.html.

3. Ernesto Che Guevara, "Man and Socialism in Cuba: Letter from Major Ernesto Che Guevara to Carlos Quijano, Editor of the Montevideo Weekly Magazine *Marcha*," trans. Margarita Zimmermann, March 1965, Guevara Internet Archive (marxists.org), 1999, https://www.marxists.org/archive/guevara/1965/03/man-socialism-alt.htm.

4. Karl Marx and Friedrich Engels, *The Communist Manifesto* (1888), https://www.gutenberg.org/files/61/61-h/61-h.htm.

5. Paul Kengor, *The Devil and Karl Marx* (Gastonia, North Carolina: TAN Books, 2020), 72.

6. Mike Gonzalez, "Socialism and Family," The Heritage Foundation, March 1, 2022, https://www.heritage.org/marriage-and-family/commentary/socialism-and-family.

7. Guevara, "Man and Socialism in Cuba."

8. Ada Ferrer, *Cuba: An American History* (New York: Scribner, 2021), 386.

9. Dylan M. Palmer and Will Flanders, "Education Schools Are Pushing the Classroom Leftward," RealClearEducation, September 2, 2022, https://www

.realcleareducation.com/articles/2022/09/02/education_schools_are_
pushing_the_classroom_leftward_110759.html.

10. Ibid.

11. Vincent Lloyd, "A Black Professor Trapped in Anti-Racist Hell," Compact, February 10, 2023, https://compactmag.com/article/a-black-professor -trapped-in-anti-racist-hell.

12. Ibid.

13. Ibid.

14. Project Veritas (@Project_Veritas), "BREAKING: @TeachingLabHQ Director @DrQuintinBostic Admits...," Twitter, January 17, 2023, 6:00 p.m., https://twitter.com/Project_Veritas/status/1615484136197701632.

15. Christopher F. Rufo, "Woke Elementary," *City Journal*, January 13, 2021, https://www.city-journal.org/article/woke-elementary.

16. Divya Kishore, "'All Whites Perpetuate Racism,' Teach NY Public Schools with Dramatized Videos of Dead Black Kids: Whistleblower," MEAWW, February 25, 2021, https://meaww.com/ny-public-schools-teach-all-white -people-perpetuate-systemic-racism-videos-of-dead-black-kids.

17. Joshua Rhett Miller, "Teacher Removed US Flag from Class, Encouraged Students to Pledge to Gay Pride Banner," *New York Post*, August 30, 2021, https://nypost.com/2021/08/30/ca-teacher-encouraged-students-to-pledge -gay-pride-flag-video/.

18. Ronn Blitzer, "Biden Says Students Are like Teachers' Children When in Classroom," Fox News, April 28, 2022, https://www.foxnews.com/politics /biden-students-like-teachers-children-when-in-classroom.

19. "Seattle Public Schools: K–12 Math Ethnic Studies Framework," Washington Office of Superintendent of Public Instruction, August 20, 2019, https://www .k12.wa.us/sites/default/files/public/socialstudies/pubdocs/Math%20SDS %20ES%20Framework.pdf.

20. Maia Kobabe, *Gender Queer* (Portland, Oregon: Oni Press, 2019); Alexandra Alter, "How a Debut Graphic Memoir Became the Most Banned Book in the Country," *New York Times*, May 1, 2022, updated June 22, 2023, https:// www.nytimes.com/2022/05/01/books/maia-kobabe-gender-queer-book-ban. html.

21. Jonathan Evison, *Lawn Boy* (Chapel Hill, North Carolina: Algonquin Books, 2019); Lewis Pennock, "Author of LGBT Book 'Lawn Boy' Which Describes Two 10-Year-Old Boys Giving Each Other Oral Sex Admits Graphic Story Was NEVER Meant for School Libraries—as Livid Parents Force Woke Teachers to Pull It from Shelves in US," *Daily Mail*, January 5,

2023, https://www.dailymail.co.uk/news/article-11604233/Author-banned
-book-describes-sex-act-children-says-never-meant-children.html.

22. Erika Moen and Matthew Nolan, *Let's Talk about It: The Teen's Guide to Sex, Relationships, and Being a Human* (New York: Random House Graphic, 2021); Iain Woessner, "Library, Leaders, Unaware of Explicit Book in Young Adult Section," *Valley City Times Record*, September 14, 2022, https://www.times-online.com/news/library-leaders-unaware-of-explicit
-book-in-young-adult-section/article_56373c58-339d-11ed-b175-1f553688d9
b1.html; "Broward County Public Schools Improperly Removes Sex Ed Book during Review Process," National Coalition against Censorship, February 24, 2023, https://ncac.org/letters/broward-county-public-schools
-improperly-removes-sex-ed-book-during-review-process.

23. Howard Zinn, *A People's History of the United States* (New York: Harper Perennial Modern Classics, 2015).

24. James Axtell, "Who Invented Scalping?," *American Heritage* 28, no. 3 (April 1977), https://www.americanheritage.com/who-invented-scalping.

25. Jessica Chasmar, "Loudoun County Father Arrested at School Board Event Says School Tried to Cover Up Daughter's Bathroom Assault," Fox News, October 12, 2021, https://www.foxnews.com/politics/loudoun-county-father
-school-cover-up-bathroom-assault-daughter.

26. Tyler O'Neil, "Loudoun County Public Schools Removes Book for 'Sexual Content' While Fairfax Insists It's Not Obscene," Fox News, January 16, 2022, https://www.foxnews.com/politics/loudoun-county-public-schools
-removes-book-for-sexual-content-while-fairfax-defends-it.

Chapter Three: The Newsroom Revolution

1. "Nidal Malik Hasan" (aggregation of articles), *New York Times*, November 5, 2009–December 6, 2019, https://www.nytimes.com/topic/person/nidal
-malik-hasan.

2. Manny Fernandez and Alan Blinder, "At Fort Hood, Wrestling with Label of Terrorism," *New York Times*, April 8, 2014, https://www.nytimes.com
/2014/04/09/us/at-fort-hood-wrestling-with-label-of-terrorism.html.

3. Robert Spencer, "Obama Administration Refuses to Tell Congress Why It Purged References to 'Islamic Terrorism' from Public Documents," Jihad Watch, June 29, 2016, https://www.jihadwatch.org/2016/06/obama
-administration-refuses-to-tell-congress-why-it-purged-references-to-islamic
-terrorism-from-public-documents.

4. Michelle Ye Hee Lee, "The Bogus Claim That a Map of Crosshairs by Sarah Palin's PAC Incited Rep. Gabby Giffords's Shooting," *Washington Post*, June 15, 2017, https://www.washingtonpost.com/news/fact-checker/wp/2017/06/15/the-bogus-claim-that-a-map-of-crosshairs-by-sarah-palins-pac-incited-rep-gabby-giffordss-shooting/; Patrick Reilly, "NYT Editors Ignored Fact Checkers before Publishing Editorial Linking Palin to Shooting: Emails," *New York Post*, February 4, 2022, https://nypost.com/2022/02/04/nyt-editors-ignored-fact-checkers-before-publishing-editorial-linking-palin-to-shooting/.

5. "Occupy Movement (Occupy Wall Street)" (aggregation of articles), *New York Times*, October 16, 2011–June 13, 2023, https://www.nytimes.com/topic/organization/occupy-movement-occupy-wall-street.

6. "The New York Times WMD Coverage," PBS, May 26, 2004, https://www.pbs.org/newshour/show/the-new-york-times-wmd-coverage; Katharine Q. Seelye, "Times Reporter Agrees to Leave the Paper," *New York Times*, November 10, 2005, https://www.nytimes.com/2005/11/10/business/media/times-reporter-agrees-to-leave-the-paper.html.

7. "If Trump Were President: Boston Globe's Fake Front Page Dares to Imagine," *The Guardian*, April 9, 2016, https://www.theguardian.com/us-news/2016/apr/10/trump-president-boston-globe-predicts-news-fake-front-page.

8. "Trump and the Russians," *New York Times*, https://www.nytimes.com/spotlight/trump-russia. I exaggerate (but only a little bit) for effect; no one was literally predicting Siberian exile.

9. "The Absurd 'Russiagate' Pulitzer of the NY Times and Washington Post," *New York Post*, February 20, 2022, https://nypost.com/2022/02/20/the-absurd-russiagate-pulitzer-of-the-ny-times-and-washington-post/.

10. Ashley Feinberg, "The New York Times Unites vs. Twitter," Slate, August 15, 2019, https://slate.com/news-and-politics/2019/08/new-york-times-meeting-transcript.html.

11. Ibid.

12. Quoted in Martin Baron, "Opinion: We Want Objective Judges and Doctors. Why Not Journalists Too?," *Washington Post*, March 24, 2023, https://www.washingtonpost.com/opinions/2023/03/24/journalism-objectivity-trump-misinformation-marty-baron/.

13. Bob Woodward and Carl Bernstein, "GOP Security Aide among Five Arrested in Bugging Affair," *Washington Post*, June 19, 1972, https://www.washingtonpost.com/wp-srv/national/longterm/watergate/articles/061972

-1.htm; Bob Woodward and Carl Bernstein, "FBI Finds Nixon Aides Sabotaged Democrats," *Washington Post*, October 10, 1972, https://www.washingtonpost.com/wp-srv/national/longterm/watergate/articles/101072-1.htm, and the like.

14. Benjamin Mullin, "Read Carl Bernstein and Bob Woodward's Remarks to the White House Correspondents' Dinner," Poynter., April 30, 2017, https://www.poynter.org/reporting-editing/2017/read-carl-bernstein-and-bob-woodwards-remarks-to-the-white-house-correspondents-association/.

15. Jeff Gerth, "The Press versus the President, Part One," *Columbia Journalism Review*, January 30, 2023, https://www.cjr.org/special_report/trumped-up-press-versus-president-part-1.php.

16. Feinberg, "The New York Times Unites."

17. Ibid.

18. Paul Farhi and Sarah Ellison, "Ignited by Public Protests, American Newsrooms Are Having Their Own Racial Reckoning," *Washington Post*, June 13, 2020, https://www.washingtonpost.com/lifestyle/media/ignited-by-public-protests-american-newsrooms-are-having-their-own-racial-reckoning/2020/06/12/be622bce-a995-11ea-94d2-d7bc43b26bf9_story.html; Sam Sanders et al., "Reckoning with Race in Journalism," NPR, July 14, 2020, https://www.npr.org/2020/07/10/889773113/reckoning-with-race-in-journalism; Alison MacAdam, "Six Ways to Run a Listening Session," NPR, February 16, 2016, https://training.npr.org/2016/02/16/six-ways-to-run-a-listening-session/; Hanaa' Tameez, "American Journalism's 'Racial Reckoning' Still Has Lots of Reckoning to Do," Nieman Lab, March 8, 2022, https://www.niemanlab.org/2022/03/american-journalisms-racial-reckoning-still-has-lots-of-reckoning-to-do/.

19. Charles Kesler, "Call Them the 1619 Riots," *New York Post*, June 19, 2020, https://nypost.com/2020/06/19/call-them-the-1619-riots/.

20. Virginia Allen, "New York Times Mum on '1619 Project' Creator Calling '1619 Riots' Moniker an 'Honor,'" The Daily Signal, June 22, 2020, https://www.dailysignal.com/2020/06/22/new-york-times-mum-on-1619-project-creator-calling-1619-riots-moniker-an-honor/.

21. Tom Cotton, "Tom Cotton: Send in the Troops," *New York Times*, June 3, 2020, https://www.nytimes.com/2020/06/03/opinion/tom-cotton-protests-military.html.

22. Marc Tracy, "James Bennet Resigns as New York Times Opinion Editor," *New York Times*, June 7, 2020, https://www.nytimes.com/2020/06/07/business/media/james-bennet-resigns-nytimes-op-ed.html.

23. Ibid.; Scott Neuman, "Head of 'New York Times' Editorial Page Steps Down amid Controversy," NPR, June 8, 2020, https://www.npr.org/2020/06/08 /871817721/head-of-new-york-times-editorial-page-steps-down-amid -controversy.

24. Shadi Hamid, "Bari Weiss and the Left-Wing Infatuation with Taking Offense," *The Atlantic*, February 17, 2018, https://www.theatlantic.com/ politics/archive/2018/02/bari-weiss-immigrants/553550/.

25. Bari Weiss, "Resignation Letter," https://www.bariweiss.com/resignation -letter.

26. Gay Talese, *The Kingdom and the Power* (Cleveland, Ohio; New York: World Publishing Company, 1969), 72.

27. Megan Brenan, "Americans' Trust in Media Remains Near Record Low," Gallup, October 18, 2022, https://news.gallup.com/poll/403166/americans- trust-media-remains-near-record-low.aspx..

28. Ari Blaff, "Matt Taibbi, Douglas Murray Dominate Trust-in-Media Debate," *National Review*, December 1, 2022, https://www.nationalreview.com/news /matt-taibbi-douglas-murray-dominate-trust-in-media-debate/; Truthspeak, "Munk Debate: Mainstream Media ft. Douglas Murray, Matt Taibbi, Malcolm Gladwell, Michelle Goldberg," YouTube, December 8, 2022, https://www.youtube.com/watch?v=nvaf7XOOFHc.

29. Leonard Downie Jr., "Opinion: Newsrooms That Move beyond 'Objectivity' Can Build Trust," *Washington Post*, January 30, 2023, https://www .washingtonpost.com/opinions/2023/01/30/newsrooms-news-reporting -objectivity-diversity/.

30. Ibid.

31. Jonathan V. Last, "What Blogs Have Wrought," *Weekly Standard*, September 27, 2004, https://www.washingtonexaminer.com/weekly-standard/what -blogs-have-wrought.

32. Salena Zito, "How 'Let's Go Brandon' Became a Swipe at Joe Biden—and National Media," *New York Post*, November 2, 2021, https://nypost.com /2021/11/02/how-lets-go-brandon-became-a-swipe-at-joe-biden-and -national-media/.

Chapter Four: Big Tech

1. Wayne Duggan, "8 Top Nancy Pelosi Stocks to Buy," U.S. News & World Report, July 11, 2023, https://money.usnews.com/investing/slideshows/top -nancy-pelosi-stocks-to-buy.

2. Leandra Bernstein, "Connections to Jeffrey Epstein Threaten Prominent Politicians," ABC7 News, July 9, 2019, https://wjla.com/news/nation-world/connections-to-jeffrey-epstein-threaten-prominent-politicians; Soo Rin Kim, "Jeffrey Epstein Donated to Several Democrats throughout 1990s and Early 2000s," ABC News, July 12, 2019, https://abcnews.go.com/Politics/jeffrey-epstein-donated-democrats-1990s-early-2000s/story?id=64255485; Brian Schwartz, "Democratic Fundraising Committees Decline to Say Whether They Will Donate or Give Back Jeffrey Epstein Contributions," CNBC, July 24, 2019, https://www.cnbc.com/2019/07/24/democratic-groups-will-not-commit-to-returning-donating-epstein-funds.html.

3. For evidence that the social media users' experiences described here are not anomalous, see Tyler O'Neil, "Google Tries to Discredit Study Showing Google News' Left-Wing Bias," The Daily Signal, March 2, 2023, https://www.dailysignal.com/2023/03/02/lean-left-most-google-news-results-skewed-one-direction-2022-election-study-claims/; Bari Weiss (@bariweiss), "THREAD: THE TWITTER FILES PART TWO. TWITTER'S SECRET BLACKLISTS . . ." (thread), Twitter, December 8, 2022, 7:15 p.m., https://twitter.com/bariweiss/status/1601007575633305600; Marco Rubio, "Rubio Demands Answers after YouTube Censors Conservative Content" (press release), Marco Rubio Senate website, August 17, 2021, https://www.rubio.senate.gov/public/index.cfm/2021/8/rubio-demands-answers-after-youtube-censors-conservative-content; Ashley Gold, "YouTube Temporarily Suspends, Demonetizes OANN," Axios, November 24, 2020, https://www.axios.com/2020/11/24/youtube-temporarily-suspends-demonetizes-oann; Ben Shapiro, "Viewpoint Discrimination with Algorithms," *National Review*, March 7, 2018, https://www.nationalreview.com/2018/03/social-media-companies-discriminate-against-conservatives/.

4. Jason Zengerle, "Ted Cruz: The Distinguished Wacko Bird from Texas," *GQ*, September 22, 2013, https://www.gq.com/story/ted-cruz-republican-senator-october-2013.

5. Angie Drobnic Holan, "Lie of the Year: 'If You Like Your Health Care Plan, You Can Keep It,'" PolitiFact, December 12, 2013, https://www.politifact.com/article/2013/dec/12/lie-year-if-you-like-your-health-care-plan-keep-it/.

6. Josh Halliday, "Twitter's Tony Wang: 'We Are the Free Speech Wing of the Free Speech Party,'" *The Guardian*, March 22, 2012, https://www.theguardian.com/media/2012/mar/22/twitter-tony-wang-free-speech.

7. Vijaya Gadde and Kayvon Beykpour, "Setting the Record Straight on Shadow Banning," Twitter (blog), July 26, 2018, https://blog.twitter.com/en_us/topics/company/2018/Setting-the-record-straight-on-shadow-banning.

8. "Sen. Cruz: Big Tech Censorship Is Marked in Darkness and Obscurity," Ted Cruz Senate website (press release), February 28, 2019, https://www.cruz.senate.gov/newsroom/press-releases/sen-cruz-big-tech-censorship-is-marked-in-darkness-and-obscurity.

9. Gadde and Beykpour, "Setting the Record Straight."

10. That growing realization would be confirmed when Elon Musk bought Twitter and released the Twitter Files in 2022. See Weiss, "THREAD: THE TWITTER FILES PART TWO."

11. Yoel Roth (@yoyoel), "Yes, that person in the pink hat . . . ," Twitter, January 22, 2017, 6:33 p.m., https://twitter.com/yoyoel/status/823312771416588288?lang=en.

12. Jessica Chasmar, "Yoel Roth's 'Gay Data' Dissertation 'Mistakenly' Blocked from UPenn Website after Elon Musk's Tweet," Fox News, December 12, 2022, https://www.foxnews.com/politics/yoel-roths-gay-data-dissertation-mistakenly-blocked-upenn-website-elon-musks-tweet.

13. Olivia Land, "Twitter Employees Donated Almost Exclusively to Democrats during Midterms," *New York Post*, December 16, 2022, https://nypost.com/2022/12/16/twitter-employees-donated-almost-exclusively-to-democrats-in-2022/.

14. See for example, Andrew Stolzle, "In Defense of Big Tech," Andrew Stolzle, January 10, 2021 (updated March 13, 2023), https://www.stolzle.me/posts/big-tech.

15. Phil Kerpen (@kerpen), "Not the usual catchall . . . ," Twitter, June 2, 2021, 12:03 a.m., https://twitter.com/kerpen/status/1399939689025609732?s=20; C. Douglas Golden, "After Fauci Email Proves Link with Zuckerberg, House Republicans Hit Facebook with One Demand That Could Change Everything," Western Journal, June 10, 2021, https://www.westernjournal.com/fauci-email-proves-link-zuckerberg-house-republicans-hit-facebook-one-demand-change-everything/.

16. "The Cost of Coronavirus," *Verdict with Ted Cruz*, March 2020, https://open.spotify.com/episode/3TFaLhNEGyyonF7xpPYoK5; "An Expert's Perspective on the Pandemic," *Verdict with Ted Cruz*, March 2020, https://open.spotify.com/episode/187mMlNxwZQ1tuTmiH5Nxo; "The Wuhan Coverup," *Verdict with Ted Cruz*, April 2020, https://open.spotify.com/episode/7hW4QMh80e3vhp9O4WEfUH; "China Must Pay," *Verdict with*

Ted Cruz, April 2020, https://open.spotify.com/episode/on4ksmJc62z Qy4FZgDrp29.

17. Kelly Laco, "These Biden Administration Agencies Have Admitted COVID Lab Leak Is Plausible," Fox News, March 4, 2023, https://www.foxnews .com/politics/these-biden-admin-agencies-have-admitted-covid-lab-leak -plausible.

18. Newley Purnell, "Facebook Ends Ban on Posts Asserting Covid-19 Was Man-Made," *Wall Street Journal*, May 27, 2021, https://www.wsj.com/ articles/facebook-ends-ban-on-posts-asserting-covid-19-was-man-made -11622094890.

19. Jacob Sullum, "Under Government Pressure, Twitter Suppressed Truthful Speech about COVID-19," *Reason*, January 2, 2023, https://reason.com /2023/01/02/under-government-pressure-twitter-suppressed-truthful-speech -about-covid-19/.

20. Charlie Kirk (@charliekirk11), "In 2018, I met with Jack Dorsey . . ." (thread), Twitter, December 8, 2022, 9:04 p.m., https://twitter.com/charliekirk11/sta tus/1601035080280915970?lang=en.

21. Bari Weiss (@bariweiss), "4. Or consider the popular right-wing talk show host . . . ," Twitter, December 8, 2022, 7:33 p.m., https://twitter.com/ bariweiss/status/1601012181138407425.

22. "Evidence Shows FBI, Biden Campaign and Twitter Worked Together to Suppress Hunter Story," *New York Post*, December 19, 2022, https://nypost .com/2022/12/19/fbi-biden-campaign-twitter-worked-together-to-suppress -hunter-story/.

23. See Nick Bilton, "In the Coronavirus Era, the Force Is Still with Jack Dorsey," *Vanity Fair*, April 20, 2020, https://www.vanityfair.com/news/2020/04/in -the-coronavirus-era-the-force-is-still-with-jack-dorsey; Isobel Asher Hamilton, Katie Canales, and Bethany Biron, "The Wild Life of Billionaire Twitter Co-Founder Jack Dorsey, Who Has Apologized for Elon Musk's Layoffs and Is Known for Eccentricities like Eating One Meal a Day, and Taking Ice Baths," Business Insider, November 5, 2022, https://www .businessinsider.com/fabulous-life-of-billionaire-jack-dorsey-taking-square -public.

24. Caroline Downey, "'Biden Team' Requested Twitter Scrub Scandalous Hunter Biden Info Days before 2020 Election," *National Review*, December 2, 2022, https://www.nationalreview.com/news/biden-campaign-requested -twitter-scrub-scandalous-hunter-biden-content-days-before-2020-election/.

25. Mark Moore, "Google, Facebook Should Be Investigated after Twitter Files on Hunter Biden Story: Rep. McCarthy," *New York Post*, December 4, 2022, https://nypost.com/2022/12/04/mccarthy-says-google-facebook-should-be -investigated/; Steve Daines, "Big Tech's Harmful Censorship of Republican Candidates," *The Hill*, May 18, 2022, https://thehill.com/blogs/congress-blog /3493394-big-techs-harmful-censorship-of-republican-candidates/; O'Neil, "Google Tries to Discredit Study."

26. Allum Bokhari, #*DELETED: Big Tech's Battle to Erase the Trump Movement and Steal the Election* (New York: Center Street, 2020), 9.

27. Ibid., 17.

28. Sheera Frenkel, "Renegade Facebook Employees Form Task Force to Battle Fake News," BuzzFeed, November 14, 2016, https://www.buzzfeednews .com/article/sheerafrenkel/renegade-facebook-employees-form-task-force-to -battle-fake-n.

29. Bokhari, #*DELETED*, 21.

30. "Twitter can not [*sic*] violate anyone's free speech or First Amendment rights. Nobody has a right to tweet whatever they desire without repercussion. Twitter owns the platform and has the right to enforce their contractual agreements with its users.... **Mark Zuckerberg doesn't care what your political views are.** He and Facebook, along with every other major social media platform want the same thing: user engagement. Like all major corporations, the end goal of social media platforms is profit so that its employees and shareholders can eat and pay their bills. . . . Individuals like Hawley argue that tech companies are secretly meeting and sharing information so that they can simultaneously shadow ban or censor posts made by Republicans. He is not the only one claiming such malfeasance.... Users enter into an agreement with Twitter. If Twitter determines that a post violates the agreement, they can hide it or surround the tweet with a warning label" [emphasis in the original]. Stolzle, "In Defense of Big Tech."

31. Renée DiResta, "Free Speech Is Not the Same as Free Reach," *Wired*, August 30, 2018, https://www.wired.com/story/free-speech-is-not-the-same-as-free -reach/.

32. Bari Weiss (@bariweiss), "THREAD: THE TWITTER FILES PART TWO...," Twitter, December 8, 2022, 7:15 p.m., https://twitter.com/ bariweiss/status/1601007575633305600?lang=en.

33. See for example, "COVID-19 Vaccine Skeptic Alex Berenson Was 'Permanently' Banned from Twitter, Until Twitter Reinstated Him," Business Insider, July 18, 2022, https://www.insider.com/alex-berenson-twitter-covid

-vaccine-posts-2021-8; Joseph De Avila, "The People Permanently Banned from Twitter: See the List," *Wall Street Journal*, updated November 3, 2022, https://www.wsj.com/story/the-people-permanently-banned-from-twitter-52b85992. See also "Hateful Conduct," Twitter, April 2023, https://help.twitter.com/en/rules-and-policies/hateful-conduct-policy; "How We Address Misinformation on Twitter," Twitter, https://help.twitter.com/en/resources/addressing-misleading-info.

34. Weiss, "THREAD: THE TWITTER FILES PART TWO"; Gadde and Beykpour, "Setting the Record Straight."

35. Aja Romano, "The 'Controversy' over Journalist Sarah Jeong Joining the New York Times, Explained," Vox, updated August 3, 2018, https://www.vox.com/2018/8/3/17644704/sarah-jeong-new-york-times-tweets-backlash-racism.

36. Zack Beauchamp, "In Defense of Sarah Jeong," Vox, August 3, 2018, https://www.vox.com/policy-and-politics/2018/8/3/17648566/sarah-jeong-new-york-times-twitter-andrew-sullivan.

37. Ibid.

38. "Sarah Jeong," Popular Net Worth, July 9, 2023, https://popularnetworth.com/sarah-jeong/ ("Throughout her writing career, the American content writer has amassed a sizable fortune. Sarah currently has a net worth of *$500k*."[emphasis in the original]); "Fairfax Schools Defending $20K Presentation from Anti-Racism Scholar," Fox5 Washington DC, September 25, 2020, https://www.fox5dc.com/news/fairfax-county-schools-defending-20k-presentation-from-anti-racism-scholar ("The $20,000 price tag means the district paid Kendi more than $300 a minute"); Gabe Kaminsky, "Exclusive: Ibram X. Kendi Raked in $45K from University of Wisconsin, Made School Delete Lecture," The Federalist, December 9, 2021, https://thefederalist.com/2021/12/09/exclusive-ibram-x-kendi-raked-in-45k-from-university-of-wisconsin-made-school-delete-lecture/; Christopher Eberhart, "Anti-Racist Author DOUBLES Speaking Fees as America Goes Woke: 'White Fragility' Writer Robin DiAngelo Charges an Average of $14,000 per Speech and Makes '$728K a Year,'" *Daily Mail*, July 2, 2021, https://www.dailymail.co.uk/news/article-9749517/An-anti-racist-author-Robin-DiAngelo-makes-728K-year-speaking-engagements.html.

39. Kelefa Sanneh, "The Fight to Redefine Racism," *New Yorker*, August 12, 2019, https://www.newyorker.com/magazine/2019/08/19/the-fight-to-redefine-racism.

40. Brian Flood, "These Five People Are Allowed to Tweet but One of America's Oldest Newspapers Can't," Fox News, October 21, 2020, https://www .foxnews.com/media/twitter-allows-farrakhan-spencer-dictators-new-york -post-censored.

41. Joe Tacopino, "Iran's Supreme Leader Screams, 'Death to America' amid Ongoing Nuclear Talks," *New York Post*, March 23, 2015, https://nypost .com/2015/03/23/irans-supreme-leader-screams-death-to-america-amid -ongoing-nuclear-talks/; Jesse O'Neil, "Salman Rushdie Breaks Silence after Attack: I Have PTSD, Nightmares," *New York Post*, February 6, 2023, https://nypost.com/2023/02/06/salman-rushdie-breaks-silence-after-attack -i-have-ptsd-nightmares/.

42. See Zabihullah (@Zabehulah_M33), "Official Twitter Account of the Spokesman of Islamic Emirate of Afghanistan . . . ," Twitter, https://twitter .com/Zabehulah_M33; Wedaeli Chibelushi, "The Taliban Has over 800K Twitter Followers—Could They Get a Blue Tick Soon?," Independent Television News (ITV), September 5, 2021, https://www.itv.com/news/2021 -09-04/the-taliban-has-over-800k-twitter-followers-could-they-get-a-blue -tick-soon.

43. "Twitter Will No Longer Enforce Its COVID Misinformation Policy," NPR, November 9, 2022, https://www.npr.org/2022/11/29/1139822833/twitter -covid-misinformation-policy-not-enforced; "Twitter Flagged Donald Trump's Tweets with Election Misinformation: They Continued to Spread Both on and off the Platform," Misinformation Review, August 24, 2021, https://misinforeview.hks.harvard.edu/article/twitter-flagged-donald-trumps -tweets-with-election-misinformation-they-continued-to-spread-both-on-and -off-the-platform/; Clare Duffy, "Twitter Removes Transgender Protections from Hateful Conduct Policy," CNN, April 19, 2023, https://www.cnn.com /2023/04/19/tech/twitter-hateful-conduct-policy-transgender-protections/ index.html.

44. Matt Taibbi (@mtaibbi), "1. Thread: THE TWITTER FILES" (thread), Twitter, December 2, 2022, 6:34 p.m., https://twitter.com/mtaibbi/status /1598822959866683394.

45. Emma-Jo Morris and Gabrielle Fonrouge, "Smoking-Gun Email Reveals How Hunter Biden Introduced Ukrainian Businessman to VP Dad," *New York Post*, October 14, 2020, https://nypost.com/2020/10/14/email-reveals -how-hunter-biden-introduced-ukrainian-biz-man-to-dad/.

46. Taibbi, "1. Thread: THE TWITTER FILES."

47. Ibid.

48. Ari Drennen, "YouTube Strips Ad Revenue from The Matt Walsh Show after Repeated Vitriol against Dylan Mulvaney," Media Matters, April 20, 2023, https://www.mediamatters.org/matt-walsh/youtube-strips-ad-revenue-matt-walsh-show-after-repeated-vitriol-against-dylan-mulvaney.

49. Yaqiu Wang, "The Problem with TikTok's Claim of Independence from Beijing," Human Rights Watch, March 24, 2023, https://www.hrw.org/news/2023/03/24/problem-tiktoks-claim-independence-beijing; Sapna Maheshwari, "Young TikTok Users Quickly Encounter Problematic Posts, Researchers Say," *New York Times*, December 14, 2022, https://www.nytimes.com/2022/12/14/business/tiktok-safety-teens-eating-disorders-self-harm.html.

50. "17 Transgender Influencers to Follow," Izea, March 29, 2023, https://izea.com/resources/trans-influencers/; "13 Trans Influencers & Activists That Inspire Us," Teen Line, December 12, 2028; https://teenlineonline.org/13-trans-influencers-activists-that-inspire-us/.

51. Abigail Shrier, "How Influencers Lure Kids into Transgender Lifestyle, Coach Them to Lie to Doctors," The Daily Caller, June 14, 2022, https://dailycaller.com/2022/06/14/influencers-lure-kids-transgender-lifestyle-youtube-social-media/.

Chapter Five: Mr. Marx Goes to Washington

1. Mariah Espada, "President Biden, His Corvette, and the Latest Stash of Classified Documents," *Time*, January 12, 2023, https://time.com/6246994/biden-classified-documents-delaware-corvette/.

2. "Former U.S. National Security Adviser Sandy Berger Dies," Reuters, December 2, 2015, https://www.reuters.com/article/us-people-sandyberger-obituary/former-u-s-national-security-adviser-sandy-berger-dies-idUSKBN0TL1OL20151203.

3. Gigi Sohn (@gigibsohn), "For all my concerns about #Facebook, I believe…," Twitter, October 28, 2020, 10:18 a.m., https://twitter.com/gigibsohn/status/1321456221740847106?lang=en.

4. Gigi Sohn (@gigibsohn), "I agree that scrutiny of big tech is essential…," Twitter, September 4, 2019, 12:53 p.m., https://twitter.com/gigibsohn/status/1169292338277093377.

5. Sean Moran, "Biden's Controversial FCC Nominee Gigi Sohn to Face Scrutiny over Calls for Censorship, Leftist Advocacy," Breitbart, January 30, 2023, https://www.breitbart.com/politics/2023/01/30/biden-fcc-nominees

-controversial-nominee-gigi-sohn-to-face-scrutiny-over-calls-for-censorship -leftist-advocacy/.

6. "Federal Communications Commission Commissioner Confirmation Hearing," C-SPAN, February 14, 2023, https://www.c-span.org/video/?525970-1/federal-communications-commission-commissioner-confirmation-hearing.

7. "Stand with Ted Cruz," tedcruzhatesfreespeech.com.

8. Todd Shields and Zach C. Cohen, "FCC Nominee Gigi Sohn Withdraws, Citing Opposition from 'Dark Money' Groups," Bloomberg, March 7, 2023, https://www.bloomberg.com/news/articles/2023-03-07/biden-fcc-nominee -takes-blow-as-senator-manchin-opposes-her#xj4y7vzkg.

9. Joseph Rhee, Gerry Wagschal, and Jinsol Jung, "How Boeing 737 Max's Flawed Flight Control System Led to 2 Crashes That Killed 346," ABC News, November 27, 2020, https://abcnews.go.com/US/boeing-737-maxs-flawed -flight-control-system-led/story?id=74321424.

10. "Confirmation Hearing for FAA Administrator Nominee," C-SPAN, March 1, 2023, https://www.c-span.org/video/?526360-1/confirmation-hearing-faa -administrator-nominee.

11. Kerry Lynch, "Phil Washington Withdraws from FAA Administrator Consideration," AINonline, March 26, 2023, https://www.ainonline.com/ aviation-news/air-transport/2023-03-26/phil-washington-withdraws-faa -administrator-consideration.

12. "Ann E. Carlson," UCLA Law, https://law.ucla.edu/faculty/faculty-profiles/ ann-e-carlson; "Beyond the Courtroom: Climate Tort Litigation in the United States," Manufacturers' Accountability Project, https://mfgaccountability project.org/wp-content/uploads/2021/12/MAP-Beyond-the- Courtroom-122821-1.pdf, 12.

13. "Ann Carlson to Serve as Chief Counsel of the National Highway Traffic Safety Administration," UCLA Newsroom, January 25, 2021, https:// newsroom.ucla.edu/dept/faculty/ann-carlson-chief-counsel-national-highway -traffic-safety-administration.

14. Peter Aitken, "Biden Comptroller Pick Saule Omarova Refuses to Turn Over Moscow State University Thesis on Marxism," Fox Business, October 16, 2021, https://www.foxbusiness.com/politics/biden-comptroller-omarova -moscow-state-university-thesis-marxism.

15. Bradford Betz, "Biden's Pick to Regulate National Banks Received 'Lenin' Award, Praised USSR for Gender Equality," Fox News, September 29, 2021, https://www.foxnews.com/politics/bidens-pick-regulate-national-banks-lenin -award-praised-ussr-gender-equality.

16. Tyler Olson, "Biden Treasury Nominee Omarova Was Member of Marxist Facebook Group as Recently as 2019, Post Indicates," Fox News, October 23, 2021, https://www.foxbusiness.com/politics/saule-omarova-comptroller-currency-marxist-facebook.

17. "Marxist Analysis and Policy" Facebook, https://www.facebook.com/groups/348333265593636/.

18. "User Clip: Sen Kennedy Omarova," C-SPAN, November 18, 2021, https://www.c-span.org/video/?c4987304/user-clip-sen-kennedy-omarova.

19. Joseph R. Biden Jr., "Executive Order on Advancing Racial Equity and Support for Underserved Communities through the Federal Government," White House, January 20, 2021, https://www.whitehouse.gov/briefing-room/presidential-actions/2021/01/20/executive-order-advancing-racial-equity-and-support-for-underserved-communities-through-the-federal-government/.

20. Ibid.

21. "Equity vs. Equality: What's the Difference?," Milken Institute School of Public Health, George Washington University, November 5, 2020, https://onlinepublichealth.gwu.edu/resources/equity-vs-equality/.

22. Ben Wilterdink, "Racial Disparities and the High Cost of Low Debates," Independent Institute, May 8, 2018, https://www.independent.org/news/article.asp?id=10489.

23. National Review, "Bernie Sanders Can't Explain Difference between Equality and Equity," YouTube, March 6, 2023, https://www.youtube.com/watch?v=bgt8PlKTVNQ.

24. Chris Riotta, "Pete Buttigieg Says There Is 'Racism Physically Built into' America's Ailing Infrastructure System," *The Independent*, April 8, 2021, https://www.independent.co.uk/news/world/americas/us-politics/pete-buttigieg-racism-america-infrastructure-b1828621.html.

25. Vincent J. Cannato, "Buttigieg's 'Systemic Racism' Claim Is the Leftist Myth about Robert Moses," *New York Post*, November 14, 2021, https://nypost.com/2021/11/14/buttigiegs-systemic-racism-claim-is-the-the-leftist-myth-about-robert-moses/.

26. Vincent J. Cannato, "A Bridge Too Far," *City Journal*, November 12, 2021, https://www.city-journal.org/article/a-bridge-too-far-2.

27. Glenn Kessler (@GlennKesslerWP), "This is detailed at length in Robert Caro's…," Twitter, November 8, 2021, 3:36 p.m., https://twitter.com/GlennKesslerWP/status/1457809268971868162.

28. Glenn Kessler, "Robert Moses and the Saga of the Racist Parkway Bridges," *Washington Post*, November 10, 2021, https://www.washingtonpost.com/politics/2021/11/10/robert-moses-saga-racist-parkway-bridges/.

29. Char Adams, "Black People Are More Likely to Die in Traffic Accidents. Covid Made It Worse.," NBC News, June 22, 2021, https://www.nbcnews.com/news/nbcblk/black-people-are-more-likely-die-traffic-accidents-covid-made-n1271716.

30. Rachel Crowell, "Modern Mathematics Confronts Its White, Patriarchal Past," *Scientific American*, August 12, 2021, https://www.scientificamerican.com/article/modern-mathematics-confronts-its-white-patriarchal-past/.

31. Lornett Vestal, "The Unbearable Whiteness of Hiking and How to Solve It," Sierra Club, December 7, 2016, https://www.sierraclub.org/outdoors/2016/12/unbearable-whiteness-hiking-and-how-solve-it.

32. Sasha Mistlin, "'I've Never Experienced Such Abject Racism': What It's Really Like to Work in TV as a Person of Colour," *The Guardian*, December 2, 2021, https://www.theguardian.com/tv-and-radio/2021/dec/02/ive-never-experienced-such-abject-racism-what-its-really-like-to-work-in-tv-as-a-person-of-colour.

33. Ashish Ghadiali, "Nice Racism by Robin DiAngelo Review—Appearances Can Be Deceptive," review of *Nice Racism: How Progressive White People Perpetuate Racial Harm*, by Robin DiAngelo, *The Guardian*, July 11, 2021, https://www.theguardian.com/books/2021/jul/11/nice-racism-by-robin-diangelo-review-appearances-can-be-deceptive.

34. Nathaniel G. Chapman and David L. Brunsma, *Beer and Racism: How Beer Became White, Why It Matters, and the Movements to Change It* (Bristol, England: Bristol University Press, 2020).

35. Jeffrey W. Bethel, Sloane C. Burke, and Amber F. Britt, "Disparity in Disaster Preparedness between Racial/Ethnic Groups," *Disaster Health* 1, no. 2, (November 8, 2013): 110–16, https://www.ncbi.nlm.nih.gov/pmc/articles/PMC5314923/.

36. Tasos Kokkinidis, "Princeton Removes Greek, Latin for Classics Majors to Combat Racism," Greek Reporter, May 31, 2021, https://greekreporter.com/2021/05/31/princeton-removes-greek-latin-for-classics-majors-to-combat-racism/.

37. Alex Ross, "Black Scholars Confront White Supremacy in Classical Music," *New Yorker*, September 14, 2020, https://www.newyorker.com/magazine/2020/09/21/black-scholars-confront-white-supremacy-in-classical-music.

38. Brad Plumer and Nadja Popovich, "How Decades of Racist Housing Policy Left Neighborhoods Sweltering," *New York Times*, August 24, 2020, https://www.nytimes.com/interactive/2020/08/24/climate/racism-redlining-cities-global-warming.html.

39. Associated Press, "Pete Buttigieg Launches $1B Pilot to Build Racial Equity in America's Roads," NPR, June 30, 2022, https://www.npr.org/2022/06/30/1108852884/pete-buttigieg-launches-1b-pilot-to-build-racial-equity-in-americas-roads.

40. Azeen Ghorayshi, "Report Reveals Sharp Rise in Transgender Young People in the U.S.," *New York Times*, June 10, 2022, https://www.nytimes.com/2022/06/10/science/transgender-teenagers-national-survey.html.

41. See for example, "New HHS Report Released on Transgender Day of Visibility Offers Updated, Evidence-Based Roadmap for Supporting and Affirming LGBTQI+ Youth," U.S. Department of Health and Human Services, March 31, 2023, https://www.hhs.gov/about/news/2023/03/31/new-hhs-report-released-transgender-day-visibility-offers-updated-evidence-based-roadmap-supporting-affirming-lgbtqi-youth.html; "HHS Notice and Guidance on Gender Affirming Care, Civil Rights, and Patient Privacy," U.S. Department of Health and Human Services, March 2, 2022, https://www.hhs.gov/sites/default/files/hhs-ocr-notice-and-guidance-gender-affirming-care.pdf; Brad Brooks, "Judge Blocks Biden Administration's Directives on Transgender Athletes, Bathrooms," Reuters, July 18, 2022, https://www.reuters.com/world/us/judge-blocks-biden-admin-directives-transgender-athletes-bathrooms-2022-07-16/.

42. Sade Strehlke, "See How a Gender Reassignment Surgery Actually Works," *Teen Vogue*, December 9, 2015, https://www.teenvogue.com/story/male-female-gender-reassignment-surgery.

43. Abigail Shrier, *Irreversible Damage* (Washington, D.C.: Regnery Publishing, 2020), 6.

44. Jon Brooks, "The Controversial Research on 'Desistance' in Transgender Youth," KQED, May 23, 2018, https://www.kqed.org/futureofyou/441784/the-controversial-research-on-desistance-in-transgender-youth.

45. See, for example, Dora TheExorcista, "Being trans is the worst thing that's ever happened to me. What should I do?," Reddit, 2018, https://www.reddit.com/r/ask_transgender/comments/a2uogr/being_trans_is_the_worst_thing_thats_ever/.

46. Ashley Austin, Shelley L. Craig, Sandra D'Souza, and Lauren B. McInroy, "Suicidality among Transgender Youth: Elucidating the Role of Interpersonal

Risk Factors," *Journal of Interpersonal Violence* 37, nos. 5–6 (March 2022): NP2696–NP2718, first published April 29, 2020, https://pubmed.ncbi.nlm .nih.gov/32345113/.

47. "Gender Dysphoria Diagnosis History," American Psychiatric Association, https://www.psychiatry.org/psychiatrists/diversity/education/transgender-and -gender-nonconforming-patients/gender-dysphoria-diagnosis.

48. Susannah Luthi, "California Bill Would Punish Parents Who Don't 'Affirm' Their Child's Gender Identity," Washington Free Beacon, June 8, 2023, https://freebeacon.com/california/california-bill-would-punish-parents-who -dont-affirm-their-childs-gender-identity/.

49. Ed Komenda, "Transgender Minors Protected from Estranged Parents under Washington Law," PBS, May 9, 2023, https://www.pbs.org/newshour/ politics/transgender-minors-protected-from-estranged-parents-under -washington-law.

50. Bigad Shaban et al., "Transgender Kids Could Get Hormone Therapy at Earlier Ages," NBC Bay Area, September 13, 2017, https://www.nbcbayarea .com/news/local/transgender-kids-eligible-for-earlier-medical-intervention -under-new-guidelines/19909/; "More Gender Diversity Should Mean Fewer Drugs and Surgeries," Genspect, https://genspect.org/more-gender-diversity -should-mean-fewer-drugs-and-surgeries/.

51. Benji Jones, "The Staggering Costs of Being Transgender in the US, Where Even Patients with Health Insurance Can Face Six-Figure Bills," Insider, July 10, 2019, https://www.businessinsider.com/transgender-medical-care-surgery -expensive-2019-6; Associated Press, "Governor Wants Probe of Vandy Hospital after Doctor Touts Trans Procedures as 'Money Makers,'" Health News Florida, September 22, 2022, https://health.wusf.usf.edu/health-news -florida/2022-09-22/governor-wants-probe-of-vandy-hospital-after-doctor -touts-trans-procedures-are-money-makers; "U.S. Sex Reassignment Surgery Market Size, Share & Trends Analysis Report by Gender Transition (Male to Female, Female to Male), and Segment Forecasts, 2022–2030," Grand View Research, https://www.grandviewresearch.com/industry-analysis/us -sex-reassignment-surgery-market.

52. "FBI Falsely Claims Agency Never Investigated Parents at School Board Meetings," The Post Millennial, July 14, 2023, https://thepostmillennial.com /fbi-falsely-claims-agency-never-investigated-parents-at-school-board -meeting; "U.S. House Judiciary Republicans: DOJ Labeled Dozens of Parents as Terrorist Threats" (press release), House of Representatives

Judiciary Committee, https://judiciary.house.gov/media/press-releases/us
-house-judiciary-republicans-doj-labeled-dozens-of-parents-as-terrorist.

53. Brooks, "Judge Blocks Biden Administration's Directives."

54. Justin Jouvenal, "Loudoun Teen Whose Assaults Caused Political Firestorm Will Be Put on Sex Offender List," *Washington Post*, January 12, 2022, https://www.washingtonpost.com/dc-md-va/2022/01/12/loudoun-bathroom -sex-assault-sentence/.

55. Joe Bukuras, "Acquitted Pro-Life Activist Mark Houck Reveals Details of 'Reckless' FBI Raid; Will Press Charges," Catholic News Agency, February 1, 2023, https://www.catholicnewsagency.com/news/253523/acquitted-pro -life-activist-mark-houck-reveals-details-of-fbi-raid-will-press-charges.

56. Hans A. von Spakovsky and Charles "Cully" Stimson, "FBI, Justice Department Twist Federal Law to Arrest, Charge Pro-Life Activist," Heritage Foundation, September 28, 2022, https://www.heritage.org/crime-and- justice/commentary/fbi-justice-department-twist-federal-law-arrest -charge-pro-life.

57. "Protecting Patients and Health Care Providers," Civil Rights Division, U.S. Department of Justice, https://www.justice.gov/crt/protecting-patients-and -health-care-providers.

58. Bukuras, "Acquitted Pro-Life Activist Mark Houck Reveals Details."

59. Greg Norman, "Nashville Pregnancy Center Hit with Molotov Cocktail, 'Jane's Revenge' Graffiti," Fox News, July 1, 2022, https://www.foxnews .com/us/nashville-pregnancy-center-hit-molotov-cocktail-janes-revenge -arson-graffiti.

60. Mary Margaret Olohan, "Republicans to Hold Hearing on DOJ Targeting Pro-Lifers," The Daily Signal, May 12, 2023, https://www.dailysignal.com /2023/05/12/republicans-hold-hearing-doj-targeting-pro-lifers/.

61. "Justice Department Oversight Hearing," C-SPAN, March 1, 2023, at 1:41:17, https://www.c-span.org/video/?526249-1/justice-department -oversight-hearing.

62. Ken Dilanian and Corky Siemaszko, "Merrick Garland Calls Justice Department's Jan. 6 Probe the 'Most Wide-Ranging Investigation in Its History,'" NBC News, July 26, 2022, https://www.nbcnews.com/politics /2020-election/merrick-garland-not-rule-prosecuting-trump-jan-6-rcna40092.

63. Meg Anderson and Nick McMillan, "1,000 People Have Been Charged for the Capitol Riot. Here's Where Their Cases Stand," NPR, March 25, 2023, https://www.npr.org/2023/03/25/1165022885/1000-defendants-january -6-capitol-riot; Dinah Voyles Pulver and Doug Caruso, "More than 950

People Have Been Charged in Jan. 6 Capitol Riot, but Investigation 'Far from Over,'" *USA Today*, January 6, 2023, https://www.usatoday.com/story/news /politics/2023/01/06/how-many-people-charged-jan-6-riot/10965483002/#; Courtney Hessler, "After Prison Sentence for Capitol Riot, Hurricane Woman Looks to Future," *Coal Valley News*, September 14, 2022, https:// www.coalvalleynews.com/news/after-prison-sentence-for-capitol-riot -hurricane-woman-looks-to-future/article_05e59d4b-3795-58da-a906 -f989e645a0b2.html.

Chapter Six: The Long March Reaches the Boardroom

1. Clark Mindock, "Bank of America Will No Longer Do Business with Gun Companies That Manufacture AR-15s and Similar Assault Weapons," *The Independent*, April 11, 2018, https://www.independent.co.uk/news/world/ americas/bank-of-america-ar-15s-no-business-baml-gun-control-arms -manufacturers-assault-rifles-a8299981.html.

2. Ed Skyler, "Announcing Our U.S. Commercial Firearms Policy," Citigroup, March 22, 2018, https://www.citigroup.com/global/news/perspective/2018/ announcing-our-us-commercial-firearms-policy.

3. See, for example, Louis Jacobson, "Fact-Check: Did Democrats Filibuster Gun-Related Legislation in 2013?," *Austin American-Statesman*, June 1, 2022, https://www.statesman.com/story/news/politics/politifact/2022/06/01 /fact-check-did-2013-democrats-filibuster-gun-related-legislation/745606 2001/. Even the notoriously disingenuous PolitiFact has to admit that "a review of the legislative wrangling from 2013 shows that Cruz accurately explained the voting on the Grassley-Cruz amendment" when "Cruz cited an amendment he sponsored along with Sen. Chuck Grassley, R-Iowa":

    In 2013, I introduced legislation called Grassley-Cruz which targeted felons and fugitives and those with serious mental illness. It directed the Department of Justice to do an audit of federal convictions to make sure felons are in the database. It directed the Department of Justice to prosecute and put in jail felons and fugitives who try to illegally buy firearms.

    In the Harry Reid Democrat(ic) Senate, a majority of the Senate voted in favor of Grassley-Cruz, but the Democrats filibustered it. They demanded 60 votes. They defeated it, because they wanted to go after law-abiding citizens instead of stopping the bad guys.

4. John R. Lott Jr., *More Guns, Less Crime: Understanding Crime and Gun Control Laws* (Chicago: University of Chicago Press, 1998).

5. "Sen. Cruz: 'The Bill of Rights Should Not Be Subject to Corporate Pressure or Financial Coercion'" (press release), Ted Cruz Senate website, May 4, 2018, https://www.cruz.senate.gov/newsroom/press-releases/sen-cruz-and-lsquothe-bill-of-rights-should-not-be-subject-to-corporate-pressure-or-financial-coercion-and-rsquo.

6. David Benoit, "Inside Citigroup's Attempt to Rally Wall Street to Pressure Gun Sellers," *Wall Street Journal*, updated June 25, 2022, https://www.wsj.com/articles/citigroup-tried-and-failed-to-rally-banks-to-pressure-gun-sellers-11656124086.

7. Alexa Ura, "After Drastic Changes Made behind Closed Doors, and an Overnight Debate, Texas Senate Approves Voting Bill," The Texas Tribune, May 30, 2021, https://www.texastribune.org/2021/05/30/texas-voting-restrictions-senate/.

8. "Statement from James Quincey on Georgia Voting Legislation," The Coca-Cola Company, April 1, 2021, https://www.coca-colacompany.com/media-center/georgia-voting-legislation.

9. David K. Li and Jane C. Timm, "MLB's All-Star Game Moved to Denver in Wake of Georgia Restricting Voter Access," NBC News, April 6, 2021, https://www.nbcnews.com/news/us-news/mlb-s-all-star-game-reportedly-moved-denver-wake-georgia-n1263029.

10. Derek Draplin, "MLB All-Star Game Expected to Bring in $190 Million in Revenue for Colorado," The Center Square, April 6, 2021, https://www.thecentersquare.com/colorado/article_8f804554-970e-11eb-9388-17c5c389e556.html.

11. Lucian Bebchuk and Scott Hirst, "The Specter of the Giant Three," *Boston University Law Review* 99, no. 721 (2019): 723–41, https://ccl.yale.edu/sites/default/files/files/BEBCHUK-HIRST-1%20(The%20Specter%20of%20the%20Giant%20Three)%20(Boston%20University%20Law%20Review)(Introduction).pdf; "The Big Three & ESG: A Guide to BlackRock, State Street, & Vanguard Proxy Voting Policies & Guidance on Key ESG Issues," Deloitte., June 5, 2023, https://www.iasplus.com/en-ca/publications/thought-leadership/2023/the-big-three-esg-a-guide-to-blackrock-state-street-vanguard-proxy-voting-policies-guidance-on-key-esg-issues.

12. Kit Rees, "BlackRock's Assets Seen Topping $15 Trillion in Five Years' Time," Bloomberg, April 17, 2023, https://www.bloomberg.com/news/articles/2023-04-17/blackrock-assets-to-top-15-trillion-in-five-years-analyst-says#xj4y7vzkg.

13. Larry Fink, "A Sense of Purpose," Harvard Law School Forum on Corporate Governance, January 17, 2018, https://corpgov.law.harvard.edu/2018/01/17/a-sense-of-purpose/.

14. Shaun J. Mathew and Sarah A. Fortt, "BlackRock's 2018 CEO Letter: A New 'Sense of Purpose' for Corporate America?," Lexology, January 24, 2018, https://www.lexology.com/firms/vinson-and-elkins-llp/shaun_j_mathew.

15. See, for example, Ricardo Martinez, Corey Goldblum, and Michael Monaco, "ESG & Climate Risk: An Introduction for Financial Services Institutions," Federal Home Loan Bank of New York, https://www.fhlbny.com/financial_intelligen/webinar-esg-climate-risk/; Jon McGowan, "Target's LGBTQ+ Pride Marketing May Be ESG-Driven," *Forbes*, May 25, 2023, https://www.forbes.com/sites/jonmcgowan/2023/05/25/targets-lgbtq-pride-marketing-may-be-esg-driven/?sh=1b18c6c531f2; Andrew Winston, "Why Business Leaders Must Resist the Anti-ESG Movement," *Harvard Business Review*, April 5, 2023, https://hbr.org/2023/04/why-business-leaders-must-resist-the-anti-esg-movement.

16. Bebchuk and Hirst, "The Specter."

17. Sanjai Bhagat, "An Inconvenient Truth about ESG Investment," *Harvard Business Review*, March 31, 2022, https://hbr.org/2022/03/an-inconvenient-truth-about-esg-investing.

18. Aneesh Raghunandan and Shivaram Rajgopal, "Do ESG Funds Make Stakeholder-Friendly Investments?," *Review of Accounting Studies*, May 27, 2022, https://papers.ssrn.com/sol3/papers.cfm?abstract_id=3826357.

19. Vivek Ramaswamy, *Capitalist Punishment: How Wall Street Is Using Your Money to Create a Country You Didn't Vote For* (New York: Broadside Books, 2023), ix.

20. Ibid., 3.

21. Ibid., 15; "BlackRock's Approach to Companies That Manufacture and Distribute Civilian Firearms" (press release), BlackRock, March 2, 2018, https://www.blackrock.com/corporate/newsroom/press-releases/article/corporate-one/press-releases/blackrock-approach-to-companies-manufacturing-distributing-firearms; "Kroger's Fred Meyer Plans to Phase Out Firearms Business," Reuters, March 19, 2018, https://www.reuters.com/article/us-usa-guns-kroger/krogers-fred-meyer-plans-to-phase-out-firearms-business-idUSKBN1GV2RL; Rachel Siegel, "BlackRock Unveils Gun-Free Investment Options," *Washington Post*, April 6, 2018, https://www

.washingtonpost.com/news/business/wp/2018/04/06/blackrock-unveils-gun -free-investment-options/.

22. Ramaswamy, *Capitalist Punishment*, 15.

23. Dana Kennedy, "Inside the CEI System Pushing Brands to Endorse Celebs Like Dylan Mulvaney," *New York Post*, April 7, 2023, https://nypost.com/2023/04 /07/inside-the-woke-scoring-system-guiding-american-companies/.

24. Aryn Fields, "The Human Rights Campaign Honors Human Rights Day with Grants to Global LGTBQ Advocates" (press release), Human Rights Campaign, December 10, 2020, https://www.hrc.org/press-releases/the-human-rights-campaign-honors-human-rights-day-with-grants-to-global-lgbtq-advocates; Charles "Cully" Stimson and Zack Smith, "George Soros's Prosecutors Wage War on Law and Order," Heritage Foundation, June 22, 2023, https://www.heritage.org/crime-and-justice/commentary/george-soross-prosecutors-wage-war-law-and-order.

25. Dana Kennedy, "Inside the CEI System Pushing Brands to Endorse Celebs like Dylan Mulvaney," *New York Post*, April 7, 2023, https://nypost.com/2023/04 /07/inside-the-woke-scoring-system-guiding-american-companies/.

26. Ibid.

27. Ariel Zilber, "Chick-fil-A Sparks Anti-Woke Outrage for VP of Diversity, Equity, Inclusion Post," *New York Post*, May 30, 2023, https://nypost.com /2023/05/30/chick-fil-a-sparks-anti-woke-outrage-for-hiring-vp-of-dei/.

28. "The FTX Foundation Group Launches the FTX Climate Program," PR Newswire, July 27, 2021, https://www.prnewswire.com/news-releases/the -ftx-foundation-group-launches-the-ftx-climate-program-301342380.html.

29. "Sam Bankman-Fried Becomes an ESG Truth-Teller," *Wall Street Journal*, November 18, 2022, https://www.wsj.com/articles/sam-bankman-fried-esg -truth-teller-ftx-cryptocurrency-crash-11668723808; Jon Michael Raasch, "FTX Founder Manipulated ESG to Earn 'Virtue Signaling Glow': Palantir Co-Founder," Fox Business, November 29, 2022, https://www.foxbusiness .com/markets/ftx-founder-manipulated-esg-earn-virtue-signaling-glow -palantir-co-founder.

30. "FTX.US," OpenSecrets, https://www.opensecrets.org/orgs/ftx-us/summary ?id=D000073694.

31. Sebastian Sinclair, "Cryptocurrency CEO Donated Second-Largest Amount to Joe Biden's Campaign," CoinDesk, updated September 14, 2021, https:// www.coindesk.com/markets/2020/11/05/cryptocurrency-ceo-donated -second-largest-amount-to-joe-bidens-campaign/.

32. Kelsey Piper, "Sam Bankman-Fried Tries to Explain Himself," Vox, November 6, 2022, https://www.vox.com/future-perfect/23462333/sam-bankman-fried-ftx-cryptocurrency-effective-altruism-crypto-bahamas-philanthropy.

33. Raasch, "FTX Founder Manipulated ESG."

34. Piper, "Sam Bankman-Fried Tries to Explain Himself."

35. Prarthana Prakash, "Silicon Valley Bank Had No Official Chief Risk Officer for 8 Months While the VC Market Was Spiraling," *Fortune*, March 10, 2023, https://fortune.com/2023/03/10/silicon-valley-bank-chief-risk-officer/; Katherine Donlevy, "While Silicon Valley Bank Collapsed, Top Executive Pushed 'Woke' Programs," *New York Post*, March 11, 2023, https://nypost.com/2023/03/11/silicon-valley-bank-pushed-woke-programs-ahead-of-collapse/. Note that SVB UK was "ring-fenced" off from the original SVB around the same time as the position of chief risk officer at the original bank became vacant, and that the "safe spaces" expert at SVB UK "reported to the Chief Risk Officer for the UK and would not have been involved with risk assessment for the US bank."

36. Donlevy, "While Silicon Valley Bank Collapsed."

37. William Sullivan, "Bud Light's Demise at the Hands of Credentialed Woke Millennials," American Thinker, April 28, 2023, https://www.americanthinker.com/articles/2023/04/bud_lights_demise_at_the_hands_of_credentialed_woke_millennials.html.

38. Lizette Chapman and Jason Leopold, "The FDIC Has Accidentally Released a List of Companies It Bailed Out for Billions in the Silicon Valley Bank Collapse," *Fortune*, June 23, 2023, https://fortune.com/2023/06/23/fdic-accidentally-released-list-of-companies-it-bailed-out-silicon-valley-bank-collapse/.

39. Sullivan, "Bud Light's Demise at the Hands of Credentialed Woke Millennials."

40. Alexander Hall, "Bud Light's Marketing VP Was Inspired to Update 'Fratty,' 'Out of Touch' Branding," *New York Post*, April 10, 2023, https://nypost.com/2023/04/10/bud-lights-marketing-vp-was-inspired-to-update-fratty-out-of-touch-branding/.

41. "Blackrock Inc. Ownership in Bud/Anheuser-Busch In BEV SA/NV—ADR," Fintel, https://fintel.io/so/us/bud/blackrock; "Anheuser-Busch Inbev SA," CNN Business, https://money.cnn.com/quote/shareholders/shareholders.html?symb=BUDFF&subView=institutional.

42. A dude, "Dylan Mulvaney Days of Girlhood Tiktoks," YouTube, September 14, 2022, https://www.youtube.com/watch?v=dwA_rOu-e5c; "Dylan Mulvaney (dylanmulvaney)," TikTok, https://www.tiktok.com/@dylanmulvaney?lang=en.

43. Dana Kennedy, "Who Is Trans Star Dylan Mulvaney—and Why Is She Suddenly Everywhere?," *New York Post*, April 6, 2023, and https://nypost .com/2023/04/06/inside-trans-star-dylan-mulvaneys-life-of-san-diego -privilege/.

44. Samantha Aschieris, "Cruz, Blackburn Probe Anheuser-Busch's Partnership with Dylan Mulvaney," The Daily Signal, May 19, 2023, https://www .dailysignal.com/2023/05/19/cruz-blackburn-probe-anheuser-buschs -partnership-with-dylan-mulvaney/.

45. "Barbie Doll Market Share and Size 2023 to 2030: A Comprehensive Market Research Report with 9.8% CAGR," MarketWatch, April 15, 2023, https:// www.marketwatch.com/press-release/barbie-doll-market-share-and-size -2023-to-2030-a-comprehensive-market-research-report-with-98-cagr-2023 -04-15.

46. Aschieris, "Cruz, Blackburn Probe."

47. Grace Mayer, "Bud Light Has Been Embroiled in Backlash since a Beer Promotion by a Transgender Influence. Here's a Timeline of How the Controversy Has Played Out," Business Insider, July 21, 2023, https://www .businessinsider.com/bud-light-transgender-controversy-backlash-boycotts -history; Shannon Power, "Why Dylan Mulvaney Has the Last Laugh in Bud Light Controversy," *Newsweek*, April 17, 2023, https://www.newsweek.com /bud-light-controversy-dylan-mulvaney-beer-transgender-boycott- 794798.

48. Lee Brown, "Kid Rock Shoots Bud Light Cans after Trans TikToker Dylan Mulvaney Partnership," *New York Post*, April 4, 2023, https://nypost.com /2023/04/04/kid-rock-shoots-bud-lights-amid-anger-over-trans-campaign/.

49. Ariel Zilber, "Bud Light Dethroned, Loses Title as America's Top-Selling Beer," *New York Post*, June 14, 2023, https://nypost.com/2023/06/14/bud -light-loses-title-as-americas-top-selling-beer/.

50. Shannon Thaler, "Bud Light Parent Anheuser-Busch's Stock Has Lost over $27B over Dylan Mulvaney," *New York Post*, June 2, 2023, https://nypost .com/2023/06/02/bud-light-parent-anheuser-buschs-stock-lost-27b-over -dylan-mulvaney/.

51. Amanda Holpuch and Julie Creswell, "2 Executives Are on Leave after Bud Light Promotion with Transgender Influencer," *New York Times*, April 25, 2023, https://www.nytimes.com/2023/04/25/business/bud-light-dylan

-mulvaney.html. Two months later, it was reported that the company had let both executives go but for legal reasons did not want to publicly announce firing them. David Hookstead, "Anheuser-Busch Executives Responsible for Bud Light Disaster Are Gone: Report," OutKick, June 27, 2023, https://www .outkick.com/anheuser-busch-bud-light-executives-alissa-heinerscheid-daniel -blake-gone/. Anheuser-Busch denied that they had been fired. Melissa Koenig, "Anheuser-Busch DENIES Claim It Fired Two Top Marketing Executives Responsible for Bud Light's Disastrous Dylan Mulvaney Campaign—and Maintains Pair Are on 'Leave of Absence,'" *Daily Mail*, June 27, 2023, https://www.dailymail.co.uk/news/article-12240443/ Anheuser-Busch-DENIES-report-fired-two-marketing-executives.html.

52. Lindsay Kornick and Alexa Moutevelis, "Stores Selling Bud Light for Free as Mulvaney Backlash Continues," Fox News, May 25, 2023, https://www .foxnews.com/media/stores-sell-bud-light-free-mulvaney-backlash-continues.

53. Zilber, "Bud Light Dethroned." See also Jacob Pramuk and Stefan Sykes, "Modelo Tops Bud Light as the Top-Selling Beer in the U.S. in May," NBC News, June 14, 2023, https://www.nbcnews.com/business/consumer/modelo -tops-bud-light-top-selling-beer-us-may-rcna89350.

54. Kendall Tietz, "Bud Light No Longer Ranks among America's Top 10 Beers," Fox News, July 7, 2023, https://www.foxnews.com/media/bud-light -no-longer-ranks-among-americas-top-10-beers.

55. Daniel Arkin, Mark Lavietes, and Daysia Tolentino, "Target Quietly Moves Pride Merchandise in Some Stores as Conservative Activists Declare Victory," NBC News, May 24, 2023, https://www.nbcnews.com/nbc-out/out-news/ -target-pride-merchandise-lgbtq-designers-pulled-criticism-rcna86036.

56. Jenny Goldsberry, "Target Pride Month Partner Boasts about Satanism: Satan Respects Pronouns," *Washington Examiner*, May 21, 2023, https:// www.washingtonexaminer.com/news/targets-pride-month-designer-satanic -roots.

57. Conor Murray, "Target Removes Pride Items after Conservative Firestorm— Sparking Criticism from LGBTQ Groups," *Forbes*, May 24, 2023, https:// www.forbes.com/sites/conormurray/2023/05/24/target-removes-pride-items -after-conservative-firestorm-sparking-criticism-from-lgbtq-groups/?sh= 552876cee512.

58. Brian Flood, "Target Holds 'Emergency' Meeting over LGBTQ Merchandise in Southern Stores," *New York Post*, May 23, 2023, https://nypost.com/2023 /05/23/target-holds-emergency-meeting-over-lgbtq-merchandise-in-southern -stores/.

59. James Gordon, "Target's Market Cap Slumps by $15 Billion amid Backlash over 'Tuck-Friendly' Transgender Swimsuits and Pride Clothes for Kids, as Analysts Say Retail Giant Is Hemorrhaging Customers to Walmart," *Daily Mail*, June 9, 2023, https://www.dailymail.co.uk/news/article-12179575/Targets-value-slumps-15-BILLION-shares-drop-3-26-backlash-Pride-collection.html.

60. Andrew Solender, "Republicans Vow Boycott, Retaliation against MLB over Pulled All-Star Game," *Forbes*, April 2, 2021, https://www.forbes.com/sites/andrewsolender/2021/04/02/republicans-vow-boycott-retaliation-against-mlb-over-pulled-all-star-game/?sh=2285da92787c.

61. Ted Cruz, "Texas Is Fighting Back against Big Businesses That Threaten Oil, Gas Jobs," *Fort Worth Star-Telegram*, May 4, 2021, https://www.star-telegram.com/article251136074.html.

62. "Investment Management," Teacher Retirement System of Texas ($180 billion as of December 2022), April 2023, http://www.trs.texas.gov/TRS%20Documents/imc-book-april-2023.pdf; "Annual Comprehensive Financial Report," Texas PSF (Texas Permanent School Fund, $61 billion as of August 1, 2022), https://texaspsf.org/reports/; "Performance," ERS (Employee Retirement System, $34 billion as of May 31, 2023), https://ers.texas.gov/about-ers/ers-investments-overview/performance#:~:text=ERS%20manages%20retirement%20trust%20assets,provided%20by%20the%20ERS%20Trust (https://ers.texas.gov/about-ers/ers-investments-overview/performance#:~:text=ERS%20manages%20retirement%20trust%20assets,provided%20by%20the%20ERS%20Trust); "Investing with Intention," TCDRS (Texas County & District Retirement System, $43 billion as of March 31, 2023), https://www.tcdrs.org/investments/#:~:text=We%20are%20proud%20of%20the,billion%20in%20net%20plan%20assets; "Overview," TMRS (Texas Municipal Retirement System, $37 billion as of March 31, 2023), https://www.tmrs.com/TMRS_highlights_overview.php#:~:text=than%2020%20years-,Assets,of%2012%2F31%2F2021.

63. Isla Binnie, "BlackRock's Fink Says He's Stopped Using 'Weaponised' Term ESG," Reuters, June 26, 2023, https://www.reuters.com/business/environment/blackrocks-fink-says-hes-stopped-using-weaponised-term-esg-2023-06-26/.

64. John Frank, "Larry Fink 'Ashamed' to Be Part of ESG Political Debate," Axios, June 25, 2023, https://www.axios.com/2023/06/26/larry-fink-ashamed-esg-weaponized-desantis.

65. "BlackRock's Larry Fink Stops Using Term 'ESG,' Says It's Become 'Weaponized,'" *New York Post*, June 26, 2023, https://nypost.com/2023/06/26/blackrocks-larry-fink-drops-use-of-weaponized-term-esg/.

66. Frank, "Larry Fink 'Ashamed.'"
67. Ibid.
68. Binnie, "BlackRock's Fink."

Chapter Seven: Entertainment

1. Andrew Klavan, Foreword in Christian Toto, *Virtue Bombs: How Hollywood Got Woke and Lost Its Soul* (Bombardier Books, 2022), ii–v.
2. Thomas D. Williams, "'The Office' Star Rainn Wilson Slams Hollywood's 'Anti-Christian Bias,'" Breitbart, March 15, 2023, https://www.breitbart.com/faith/2023/03/15/the-office-star-rainn-wilson-slams-hollywoods-anti-christian-bias/?utm_medium=social&utm_source=facebook.
3. Chris Edwards, "'The Office' Star Rainn Wilson Criticises 'Anti-Christian Bias' in 'The Last of Us,'" NME, March 14, 2023, https://www.nme.com/news/tv/the-office-star-rainn-wilson-criticises-anti-christian-bias-in-the-last-of-us-3413311.
4. Rainn Wilson (@rainnwilson), "I do think there is an anti-Christian bias…," Twitter, March 11, 2023, 3:50 p.m., https://twitter.com/rainnwilson/status/1634657997317361665.
5. Nicholas McEntyre, "'Jaws' Star Richard Dreyfuss Slams New Oscars Diversity Rules," *New York Post*, May 7, 2023, https://nypost.com/2023/05/07/richard-dreyfuss-slams-oscars-new-diversity-standards/.
6. Gabriel Hays, "'Jaws' Star Richard Dreyfuss Blasts Hollywood Inclusion Standards; 'They Make Me Vomit,'" Fox News, May 6, 2023, https://www.foxnews.com/media/jaws-star-richard-dreyfuss-blasts-hollywood-inclusion-standards-they-make-me-vomit.
7. It's amusing and painful to imagine how these arguments will go in the future. Trying to make the Oscar eligibility case for *Jaws*? "Well, the shark was gay!"
8. Emma Nolan, "Ted Cruz Called Out by 'Watchmen' Writer for Misunderstanding the Comic," *Newsweek*, February 2, 2021, https://www.newsweek.com/ted-cruz-watchmen-avengers-thanos-environmentalist-twitter-1566206.
9. Greg Braxton, "Watchmen's Provocative Portrait of Race in America Has Its Own Creator Worried," *Los Angeles Times*, October 20, 2019, https://www.latimes.com/entertainment-arts/tv/story/2019-10-20/hbo-watchmen-damon-lindelof-regina-king-nicole-kassell.

10. Aisha Harris, "'The Little Mermaid' Is the Latest of Disney's Poor Unfortunate Remakes," NPR, May 22, 2023, https://www.npr.org/2023/05/22/1177439851/the-little-mermaid-review-remake-disney.

11. A. J. Willingham, "Analysis: A Definitive Rebuttal to Every Racist 'Little Mermaid' Argument," CNN, September 17, 2022, https://www.cnn.com/2022/09/17/entertainment/little-mermaid-racist-backlash-halle-bailey-disney-cec/index.html.

12. Nick Romano, "*The Little Mermaid* Star Halle Bailey Responds to Racist Backlash: 'As a Black Person, You Just Expect It,'" *Entertainment Weekly*, February 23, 2023, https://ew.com/movies/the-little-mermaid-halle-bailey-racist-backlash-you-just-expect-it/.

13. Becky Burkett, "Disney's 'Woke' Film Ideology Cost the Studios Nearly $300 Million at the Box Office," DisneyDining, April 17, 2023, https://www.disneydining.com/disney-woke-film-flops-bb1/.

14. Andrew Mark Miller, "Disney Exposed: Leaked Videos Show Officials Pushing LGBT Agenda, Saying DeSantis Wants to 'Erase' Gay Kids," Fox Business, March 29, 2022, https://www.foxbusiness.com/politics/disney-officials-leaked-videos-pushing-lgbt-agenda-saying-desantis-erase-gay-kids.

15. "Stories Matter," The Walt Disney Company, https://storiesmatter.thewaltdisneycompany.com/.

16. Ibid.

17. Caroline Downey, "Disney Executive Producer Admits to 'Gay Agenda,' 'Adding Queerness' Wherever She Could," *National Review*, March 29, 2022, https://www.nationalreview.com/news/disney-executive-producer-admits-to-gay-agenda-adding-queerness-wherever-she-could/.

18. See Mary Grabar, *Debunking The 1619 Project: Exposing the Plan to Divide America* (Washington, D.C.: Regnery, 2021) for an account of prominent historians' criticisms and an examination of Hannah-Jones's manifold historical errors.

19. See David Marcus, "The New York Times' Correction to The 1619 Project Proves It Is Not Fit for Schools," The Federalist, March 13, 2020, https://thefederalist.com/2020/03/13/correction-to-the-1619-project-proves-it-is-not-fit-for-schools/ and Sean Wilentz, "A Matter of Facts," *The Atlantic*, January 22, 2020, https://www.theatlantic.com/ideas/archive/2020/01/1619-project-new-york-times-wilentz/605152/ for reporting on this original assertion, its inaccuracy, and the *Times'* modification of the claim.

20. *The 1619 Project*, season 1, episode 1, "Democracy," directed by Roger Ross Williams, Hulu, January 26, 2023, https://www.hulu.com/series/the-1619 -project-7ba3407a-299c-4a10-8310-bbcdd6ab4653.

21. *Colin in Black and White*, season 1, episode 1, "Cornrows," directed by Ava DuVernay, Netflix, October 29, 2021, https://www.netflix.com/title /80244479.

22. Michele Roberts, "Colin Kaepernick Calls Out Adoptive Parents in his New Graphic Novel," CBS News, March 10, 2023, https://www.cbsnews.com/ atlanta/news/colin-kaepernick-calls-out-adoptive-parents-in-his-new-graphic -novel/.

23. Ibid.

24. See, for example, Christian Holub, "All the Artists Who Won't Perform at Donald Trump's Inauguration," *Entertainment Weekly*, January 10, 2017, https://ew.com/music/2017/01/10/donald-trump-inauguration-artists-who -wont-perform/; Hugh McIntyre, "Here Are All the Musicians Performing at Donald Trump's Inauguration," *Forbes*, January 17, 2017, https://www .forbes.com/sites/hughmcintyre/2017/01/17/here-are-all-the-celebrities -performing-at-donald-trumps-inauguration/?sh=338ceob8184c.

25. Jacob Uitti, "Behind the Career Altering Band Name Change The Dixie Chicks to The Chicks," May 2023, American Songwriter, https:// americansongwriter.com/behind-the-career-altering-band-name-change-the -dixie-chicks-to-the-chicks/.

26. Cindy Boren, "Colin Kaepernick's Future Might Have More to Do with Football Than Free Speech," *Washington Post*, August 29, 2016, https:// www.washingtonpost.com/news/early-lead/wp/2016/08/29/colin -kaepernicks-future-might-have-more-to-do-with-football-than-free-speech/; Marc Sessler, "Kaepernick Makes Roster; Gabbert Named Started QB," NFL, September 3, 2016, https://www.nfl.com/news/kaepernick-makes -roster-gabbert-named-starting-qb-0ap3000000695093.

27. Cindy Boren, "A Timeline of Colin Kaepernick's Protests against Police Brutality, Four Years after They Began," *Washington Post*, August 26, 2020, https://www.washingtonpost.com/sports/2020/06/01/colin-kaepernick -kneeling-history/.

28. Analis Bailey, "On This Day Four Years Ago, Colin Kaepernick Began His Peaceful Protests during the National Anthem," *USA Today*, August 26, 2020, https://www.usatoday.com/story/sports/nfl/2020/08/26/colin -kaepernick-started-protesting-day-2016/3440690001/.

29. Sam Frost, "Colin Kaepernick Takes Aim at NFL and Makes Accusation over Last Six Years," *Mirror*, May 25, 2023, https://www.mirror.co.uk/sport /other-sports/american-sports/colin-kaepernick-nfl-comeback-hopes -30077753.

30. See, for example, "Bonus Time: By Sitting, Colin Kaepernick Stands with Ignorance," NBC Palm Springs News First, August 30, 2016, https:// nbcpalmsprings.com/2016/08/30/bonus-time-by-sitting-kaepernick-stands -with-ignorance/; Rich Lowry, "Colin Kaepernick's Stupid Lie about America," *National Review*, January 7, 2020, https://www.nationalreview .com/2020/01/colin-kaepernick-stupid-lie-about-america/; Wil Leitner, "Clay Travis Calls Colin Kaepernick an 'Imbecile' after Netflix Special," Fox Sports Radio, November 12, 2021, https://foxsportsradio.iheart.com/content/2021 -11-12-clay-travis-calls-colin-kaepernick-an-imbecile-after-netflix-special/.

31. Colin Kaepernick (@Kaepernick7), "What have I, or those I represent, to do with your national independence?…," Twitter, July 4, 2019, 1:03 p.m., https://twitter.com/Kaepernick7/status/1146826827593342977.

32. Ted Cruz (@TedCruz), "You quote a mighty and historic speech…" (thread), Twitter, July 4, 2019, 9:27 p.m., https://twitter.com/tedcruz/status /1146953662121615366?lang=en.

33. Ibid.

34. "NAACP Travel Advisory for the State of Florida," NAACP, https://naacp .org/resources/naacp-travel-advisory-state-florida.

35. Brianna Herlihy, "Ted Cruz Reminds AOC Her Own Democratic Party Founded KKK, Wrote Jim Crow Laws," Fox News, May 23, 2023, https:// www.foxnews.com/politics/ted-cruz-reminds-aoc-her-democrat-party -founded-kkk-wrote-jim-crow-laws.

36. Alexandria Ocasio-Cortez (@AOC), "Why don't you go ahead…," Twitter, May 23, 2023, 9:06 a.m., https://twitter.com/AOC/status/166099572 5298225152?lang=en.

37. Ryan Morik, "'Mount Rushmore' Term Is 'Offensive' and Should Be 'Retired,' ESPN's Jalen Rose Says," Fox News, August 5, 2022, https://www .foxnews.com/sports/mount-rushmore-term-offensive-retired-says-espns -jalen-rose.

38. Ryan Morik, "NBA Showcases Transgender and Nonbinary Hockey Tournament, Responds to Criticism on Twitter," Fox News, November 22, 2022, https://www.foxnews.com/sports/nhl-showcases-transgender -nonbinary-hockey-tournament-responds-criticism-twitter.

39. Houston Keene, "Twitter, NBA Make 2022 'Worst of the Woke' List, Disney, Blackrock Appear Second Year in a Row," Fox News, December 23, 2022, https://www.foxnews.com/politics/twitter-nba-make-2022-worst-woke-list -disney-blackrock-repeat-second-year-row.

40. See for example, "NBA Creates Annual Kareem Abdul-Jabbar Social Justice Award" (official release), NBA, May 13, 2021, https://www.nba.com/news/ nba-creates-kareem-abdul-jabbar-social-justice-award-official-release; "Trail Blazers Foundation," NBA, https://www.nba.com/blazers/community/ foundation; Blake Schuster, "NBA Announces Program Providing COVID- 19 Tests to Marginalized Communities," Bleacher Report, July 29, 2020, https://bleacherreport.com/articles/2902279-nba-announces-program -providing-covid-19-tests-to-marginalized-communities.

41. NBA Retweet (@RTBNA), "List of the approved social messages…," Twitter, July 3, 2020, 9:07 p.m., https://twitter.com/RTNBA/status/127922 0134532526080?lang=en.

42. Jordan Heck, "NBA Says 'Free Hong Kong' Was 'Inadvertently Prohibited' from Jerseys," The Sporting News, July 14, 2020, https://www.sportingnews .com/us/nba/news/nba-store-free-hong-kong-jerseys/vamfw17sza 9f16m8iuo6la7wt.

43. Keene, "Twitter, NBA Make 2022 'Worst of the Woke' List."

44. Jon Lewis, "NBA Ratings Deep-Dive: Where Does the League Stand?," Sports Media Watch, April 2023, https://www.sportsmediawatch.com/2023 /04/nba-ratings-viewership-past-30-years-analysis-where-league-stands/.

45. Ibid.

46. "The Passion of the Christ," Box Office Mojo, https://www.boxofficemojo .com/release/rl3781789185/.

47. Maureen Lee Lenker, *The Mandalorian* Star Gina Carano Faces Backlash for Controversial Instagram Posts," *Entertainment Weekly*, February 10, 2021, https://web.archive.org/web/20210211043551/https://ew.com/tv/ mandalorian-gina-carano-backlash-controversial-instagram-posts/.

48. Brady Langmann, "Gina Carano's *The Mandalorian* Controversy Isn't Going Anywhere," *Esquire*, February 22, 2021, https://www.esquire.com/ entertainment/tv/a35478544/gina-carano-the-mandalorian-social-media -posts-lucasfilm-controversy-fired-explained/.

49. Tatiana Siegel, "Richard Gere's Studio Exile: Why His Hollywood Career Took an Indie Turn," *Hollywood Reporter*, April 18, 2017, https://www .hollywoodreporter.com/movies/movie-features/richard-geres-studio-exile -why-his-hollywood-career-took-an-indie-turn-992258/.

50. Ibid.
51. "A Time for Choosing," CNN, October 27, 1964, http://www.cnn.com/SPECIALS/2004/reagan/stories/speech.archive/time.html.

Chapter Eight: "The Science"

1. Mallory Simon, "Over 1,000 Health Professionals Sign a Letter Saying, Don't Shut Down Protests Using Coronavirus Concerns as an Excuse," CNN, June 5, 2020, https://www.cnn.com/2020/06/05/health/health-care-open-letter-protests-coronavirus-trnd/index.html.
2. See, for example, Joseph Cesario, David J. Johnson, and William Terrill, "Is There Evidence of Racial Disparity in Police Use of Deadly Force? Analyses of Officer-Involved Fatal Shootings in 2015–2016," *Social Psychological and Personality Science* 10, no. 5 (July 2019): 586–95, https://journals.sagepub.com/doi/abs/10.1177/1948550618775108; "Poverty Explains Racial Bias in Police Shootings," Replicability-Index, September 27, 2019, https://replicationindex.com/2019/09/27/poverty-explain-racial-biases-in-police-shootings/; and the cites to numerous studies in "Obesity, Race/Ethnicity, and COVID-19," Centers for Disease Control and Prevention," https://www.cdc.gov/obesity/data/obesity-and-covid-19.html, including cites to numerous studies; also see Akilah Johnson and Dan Keating, "Whites Now More Likely to Die from Covid Than Blacks: Why the Pandemic Shifted," *Washington Post*, October 19, 2022, https://www.washingtonpost.com/health/2022/10/19/covid-deaths-us-race/.
3. Lawrence Krauss, "The Ideological Corruption of Science," *Wall Street Journal*, July 12, 2020, https://www.wsj.com/articles/the-ideological-corruption-of-science-11594572501.
4. Ibid.
5. Ibid.
6. Ibid.
7. Ibid.
8. Ibid.
9. Carlie Porterfield, "Dr. Fauci on GOP Criticism: 'Attacks on Me Quite Frankly, Are Attacks on Science,'" *Forbes*, June 9, 2021, https://www.forbes.com/sites/carlieporterfield/2021/06/09/fauci-on-gop-criticism-attacks-on-me-quite-frankly-are-attacks-on-science/?sh=68819eef4542.
10. "Brynn Holland, "7 of the Most Outrageous Medical Treatments in History," History, September 5, 2017, updated March 28, 2023, https://www.history.com/news/7-of-the-most-outrageous-medical-treatments-in-history.

11. Ibid.

12. Darragh Roche, "Fauci Said Masks 'Not Really Effective in Keeping Out Virus,' Email Reveals," *Newsweek*, June 2, 2021, https://www.newsweek .com/fauci-said-masks-not-really-effective-keeping-out-virus-email-reveals -1596703.

13. Mia Jankowicz, "Fauci Said US Government Held Off Promoting Face Masks Because It Knew Shortages Were So Bad That Even Doctors Couldn't Get Enough," Business Insider, June 15, 2020, https://www.businessinsider .com/fauci-mask-advice-was-because-doctors-shortages-from-the-start-2020 -6.

14. Samuel Chamberlain, "Fauci Emails Show His Flip-Flopping on Wearing Masks to Fight Covid," *New York Post*, June 3, 2021, https://nypost.com /2021/06/03/fauci-emails-show-his-flip-flopping-on-wearing-masks-to-fight -covid/.

15. Katherine Ross, "Why Weren't We Wearing Masks from the Beginning? Dr. Fauci Explains," The Street, June 12, 2020, https://www.thestreet.com/video /dr-fauci-masks-changing-directive-coronavirus?utm_source=aw&utm_med ium=affiliate&awc=28355_1688065369_035de72502013de44c0dd606ddo cd0a0.

16. Taylor Hatmaker, "Twitter Broadly Bans Any COVID-19 Tweets That Could Help the Virus Spread," TechCrunch, March 18, 2020, https://techcrunch .com/2020/03/18/twitter-coronavirus-covid-19-misinformation-policy/.

17. The original version traces back to Greek physician Hippocrates, who lived from 460 to 370 BC. It provided: "Neither will I administer a poison to anybody when asked to do so, nor will I suggest such a course. Similarly I will not give to a woman a pessary to cause abortion. But I will keep pure and holy both my life and my art." That language remained largely unchanged for over two thousand years.

18. Jack Dutton, "Video of Medical Students 'Chanting Critical Race Theory Mantra' Goes Viral," *Newsweek*, February 16, 2023, https://www.newsweek .com/video-medical-students-chanting-critical-race-theory-mantra-goes-viral -1781401.

19. "Advancing Health Equity: A Guide to Language, Narrative and Concepts," American Medical Association and AAMC Center for Health Justice, https:// www.ama-assn.org/system/files/ama-aamc-equity-guide.pdf, 5, 49.

20. "Woke Medical Schools Are a Threat to Your Health," *Washington Examiner*, January 16, 2023, https://www.washingtonexaminer.com/

restoring-america/equality-not-elitism/woke-medical-schools-are-a-threat
-to-your-health.

21. "Organizational Strategic Plan to Embed Racial Justice and Advance Health Equity 2021–2023," American Medical Association, 2023, https://www.ama -assn.org/system/files/ama-equity-strategic-plan.pdf.

22. Heather Mac Donald, "Woke Medical Organizations Are Hazardous to Your Health," *Wall Street Journal*, August 5, 2022, https://www.wsj.com/ articles/woke-medical-organizations-are-hazardous-to-your-health-equity -scientific-progress-social-justice-medical-organizations-11659707075.

23. Mairead Elordi, "Jordan Peterson Battles Canadian Regulator in Court over Threat to Strip His Psychologist License," The Daily Wire, June 27, 2023, https://www.dailywire.com/news/jordan-peterson-battles-canadian -regulator-in-court-over-threat-to-strip-his-psychologist-license.

24. Ibid.

25. Ibid.

26. Geoff Brumfiel, "This Doctor Spread False Information about COVID. She Still Kept Her Medical License," NPR, September 14, 2021, https://www .npr.org/sections/health-shots/2021/09/14/1035915598/doctors-covid -misinformation-medical-license.

27. Darius Tahir, "Medical Boards Get Pushback as They Try to Punish Doctors for Covid Misinformation," Politico, February 1, 2022, https://www.politico .com/news/2022/02/01/covid-misinfo-docs-vaccines-00003383.

28. Besides the complaint to the Texas Bar in my own case, see, for example, Kate Polantz, "Attorney Disciplinary Committee Recommends Rudy Giuliani Be Disbarred for 2020 Election Legal Work," CNN, updated July 7, 2023, https://www.cnn.com/2023/07/07/politics/dc-bar-rudy-giuliani/ index.html; Stefanie Dazio, Michael R. Blood, and Alanna Durkin Richer, "Trump Adviser Faces Possible Disbarment over His Efforts to Overturn 2020 Election," Associated Press, June 20, 2023, https://apnews.com/article /donald-trump-john-eastman-607f457a20ac9ed11daa546f01aa6c8d; Jaclyn Diaz, "Lin Wood, a Pro-Trump Attorney Who Challenged 2020 Election, Retires His Law License," NPR, July 5, 2023, https://www.npr.org/2023/07 /05/1186071934/lin-wood-attorney-retires-law-license-trump; Jacob Shamsian, "Trump's Lawyers Keep Getting in Trouble with Judges. Here Are the 17 Sanctioned So Far," Business Insider, updated March 14, 2023, https://www.businessinsider.com/trump-lawyers-sanctioned-by-courts -election-lawsuits-2022-12.

29. William Cummings, "'The World Is Going to End in 12 Years If We Don't Address Climate Change,' Ocasio-Cortez Says," *USA Today*, January 22, 2019, https://www.usatoday.com/story/news/politics/onpolitics/2019/01/22/ocasio-cortez-climate-change-alarm/2642481002/.

30. See, for example, "Global Warming of 1.5° C," Intergovernmental Panel on Climate Change, 2018, https://www.ipcc.ch/sr15/; Jonathan Watts, "We Have 12 Years to Limit Climate Change Catastrophe," *The Guardian*, October 8, 2018, https://www.theguardian.com/environment/2018/oct/08/global-warming-must-not-exceed-15c-warns-landmark-un-report.

31. Quoted in: Michael Shellenberger, *Apocalypse Never: Why Environmental Alarmism Hurts Us All* (New York: Harper, 2020), 1.

32. Ibid., 4.

33. Jason Plautz, "The Environmental Burden of Generation Z," *Washington Post*, February 3, 2020, https://www.washingtonpost.com/magazine/2020/02/03/eco-anxiety-is-overwhelming-kids-wheres-line-between-education-alarmism/.

34. Kerrington Powell and Vinay Prasad, "The Noble Lies of COVID-19," Slate, July 28, 2021, https://slate.com/technology/2021/07/noble-lies-covid-fauci-cdc-masks.html.

35. See, for example, Cortney O'Brien, "Viewers Demand Apology from MSNBC, Rachel Maddow for Previous COVID Vaccine Comments," Fox News, December 28, 2021, https://www.foxnews.com/media/social-media-users-demand-apology-msnbc-rachel-maddow-vaccines.

36. Alex Epstein, *The Moral Case for Fossil Fuels* (New York: Portfolio, 2014), 8.

37. Joe Hasell and Max Roser, "Famines," Our World in Data, December 7, 2017, https://ourworldindata.org/famines.

38. Epstein, *The Moral Case for Fossil Fuels*, 14–15.

39. Rachel Wallace, "Barack and Michelle Obama Buy an $11.75 Million Home on Martha's Vineyard," *Architectural Digest*, December 6, 2019, https://www.architecturaldigest.com/story/barack-and-michelle-obama-buy-a-home-on-marthas-vineyard.

40. Alex Trembath and Vijaya Ramachandran, "The Malthusians Are Back," *The Atlantic*, March 22, 2023, https://www.theatlantic.com/ideas/archive/2023/03/population-control-movement-climate-malthusian-similarities/673450/.

41. Ibid.

42. "Margaret Sanger: Ambitious Feminist and Racist Eugenicist," University of Chicago, September 21, 2022, https://womanisrational.uchicago.edu/2022 /09/21/margaret-sanger-the-duality-of-a-ambitious-feminist-and-racist -eugenicist/.

43. Naomi Oreskes, "Eight Billion People in the World Is a Crisis, Not an Achievement," *Scientific American*, March 1, 2023, https://www .scientificamerican.com/article/eight-billion-people-in-the-world-is-a-crisis -not-an-achievement/.

44. James Taylor, "Ted Cruz Embarrasses Sierra Club President in Global Warming Hearings," *Forbes*, October 8, 2015, https://www.forbes.com/sites /jamestaylor/2015/10/08/ted-cruz-embarrasses-sierra-club-president-in -global-warming-hearings/?sh=6ee45a762217.

45. Alex Epstein, "How to Answer Loaded Climate Questions," Energy Talking Points, June 29, 2023, https://energytalkingpoints.com/climate-q/.

46. Seth Whitehead, "UPDATE: U.S. Led World in CO2 Reductions for 10th Time This Century Last Year," Illinois Petroleum Resources Board, updated December 3, 2020, https://iprb.org/blog/2020/u-s-led-world-in-co2 -reductions-for-10th-time-this-century-last-year/.

47. Alex Epstein (@AlexEpstein), "Don't believe the lie...," Twitter, February 28, 2023, 11:56 a.m., https://twitter.com/alexepstein/status/163061286807166 9779?s=46&t=dgqLlnH7VN_R7u2COt5TsA.

48. Bjorn Lomborg, "Prioritizing the Best Solutions for Sustainable Development," *Forbes*, February 13, 2023, https://www.forbes.com/sites/ bjornlomborg/2023/02/13/prioritizing-the-best-solutions-for-sustainable -development/?sh=61eb66676353.

49. Alex Epstein (@alexepstein), "*Warning* Tomorrow the @washingtonpost plans to 'cancel' me and my new book Fossil Future . . ." (thread), Twitter, March 29, 2022, 11:08 a.m., https://twitter.com/AlexEpstein/status /1508823313182695428.

50. Maxine Joselow, "Advocates Promotes Fossil Fuels for Poor Nations He Once Disparaged," *Washington Post*, April 6, 2022, https://www.washingtonpost .com/climate-environment/2022/04/06/alex-epstein-climate-skeptic/.

51. Roy W. Spencer, "UAH Global Temperature Update for August, 2022: +0.28 Deg C.," Roy Spencer, Ph.D., September 1, 2022, https://www.drroyspencer .com/2022/09/uah-global-temperature-update-for-august-2022-0-28-deg-c/.

Chapter Nine: China

1. "Sen. Cruz Delivers Floor Speech Demanding Release of Mark Swidan, Wrongfully Detained in China" (press release), Ted Cruz Senate website, February 1, 2023, https://www.cruz.senate.gov/newsroom/press-releases/sen-cruz-delivers-floor-speech-demanding-release-of-mark-swidan-wrongfully-detained-in-china.

2. Amelia Pollard, "Ayn Rand, Live from Los Angeles," *Los Angeles Review of Books*, April 22, 2021, https://lareviewofbooks.org/article/ayn-rand-live-from-los-angeles/.

3. Caroline Downey, "Justice Gorsuch Accuses Colorado of Forcing Christian Baker to Undergo 'Reeducation Program,'" *National Review*, December 5, 2022, https://www.nationalreview.com/news/gorsuch-accuses-colorado-of-forcing-christian-baker-to-undergo-reeducation-program/.

4. Mairead Elordi, "Jordan Peterson Battles Canadian Regulator in Court over Threat to Strip His Psychologist License," The Daily Wire, June 27, 2023, https://www.dailywire.com/news/jordan-peterson-battles-canadian-regulator-in-court-over-threat-to-strip-his-psychologist-license.

5. Muyi Xiao et al., "How a Chinese Doctor Who Warned of Covid-19 Spent His Final Days," *New York Times*, October 6, 2022, https://www.nytimes.com/2022/10/06/world/asia/covid-china-doctor-li-wenliang.html.

6. Zhuang Pinghui, "China Confirms Unauthorised Labs Were Told to Destroy Early Coronavirus Samples," *South China Morning Post*, May 15, 2020, https://www.scmp.com/news/china/society/article/3084635/china-confirms-unauthorised-labs-were-told-destroy-early.

7. "The Cost of Coronavirus," *Verdict with Ted Cruz*, March 2020, https://open.spotify.com/episode/3TFaLhNEGyyonF7xpPYoK5; "An Expert's Perspective on the Pandemic," *Verdict with Ted Cruz*, March 2020, https://open.spotify.com/episode/187mMlNxwZQ1tuTmiH5Nxo; "The Wuhan Coverup," *Verdict with Ted Cruz*, April 2020, https://open.spotify.com/episode/7hW4QMh8oe3vhp9O4WEfUH; "China Must Pay," *Verdict with Ted Cruz*, April 2020, https://open.spotify.com/episode/0n4ksmJc62zQy4FZgDrp29.

8. Ibid.; Pinghui, "China Confirms Unauthorised Labs Were Told to Destroy."

9. Olafimihan Oshin, "Washington Post Issues Correction on 2020 Report on Tom Cotton, Lab-Leak Theory," *The Hill*, June 1, 2021, https://thehill.com/homenews/media/556418-washington-post-issues-correction-on-2020-report-on-tom-cotton-lab-leak-theory/.

10. "Hogan Top COVID Advisor Redfield Tosses Viral Kindling on Anti-Asian Fires," *Baltimore Sun*, March 30, 2021, https://www.baltimoresun.com/opinion/editorial/bs-ed-0331-wuhan-virus-redfield-20210330-lvmibefshbgu zhrscwkdehh3ue-story.html.

11. Phil Kerpen (@kerpen), "Not the usual catchall . . . ," Twitter, June 2, 2021, 12:03 a.m., https://twitter.com/kerpen/status/1399939689025609732?lang=en; C. Douglas Golden, "After Fauci Email Proves Link with Zuckerberg, House Republicans Hit Facebook with One Demand That Could Change Everything," The Western Journal, June 10, 2021, https://www.westernjournal.com/fauci-email-proves-link-zuckerberg-house-republicans-hit-facebook-one-demand-change-everything/.

12. Emma Bowman, "Facebook Steps Up Efforts to Combat the Spread of Coronavirus Misinformation," NPR, March 26, 2020, https://www.npr.org/sections/coronavirus-live-updates/2020/03/26/822245048/facebook-steps-up-efforts-to-combat-the-spread-of-coronavirus-misinformation.

13. Anumita Kaur and Dan Diamond, "FBI Director Says Covid-19 'Most Likely' Originated from Lab Incident, *Washington Post*, February 28, 2023, https://www.washingtonpost.com/nation/2023/02/28/fbi-director-christopher-wray-wuhan-lab/.

14. Ibid.

15. Robert R. Redfield, "Written Statement of Dr. Robert R. Redfield before the House Select Subcommittee on the Coronavirus Crisis," March 8, 2023, https://oversight.house.gov/wp-content/uploads/2023/03/2023.03.08-Statement-of-Dr.-Robert-R-Redfield88.pdf.

16. James Fallows, "On Uighurs, Han, and General Racial Attitudes in China," *The Atlantic*, July 13, 2009, https://www.theatlantic.com/technology/archive/2009/07/on-uighurs-han-and-general-racial-attitudes-in-china/21137/.

17. Jim Geraghty, "Hunter Biden: The Most Comprehensive Timeline," *National Review*, September 30, 2019, https://www.nationalreview.com/2019/09/hunter-biden-comprehensive-timeline/.

18. Miranda Devine, "Hunter Biden's Biz Partner Called Joe Biden 'the Big Guy' in Panicked Message after Post's Laptop Story," *New York Post*, July 27, 2022, https://nypost.com/2022/07/27/hunter-bidens-biz-partner-called-joe-biden-the-big-guy-in-panic-over-laptop/; Jessica Chasmar and Cameron Cawthorne, "Biden's Claim to Have No Knowledge of Hunter's Business Dealings Is Becoming Harder to Maintain," Fox News, April 13, 2023, https://www.foxnews.com/politics/bidens-claim-no-knowledge-hunters-business-dealings-harder-maintain; Miranda Devine, "Why Hunter's

Dealings with China Aren't a 'Big Fat Nothing' for His President Father," *New York Post*, June 27, 2022, https://nypost.com/2022/06/27/why-hunters-dealings-with-china-arent-a-big-fat-nothing-for-his-president-father/.

19. Josh Christenson, "Hunter Biden Used Dad Joe as Leverage in China Business Dispute: Text Message," *New York Post*, June 22, 2023, https://nypost.com/2023/06/22/hunter-biden-used-joe-as-leverage-in-china-biz-deal-text/.

20. Peter Schweizer, *Red-Handed: How American Elites Get Rich Helping China Win* (New York: Harper, 2022), 126.

21. "Nancy Pelosi's Son, Who Tagged Along on Tech Trip, Is Investor in Chinese Tech Firm: Report," *New York Post*, August 11, 2022, https://nypost.com/2022/08/11/nancy-pelosis-son-is-investor-in-chinese-tech-firm-report/.

22. Adam Sabes, "Eric Swalwell Denies Wrongdoing in Chinese Spy Scandal," Fox News, January 18, 2023, https://www.foxnews.com/politics/eric-swalwell-denies-wrongdoing-chinese-spy-scandal.

23. Harry Robertson, "Ray Dalio Says China Is Winning the Economic Race against the US, as the Billionaire Investor Doubles Down on Controversial Stance," Business Insider, December 10, 2021, https://markets.businessinsider.com/news/stocks/ray-dalio-billionaire-investor-bridgewater-china-us-economic-competition-investing-2021-12.

24. John Frank, "Larry Fink 'Ashamed' to Be Part of ESG Political Debate," Axios, June 25, 2023, https://www.axios.com/2023/06/26/larry-fink-ashamed-esg-weaponized-desantis.

25. Sarah Weaver, "Analysis: The Massive Woke Company Selling Out Americans to China," The Daily Caller, June 28, 2022, https://dailycaller.com/2022/06/28/analysis-massive-woke-company-selling-out-americans-china-blackrock-larry-fink/.

26. See, for example, the hundred-plus members of Congress co-sponsoring "H.Res.109—Recognizing the Duty of the Federal Government to Create a Green New Deal," 116th Congress, 2019–2020, https://www.congress.gov/bill/116th-congress/house-resolution/109/cosponsors.

27. "What Countries Are the Top Producers and Consumers of Oil?," U.S. Energy Information Administration, May 1, 2023, https://www.eia.gov/tools/faqs/faq.php?id=709&t=6; "Dry Natural Gas Annual," U.S. Energy Information Administration, 2021, https://www.eia.gov/international/data/world/natural-gas/dry-natural-gas-production?pd=3002&p=00g&u=0&f=A&v=mapbubble&a=-&i=none&vo=value&vb=10&t=C&g=000000000000000000000000000000000000000000000000001&l=249-

ruvvvvvfvtvnvvIvrvvvvfvvvvvvvfvvvou2oevvvvvvvvvvvvvnvvvsooo8&s=315
532800000&e=1609459200000&ev=false.

28. "The U.S. Shale Revolution," Strauss Center for International Security and
Law, https://www.strausscenter.org/energy-and-security-project/the-u-s-
shale-revolution/; "U.S. Energy Facts Explained," U.S. Energy Information
Administration, June 10, 2022, https://www.eia.gov/energyexplained/
us-energy-facts/.

29. "Nonfossil Fuel Energy Sources Accounted for 21% of U.S. Energy
Consumption in 2022," U.S. Energy Information Administration, June 29,
2023, https://www.eia.gov/todayinenergy/detail.php?id=56980.

30. David W. Kreutzer and Paige Lambermont, "The Environmental Quality
Index: Environmental Quality Weighted Oil and Gas Production," Institute
for Energy Research, February 2023, https://www.instituteforenergyresearch.
org/wp-content/uploads/2023/02/IER-EQI-2023.pdf; M. J. Wolf et al.,
*Environmental Performance Index 2022: Ranking Country Performances
on Sustainability Issues* (New Haven, Connecticut: Yale Center for
Environmental Law & Policy, 2022), https://epi.yale.edu/downloads/
epi2022report06062022.pdf.

31. Rodrigo Castillo and Caitlin Purdy, "China's Role in Supplying Critical
Minerals for the Global Energy Transmission," Brookings Institution, July
2022, https://www.brookings.edu/wp-content/uploads/2022/08/LTRC_
ChinaSupplyChain.pdf, 6; "Rare Earths: Vital Elements of the Energy
Transition," Wood Mackenzie, March 23, 2022, https://www.woodmac.
com/news/opinion/rare-earths-vital-elements-of-the-energy-transition/.

32. "The World Needs More Diverse Solar Panel Supply Chains to Ensure
a Secure Transition to Net Zero Emissions" (press release), International
Energy Agency, July 7, 2022, https://www.iea.org/news/the-world-
needs-more-diverse-solar-panel-supply-chains-to-ensure-a-secure-
transition-to-net-zero-emissions.

33. Sun Chi, "China Tops Offshore Wind Power Worldwide," *China Daily*,
August 10, 2023, https://www.chinadaily.com.cn/a/202308/10/
WS64d4533aa31035260b81b58e.html; Wang Lee Yen, "How China Is
Leading the World in Clean Energy," CEO Magazine, November 15, 2022,
https://www.theceomagazine.com/business/innovation-technology/
china-clean-energy-investment/.

34. Castillo and Purdy, "China's Role," 13.

35. Morgan D. Bazilian, Emily J. Holland, and Joshua Busby, "America's Military
Depends on Minerals That China Controls," *Foreign Policy*, March 16, 2023,
https://foreignpolicy.com/2023/03/16/us-military-china-minerals-
supply-chain/.

36. Shirley Li, "How Hollywood Sold Out to China," *The Atlantic*, September 10, 2021, https://www.theatlantic.com/culture/archive/2021/09/how -hollywood-sold-out-to-china/620021/; FH Ledger, "Bohemian Rhapsody—I Think I'm Bisexual," YouTube, April 22, 2019, https://www.youtube.com/ watch?v=1Y8VCZSxJso.

37. Waiyee Yip, "'Top Gun: Maverick' Risks China's Anger after for [*sic*] Keeping Taiwan's Flag on the Iconic Bomber Jacket Worn by Tom Cruise's Character," Business Insider, June 2, 2022, https://www.insider.com/top-gun-maverick -china-anger-taiwan-flag-jacket-cross-strait-2022-6.

38. See, for example, Jordan Weissmann, "Waking the Sleeping Dragon," Slate, September 28, 2016, https://slate.com/business/2016/09/when-china-joined -the-wto-it-kick-started-the-chinese-economy-and-roused-a-giant.html.

39. See, for example, Bruce Jones and Andrew Yeo, "China and the Challenge to Global Order," Brookings, November 2022, https://www.brookings.edu /articles/china-and-the-challenge-to-global-order/.

40. David Crawshaw and Alicia Chen, "'Heads Bashed Bloody': China's Xi Marks Communist Party Centenary with Strong Words for Adversaries," *Washington Post*, July 1, 2021, https://www.washingtonpost.com/world/ asia_pacific/china-party-heads-bashed-xi/2021/07/01/277c8f0c-da3f-11eb-8c87-ad6f27918c78_story.html.

41. Julia Hollingsworth and Yong Xiong, "The Truthtellers," CNN, February 2021, https://www.cnn.com/interactive/2021/02/asia/china-wuhan-covid -truthtellers-intl-hnk-dst/.

42. Vincent Ni, "John Cena 'Very Sorry' for Saying Taiwan Is a Country," *The Guardian*, May 25, 2021, https://www.theguardian.com/world/2021/may /26/john-cena-very-sorry-for-saying-taiwan-is-a-country.

43. Ibid.; Guardian News, "John Cena Apologises for Saying Taiwan Is a Country amid Backlash," YouTube, May 26, 2021, https://www.youtube .com/watch?v=z88zeQ25pjQ.

44. Mark Fischer, "LeBron James Rips Daryl Morey over NBA's China Controversy," *New York Post*, October 14, 2019, https://nypost.com/2019 /10/14/lebron-james-rips-daryl-morey-over-nbas-china-controversy/.

45. See, for example, LeBron James (@KingJames), "We're literally hunted . . . ," Twitter, May 6, 2020, 6:06 p.m., https://twitter.com/kingjames/status /1258156220969398272?lang=ur; LeBron James (@KingJames), "Why Doesn't America Love US!!!!!????. . . ," Twitter, May 31, 2020, 3:32 a.m., https://twitter.com/KingJames/status/1266995951853395968?lang=en; LeBron James (@KingJames), "Everyone talking about 'how do we fix this?'.

.., " Twitter, June 9, 2020, 3:08 p.m., https://twitter.com/KingJames/status/1270432672544784384.

46. Rebecca Cohen and Meredith Cash, "LeBron James Questions Why Brittney Griner Would 'Want to Go Back to America' after Slow Response from US Government," Business Insider, July 12, 2022, https://www.insider.com/lebron-james-asks-why-brittney-griner-would-want-to-go-back-to-america-2022-7.

47. See, for example, "China Bashes US over Racism, Inequality, Pandemic Response," Al-Jazeera, March 24, 2021, https://www.aljazeera.com/news/2021/3/24/china-bashes-us-over-racism-inequality-pandemic-response.

48. Michelle Nichols, "U.S. and China Spar over Racism at United Nations," Reuters, March 19, 2021, https://www.reuters.com/article/us-usa-china-un/u-s-and-china-spar-over-racism-at-united-nations-idUSKBN2BB29E.

49. Josh Rogin, "Biden's U.N. Ambassador Nominee to Face Criticism for Past Praise of China," *Washington Post*, January 27, 2021, https://www.washingtonpost.com/opinions/2021/01/27/linda-thomas-greenfield-china-biden-united-nations-ambassador/.

50. John Feng, "Linda Thomas-Greenfield Says She Regrets Positive China Speech in Senate Grilling," *Newsweek*, January 28, 2021, https://www.newsweek.com/linda-thomas-greenfield-says-she-regrets-positive-china-speech-senate-grilling-1565098; "Sen. Cruz on Linda Thomas-Greenfield: I Have No Confidence This Nominee Will Stand Up to China" (press release), Ted Cruz Senate website, February 4, 2021, https://www.cruz.senate.gov/newsroom/press-releases/sen-cruz-on-linda-thomas-greenfield-i-have-no-confidence-this-nominee-will-stand-up-to-china; "Vote Summary: Question: On the Nomination (Confirmation: Linda Thomas-Greenfield, of Louisiana, to be the Representative of the United States of America to the United Nations and the Representative of the United States of America in the Security Council of the United Nations)," United States Senate, February 23, 2021, https://www.senate.gov/legislative/LIS/roll_call_votes/vote1171/vote_117_1_00061.htm.

51. "Sen. Ted Cruz Calls China Greatest Geopolitical Threat Facing the U.S." (video), *Washington Post*, August 5, 2020, https://www.washingtonpost.com/video/washington-post-live/wplive/sen-ted-cruz-calls-china-greatest-geopolitical-threat-facing-the-us/2020/08/05/9dcd6d86-14b8-44da-b9d6-62b3fed7d6c8_video.html.

52. "Sen. Cruz: When America Doesn't Lead the World Is a More Dangerous Place" (press release), Ted Cruz Senate website, September 11, 2013, https://

www.cruz.senate.gov/newsroom/press-releases/sen-cruz-when-america
-doesn-and-146t-lead-the-world-is-a-more-dangerous-place.

53. Chris Fuchs, "New Bill Seeks to Rename Plaza in DC after Chinese Dissident," *NBC News*, February 4, 2016, https://www.nbcnews.com/news /asian-america/new-bill-seeks-rename-plaza-dc-after-chinese-dissident -n511156.

54. Spyridon Mitsotakis, "Dianne Feinstein Loses Bid to Stop Cruz-Sponsored Move to Honor Chinese Dissident," Breitbart, February 17, 2016, https:// www.breitbart.com/politics/2016/02/17/red-chinas-pet-democrat-why-is-she -so-upset-with-ted-cruzs-support-for-human-rights/.

55. Jonathan Watts and Matthew Weaver, "Liu Xiaobo's Wife under House Arrest," *The Guardian*, October 11, 2010, https://www.theguardian.com/ world/2010/oct/11/liu-xiaobo-wife-house-arrest.

56. Jane Perlez, "Liu Xia, Detained Widow of Nobel Peace Prize Laureate, Leaves China," *New York Times*, July 10, 2018, https://www.nytimes.com/2018/07 /10/world/asia/china-liu-xia-released.html.

57. Lily Kuo and Philip Oltermann, "Liu Xia: Widow of Nobel Laureate Arrives in Berlin after Release from China," *The Guardian*, July 10, 2018, https:// www.theguardian.com/world/2018/jul/10/liu-xia-nobel-laureates-widow -allowed-to-leave-china-for-europe.

58. "Senate Bill 376," Bill Sponsor, https://www.billsponsor.com/bills/430985/ senate-bill-376-congress-118.

59. "Video: Sen. Cruz Highlights 'Friends and Allies Tour' throughout Indo-Pacific" (press release), Ted Cruz Senate website, October 18, 2019, https:// www.cruz.senate.gov/newsroom/press-releases/video-sen-cruz-highlights -and-039friends-and-allies-tour-and-039-throughout-indo-pacific.

60. "Cruz Provision Assessing China's Exploitation of Hong Kong's Autonomy Advances Out of Committee" (press release), Ted Cruz, September 25, 2019, https://www.cruz.senate.gov/newsroom/press-releases/cruz-provision -assessing-china-and-146s-exploitation-of-hong-kong-and-146s-autonomy -advances-out-of-committee.

61. Naima Green-Riley, "The State Department Labeled China's Confucius Programs a Bad Influence on U.S. Students. What's the Story?," *Washington Post*, August 25, 2020, https://www.washingtonpost.com/politics/2020/08 /24/state-department-labeled-chinas-confucius-programs-bad-influence-us -students-whats-story/.

62. Gabe Kaminsky, "Biden Classified Documents: UPenn Took Cash from China Donors Tied to Hunter Biden Deals and Beijing," Washington

Examiner, May 16, 2023, https://www.washingtonexaminer.com/news/white-house/biden-classified-documents-u-penn-china-hunter-laptop.

63. "S.2226 – National Defense Authorization Act for Fiscal Year 2024," 118th Congress (2023–2024), https://www.congress.gov/bill/118th-congress/senate-bill/2226/text?s=1&r=3.

64. Gabriel Hays, "Defense Department Declares It Won't Work with Hollywood Films That Bow to Chinese Censorship: Report," Fox News, June 30, 2023, https://www.foxnews.com/media/defense-department-declares-wont-work-hollywood-films-that-bow-chinese-censorship-report.

65. "Sen. Cruz Secures Passage of Amendment Blocking China from Controlling U.S. Radio Stations," Ted Cruz Senate website, May 12, 2021, https://www.cruz.senate.gov/newsroom/press-releases/sen-cruz-secures-passage-of-amendment-blocking-china-from-controlling-us-radio-stations.

66. Cissy Zhou, "China Debates Cutting US Access to Drugs as Hostilities Spike," *South China Morning Post*, September 10, 2020, https://www.scmp.com/economy/global-economy/article/3100880/china-debates-cutting-us-access-drugs-hostilities-spike.

67. "S.6394 – ORE Act," 116th Congress, https://www.congress.gov/bill/116th-congress/senate-bill/3694/text.

68. Jimmy Quinn, "John Kerry on Mass Atrocities: 'That's Not My Lane,'" *National Review*, November 11, 2021, https://www.nationalreview.com/2021/11/john-kerry-on-mass-atrocities-thats-not-my-lane/.

69. Dillon Burroughs, "Cruz: 'John Kerry Is the Customer of the Year for Chinese Concentration Camps,'" The Daily Wire, December 8, 2021, https://www.dailywire.com/news/cruz-john-kerry-is-the-customer-of-the-year-for-chinese-concentration-camps.

Index